Praise for *The Complete Guide to* *the Christian Novel*

"*The Complete Guide to Writing & Selling the Christian Novel*
is the essential book for both novices and advanced writers of
Christian fiction. In a genre that is growing rapidly in both size
and quality, Penelope Stokes establishes high standards. Perhaps
her most important contribution in these pages is to help writers
discover natural and profound ways of portraying spiritual
truth. Stokes's experience as a successful writer of Christian fiction and as the editor of many of the prominent novelists in the
Christian market shines through every page of this book. *The
Complete Guide to Writing & Selling the Christian Novel*
should be on every fiction writer's resource shelf."
> —Ken Petersen, acquisition director,
> Tyndale House Publishers

"Penelope Stokes offers the best combination of instruction and
inspiration. Anyone who loves to read good writing about good
writing should read this book. Anyone who is serious about
writing fiction for the Christian market must read this book."
> —Judith Markham, writer & editor,
> Blue Water Ink

"What can I say? Penny has covered the information logically
and beautifully. Because she's been an editor as well as a writer,
Penny's comments can be trusted. She looks at both sides of the
same coin and gives practical and helpful counsel for cracking
this specialized market from the unique perspective of her Christian faith—a key ingredient for writing in this market. Her book
should be a 'must read' for all CBA writers—including those
who are already published."
> —Lurlene McDaniel, author of
> *I'll Be Seeing You* and *Saving Jessica*

THE COMPLETE GUIDE TO

Writing &
Selling the
Christian
Novel

Penelope J. Stokes, Ph.D.

WRITER'S DIGEST BOOKS
CINCINNATI, OHIO

Other fine Writer's Digest Books are available from your local bookstore or
direct from the publisher.

02 01 00 99 98   5 4 3 2 1

Library of Congress Cataloging-in-Publication Data

Stokes, Penelope J.
    The complete guide to writing & selling the Christian novel / Penelope J.
Stokes.—1st ed.
        p.   cm.
    Includes bibliographical references and index.
    ISBN 0-89879-810-8 (alk. paper)
    1. Christian fiction—Authorship. 2. Christian fiction—Marketing. I. Title.
PN3377.5.C47S76   1998
808.3—dc21   97-32910
                                                                  CIP

Edited by Roseann Biederman and Bruce Stoker
Production edited by Michelle Howry
Cover design by Chad Planner and Angela Wilcox

Dedication

To all my friends in Christian publishing

who gave me a chance,
helped me grow,
and cheered me on. . . .

And to all the writers waiting in the wings—

your day in the sun is coming
sooner than you think . . . .

ACKNOWLEDGMENTS

A book—especially a book like this—is never the work of a single writer. It is the product of years of inspiration, instruction, and encouragement by countless teachers, friends, family members and professional colleagues. To all who have believed in me and given me a chance, a pat on the back, a shove in the right direction, a prayer or a word of hope, I say thank you, and may God give you grace in full measure, pressed, shaken together and running over, as you have given freely to me.

Thanks, too, to the following writers and editors who generously gave of their time to answer a long questionnaire. Your responses helped bring a variety of perspectives to the issues covered in this book. Lisa Bergren, executive editor, WaterBrook Press; Carol Johnson, editorial director, Bethany House Publishers; Judith Markham, Blue Water Ink; Sally Stuart, *Christian Writers' Market Guide*; B.J. Hoff; Angela Elwell Hunt; Jerry Jenkins; Lurlene McDaniel; Janette Oke; Judith Pella; Francine Rivers; Gayle Roper and Patricia H. Rushford.

ABOUT THE AUTHOR

Unless you frequent Christian writing conferences, you may never have heard of Penelope J. Stokes. But chances are, the publishers you want to write for have.

For the past fifteen years, Dr. Stokes has worked as a freelance editor with some of the biggest names in Christian publishing—companies such as Tyndale, Bethany House, Zondervan, Harvest House, Servant, David C. Cook and WaterBrook. Books under her editorial direction regularly appear on the best-seller list, and she has edited at least ten Gold Medallion winners.

Her experience, however, is not limited to editing other people's work. An accomplished author in her own right, Stokes has written a dozen books, including *Faith: The Substance of Things Unseen* (Tyndale House), *Turner's Crossroads* and a trilogy of World War II home front novels that includes *Home Fires Burning, Till We Meet Again* and *Remembering You.*

Penelope J. Stokes holds a Ph.D. in Renaissance literature, and for twelve years worked as a college professor teaching writing and literature. In 1986, she left teaching to begin a full-time career in freelance writing and editing. During her years as a freelancer, she has edited more than one hundred fifty novels and nonfiction books for the CBA market, and has been actively involved in writing both fiction and nonfiction.

A popular speaker at Christian writing conferences, Stokes is a member of the Academy of Christian Editors and Phi Kappa Phi, and is listed in *Who's Who in U.S. Writers, Editors, and Poets.*

TABLE OF CONTENTS

"Let your words always be full of grace. . . ."
—Colossians 4:6

INTRODUCTION: READ THIS FIRST

This is a book I never planned to write.

Frankly, I was too busy writing and editing to consider the possibility of writing about writing and editing. And there are plenty of other books about writing on the market—even a few specifically about writing fiction for the Christian market.

Then some authors and editors with whom I work began to press the issue. They pointed out—quite vehemently, in some cases—that upcoming fiction writers in the Christian market need quality instruction, and that the writing books which do exist for writers in the Christian market are almost exclusively written from an author's perspective, not an editor's.

Thus the idea for *The Complete Guide to Writing & Selling the Christian Novel* was conceived.

It began with a simple request from Carol Johnson of Bethany House, asking me to compile some notes to be used to help their authors learn techniques for maintaining consistent point of view. Before I knew what had happened, I had written an entire handbook specifically designed to help writers learn the basics of novel writing for the Christian market—a book called *Essentials of Quality Fiction*. A few writers and editors, myself included, made it available at writing conferences. Requests began coming in the mail, and finally Writer's Digest Books—a company with a vision for helping writers—offered a contract for a new, expanded handbook, a book that would address the unique perspective of the novelist writing from a Christian worldview and life view.

So what makes *The Complete Guide to Writing & Selling the Christian Novel* different from the scores of other books on fiction writing?

For one thing, it is based on fifteen years of editing experience, primarily in the field of Christian fiction. The principles in this handbook have been gleaned from my work on over 150 books by some twenty-five or thirty individual authors—many of those books best-sellers, and a number of them winners of the Gold Medallion, the most prestigious book award in Christian publishing.

Second, this book is written primarily from a problem-solving perspective. For years I have earned my living helping fiction writers solve problems of timing, motivation, point of view and dialogue. If we can learn how to deal with such difficulties up front, the editorial process will be infinitely easier, and the level of excellence in Christian fiction will be higher.

My intent in *The Complete Guide to Writing & Selling the Christian Novel*, then, was to identify and focus on issues that present repetitive problems for fiction writers. As I began this project, I asked myself: "What do writers need to know to succeed in the world of Christian fiction?"

I came up with a number of areas—some of them specific, practical and down-to-earth issues such as Plot Development, Characterization, Dialogue and Point of View, and some more personal issues, such as understanding how the Christian writing market works, which genres are most likely to be acquired by evangelical publishers, how to prepare in advance for the pressures that success inevitably brings, and spiritual issues that affect the Christian writer.

I began work on this project by sending out a survey to well-known writers and editors in the field of Christian fiction. Some did not have time to respond, but many did, and their comments and perspectives are included here. I have also made reference throughout the book to my own process in writing fiction—not because I want to promote my books, but because I know from the inside out what kinds of challenges and dilemmas faced me as I wrote my novels.

You may be tempted to approach this handbook like a smorgasbord, skipping over to the sections that seem most vital to your present writing dilemmas. And while this is a reference book, designed to be used and reused for instruction and reminder, I'd like to recommend that, on your first reading, you begin at the beginning. Experience bears out the truth that even published writers don't always have a clear grasp of the differences in genres or of the issues that distinguish Christian fiction from fiction in the general market.

Successful writing is based on a number of factors: gift, calling, skill, hard work and a teachable attitude. The best writers I know are those who acknowledge their gift and calling, develop their skills, and never stop learning or working to improve their craft. They actively seek out the expertise of their editors and struggle through rewrites without complaint. They know when to stick to their guns and when to compromise. And they listen.

The Complete Guide to Writing & Selling the Christian Novel is not a rule book—it is an exposition of principles that have been proven to work. My prayer is that this handbook will be of service to you in your own quest for excellence and continued growth in your writing. May your work be a testament to God's grace and a reflection of the creative Spirit of the One who created us.

PART ONE

Prayer, Planning and Preparation

Chapter One

For God, Gold or Glory?

The Motive Behind Christian Fiction

Jesus," Madeleine L'Engle says in *Walking on Water*, "was not a theologian. He was God who told stories."

And good stories they were, too—stories that shook the religious status quo to its foundations, stories that made people think, that made them wonder and question and reevaluate their own relationships with God. Sometimes they were stories that made his listeners angry. Stories about death and rebirth, about sin and redemption, about a God who cares enough to go after one wandering sheep or to search the entire house for a single lost coin. Stories about an outcast who becomes a model of godliness by helping a wounded enemy. Stories about a father who forgives even before his wayward son has repented. Intriguing stories. Disturbing stories. Stories that comforted the afflicted—and afflicted the comfortable.

If you don't believe stories have power, watch what happens in your church on some sleepy Sunday morning. The pastor drones on about justification and sanctification and nearly every other religious term you can think of, and then suddenly says, "Let me tell you a story." Heads pop up, spines straighten and eyes open. Ah, here it is. Not doctrine or law or history, but a *story*. We can relate to a story. We can hear it, glean its meaning and make our own applications. We can find our own truth in its words—truth that may have more influence for change than all the *shoulds* in Christendom.

THE POWER OF STORY

Herein lies the essential difference between fiction and nonfiction: Nonfiction tells us what is wrong and how to fix it; fiction holds a mirror up to our lives and allows us to apply the truth in an infinite number of individual ways.

Nonfiction lays out plans and strategies for right living, for change, for spiritual growth and development: *Three Thousand, Eight Hundred and Seventy-Five Easy Steps to Christian Perfection.* Fiction shows us people like ourselves—people in conflict who resolve (or fail to resolve) their problems, who trust (or fail to trust), who live, love, work, struggle and die in the real world, and whose experiences bring us to a deeper understanding of ourselves.

The power of story is undeniable. Entire cultural identities are based around the *mythos* of the people—those stories handed down from generation to generation that become the bedrock of our societies. Stories have the power to define us, to motivate us, to govern our actions and mold our perceptions. When we connect and identify with a character on the page, we come away different somehow, with a deeper insight or a nobler purpose.

A few years ago I stumbled across the fascinating legend of St. Sebaldus, whose feast day is celebrated on August 9. According to legend, Sebaldus studied for the priesthood in Rome and then returned to bring the gospel to his Germanic tribe. Caught in a blizzard, Sebaldus sought shelter at the home of a peasant; when he was refused, he went into the woods and built a fire out of icicles—a clear image of the love of Christ melting the frigid heart of the unbeliever. "The legend is an allegory, not history," author Howard V. Harper concludes in *Days and Customs of All Faiths.* "That is what legends are for, to tell the truth, not the facts."

And that, at the bottom line, is what Christian fiction is about—telling the *truth*, not the facts. Fiction, by its very nature, derives from the heart, mind and experience of the writer. A story may be based on a factual occurrence, and yet the essence of the tale is not the event itself, but the truth that underlies the event.

Christian writers have a unique perspective on truth. We believe in a God who is intimately involved in people's lives, a Creator who cares about our joys and struggles, who hears our prayers and responds, who gives us direction and comfort, whose presence infuses eternal meaning into our temporal lives. And as we spin stories out of that significant interaction between the Creator and the created, our work has the potential of becoming a catalyst for God's work in our readers' lives.

WHY CHRISTIAN FICTION?

In the past decade, the Christian publishing industry has experienced an unprecedented growth in the popularity and sales of Christian fiction. After a long history of perceiving spiritual fiction as somehow suspect and inferior, readers and publishers alike are beginning to acknowledge the value of strong, creative, spiritually oriented novels. Business is booming. New markets are opening up for prospective novelists, and the opportunities have never been greater.

But before we get too excited about the potential for success in this burgeoning market, we might do well to raise a few significant questions—practical questions, certainly, but spiritual challenges as well. What differentiates a "Christian" novel from any other kind? And what is the motivation for writing one?

What Is a Christian Novel?

For the record, let me begin by saying that the so-called "secular" market includes countless numbers of fine novels written by authors who obviously hold their own personal faith in high regard. The thrillers of John Grisham, the mysteries of Mary Higgins Clark and the character novels of Gail Godwin, Maeve Binchy, Jon Hassler, Andrew Greeley, Chaim Potok and John Irving cannot be found in most "Christian" bookstores, and yet their books reflect the reality of God and the depth of their own spiritual experience in ways often untouched by current "Christian" fiction. By the same token, certain "Christian" bookstores do not carry the works of acknowledged spiritual leaders such as Madeleine L'Engle and Frederick Buechner because their books are not sufficiently evangelical in nature.

We need to understand that what is commonly called "Christian fiction" might more properly be labeled "evangelical fiction." What differentiates this kind of novel from a general-market book is not simply the faith of the writer or the acknowledgment of God, but a distinctly religious viewpoint, usually marked by the personal conversion of one or more characters. We'll get into the distinctive features of evangelical fiction and what publishing companies expect in a Christian novel, but for the moment we can simply define the Christian novel as a work of fiction that derives from a conservative evangelical perspective.

Why Write Evangelical Fiction?

The reasons for writing a Christian novel are probably as varied as the people who write them. Some do it for high moral purposes—to convert their readers to Christian faith or to proclaim a message of God's truth to the unbelieving masses. Others have jumped on the bandwagon for less noble motives—because the sales figures far exceed the sales figures for nonfiction books. Still other writers simply want to tell their stories in an environment where they are not expected to water down the intensity of their faith.

From my experience with a wide variety of authors, from the famous to the unknown, I find that writers of Christian fiction choose this genre for several reasons.

1. *Ministry:* "I want my writing to reach people, to proclaim the truth of Jesus Christ and to lead other people to the Savior."
2. *Message:* "I have something important to say, principles that will change people's lives for the better."
3. *Money:* "I have a better chance of success in the smaller Christian market than I do in the general market, and I want to make a living."
4. *Motivation:* "The story I have to tell can only be told from a spiritual perspective."

Whatever the reason, fiction writing has become extremely popular—and profitable—for Christian authors and their publishers, and the upsurge of interest has proved to be both a blessing and a curse. Fiction classes at writers conferences are swamped with budding authors wanting shortcuts to success. Acquisitions editors are inundated with manuscripts, proposals and ideas. Television personalities, preachers and spiritual leaders known for their nonfiction are turning to fiction as a vehicle for their message.

It's true that fiction is a good way to get a point across—to get in the back door of a reader's mind and heart and bring about change. It's also true that a successful writer can make a living wage in the Christian market. But we must never forget that fiction is, first and foremost, about telling a story, not about preaching a sermon.

THE PURPOSE OF FICTION

A few years ago, a friend attended a debate on the subject of "Spirituality in Fiction." The principal speakers were Chaim Potok, the famous Jewish author of *My Name is Asher Lev* and *The Chosen*, and Andrew Greeley, a priest and the author of *The Cardinal Sins* and *Irish Gold*. A voice from the audience asked Potok a probing question: "Why do your Jewish novels find an audience even among atheists and agnostics, while novels from a Christian perspective rarely see the light of day in the general market?"

Potok's response: "Because Jewish authors do not proselytize."

It's a telling statement, and one we'd all do well to remember. The purpose of fiction—even evangelical fiction—is not to convert readers, but to draw them into a world of our creation, to connect them with the joys and heartaches of our characters and to let them decide for themselves what spiritual applications are appropriate. We may have high and noble visions of spreading the gospel to the world, but in most cases evangelical novels are read by other evangelicals; only rarely does a religious novel find an audience among the unconverted.

Before we begin, then, we need to examine our motives and understand why we are writing in the first place. And we need to be realistic. Novel writing is hard, lonely, high-pressure work, not a job for the lazy, the impatient or the faint of heart. But for those who have been called and who are willing to pay the price, it can be the most fulfilling, most meaningful career on earth.

UNDERSTANDING THE CBA

In the world of Christian fiction, CBA is often used as shorthand to refer to the complex and multifaceted system of Christian publishing. CBA stands for the Christian Booksellers' Association, an organization of book distributors (both independent booksellers and large distributing houses such as Parable and Spring Arbor) who specialize in marketing books for the Christian audience. Publishing companies associated with CBA (and there are thousands of them!) produce fiction, nonfiction, children's books, Bibles and other materials specifically for that target audience.

The history differs from one company to another, but many of these book publishers originally began their publishing efforts as denominational publishers, producing church-oriented materials such as reference works and Sunday School curricula. Thus, doctrinal differences abound; the membership of CBA includes companies with roots in every religious tradition from Roman Catholicism to the Pentecostal movement.

Every year, CBA hosts a national convention for booksellers —an opportunity for publishers to display their new products and compete for the limited shelf space in the thousands of Christian bookstores across the country. One trip to the CBA convention will convince any prospective writer of the overwhelming diversity in religious publishing. But a single common thread connects these widely divergent publishers: For the most part, they produce books *by* Christians, *for* Christians. And over the years, the audience has narrowed from a wide range of religious perspectives to a target market that expects primarily conservative Christian values and beliefs. Thus, the booksellers who stock CBA books rely on the fact that products from CBA publishing houses are conservatively Christian, theologically sound and appropriate for their customers.

This distinction is important for a writer who hopes to produce and sell fiction for the Christian market. The so-called "Christian" market is not simply generically spiritual or religious, but specifically geared toward a conservative Christian worldview and life view. Later in this chapter we will discuss some of the distinctive features of fiction produced for the CBA market, but for now we simply need to understand that the market we are writing for has certain expectations of its authors and of the books they produce.

WHO PUBLISHES CHRISTIAN FICTION?

One glance at Sally Stuart's *Christian Writers' Market Guide* will give you enough information about Christian book publishers to get you started—or to overwhelm you. The numbers are legion, from small houses that produce a dozen books a year to the big, multifaceted corporations, such as Tyndale, Bethany, Zondervan, Cook and Nelson, that produce hundreds of titles annually under dozens of different imprints.

Unlike general-market publishers, which for the most part line the Avenue of the Americas in New York City, CBA publishers can be found all over the map. Bethany House and Augsburg have their offices and production facilities in Minneapolis; Abingdon, Broadman, and Thomas Nelson are in Nashville, as is Nelson's sister corporation, Word. Zondervan, Servant and Baker Book House are located in the Grand Rapids/Ann Arbor area of Michigan; Questar and Harvest House are in Oregon. For many years, the epicenter of Christian publishing was the Wheaton/Carol Stream suburb of Chicago (Moody, Tyndale, Harold Shaw and InterVarsity Press), but in recent years that center has shifted westward to the Denver/Colorado Springs area, now home to Cook Communications (including the Chariot/Victor line), Accent, Focus on the Family, NavPress and the new WaterBrook imprint from Doubleday.

Just as Christian publishers can be found in almost every area of the country, they also represent almost every area of Christian belief and doctrine. Publishers who are members of the CBA run the gamut of doctrinal perspective, from conservative to liberal, and from houses controlled by specific denominational guidelines to more mainstream publishers who no longer have any denominational ties. You can find every conceivable kind of publisher within the membership of CBA, and no matter what brand of religious nonfiction you want to write, from reactionary to revolutionary, you can probably locate a publisher who shares your belief system and is willing to publish your work.

Fiction, however, is another matter. Most of the CBA houses that publish fiction tend to be clustered on the conservative end of the doctrinal scale—even those which have their roots in denominations that are perceived as "liberal." The reasons may largely pertain to the readership of Christian fiction—that is, the perspectives of the customers and what they expect from a Christian novel—but we'll get into that issue in a moment. For now, we simply need to realize that the major publishers of Christian fiction tend to be evangelical, conservative and cautious.

What kind of fiction do these publishers turn out? The answer to that question varies from one publisher to another, depending upon each organization's current publication needs. In recent years, Tyndale and Bethany House have been leaders in historical fiction, nostalgic romance (such as Janette Oke's books) and western titles. Nelson/Word and Zondervan produce a variety of mainstream titles. Cook, which includes Chariot/Victor and the British company Lion Publishers, has been successful with Jan Karon's nostalgic Mitford series and Angela Elwell Hunt's *Tale of Three Trees*. Palisades and Harvest House specialize in romance, but those doors are now open with many other publishers as well.

No matter what particular genres these houses publish, they all have one thing in common: They are looking for fiction that reflects the prevailing values of the CBA market, and for writers who can produce excellent novels within the established parameters. Slipshod writers who have all the evangelical elements in place, or excellent writers who diverge from the expected norms, will probably not find a place for their work among CBA publishers. A writer who produces a fine story containing the elements necessary for Christian fiction has a good chance of succeeding in this market.

WHO WRITES CHRISTIAN FICTION?

If the Christian fiction market is primarily evangelical and conservative in its constituency, it stands to reason that only conservative evangelical writers can make it as successful novelists in that market, doesn't it? This argument appears sound, but thankfully, it is far from true. Successful writers of Christian fiction come from all sorts of religious backgrounds—they can be Catholic, Episcopalian, mainline Protestant, Seventh-Day Adventist, Church of Christ, evangelical, charismatic or Pentecostal. Name a branch of Christianity, and you'll probably find Christian novelists who are part of it.

The common denominator is not religious background or even current religious affiliation, but the ability to produce novels that reflect the prevailing values of the market. The name of the game is *compromise*.

Before you begin to write angry letters telling me that you will never compromise your beliefs, let me explain what I mean by compromise. Donald Maass, a New York agent who has also written some fourteen novels, discusses necessary compromise in his excellent book *The Career Novelist*. Maass writes from the perspective of the New York markets, but his advice is valuable for Christian writers as well. He emphasizes that our "market, our customers," if you will, are our readers. "Authors without a sense of their readers," Maass says, "do not understand the reason for their success. These authors risk failure, too, for they know nothing of their customers' needs."

Our primary "customers" are not the publishers or the booksellers, but the readers who come into the Christian bookstore or open a catalog to place an order. Ultimately they are the people who determine what will sell and what will languish on the shelves. But we must understand that before we can get to the readers, we must first convince the publisher and the bookseller that what we are offering is what the customers want.

And who are those customers we ultimately want to reach? Let's be honest here. Our customers are not, by and large, bright-eyed, eager, deeply spiritual intellectuals who want to be challenged, educated and stretched. They are ordinary people—usually women and usually middle-aged—who want a good story with strong values, likable characters, a fast-moving plot and a satisfying ending. The stretching or challenging that takes place in a novel usually happens between the lines, not on them. You can be a brilliant, avant-garde writer with the Great American Novel under your belt and a Pulitzer on the horizon, but you may find yourself bussing tables for a living if you don't satisfy your customers.

Too many writers enter into the profession thinking they know better than the publisher what will sell and what won't. But most of these publishers have a long track record of success—they know the market. We need to learn to listen to them, and then to craft our work to meet the needs of the customer.

This does not mean that you can or should water down your specific religious beliefs just to find a publisher. It does mean, however, that if you understand the evangelical mindset and can in good conscience write fiction that reflects those conservative Christian values, you can write and publish successfully in the CBA market.

FINDING THE COMMON GROUND
What, then, is the starting point for all Christian novelists, no matter what their personal religious practices or backgrounds?

What is the bottom line?

The baseline for any Christian writer, I believe, is a commitment to God, faith in Jesus Christ, and an awareness of God's work in the world and in individual lives. Those are pretty basic tenets of belief, but they are vitally important. No matter how brilliant writers may be, they cannot write successful novels for the Christian market based on "secondhand" or "vicarious" faith. If one of the primary commandments of good writing is "Write what you know," then you must know God in some personal way, or that lack of relationship will be evident in your novel.

Does this mean that you must be able to cite a date and time of your "decision for Christ" to write for a publisher who believes in being born again? Of course not. Whether you grew into it over a period of years or made a decision at a Billy Graham Crusade is not the crucial issue: The crucial issue is that you understand what it is to have that personal relationship.

Does it mean that you have to be able to cite scripture passages from memory, or write in the jargon of the evangelical world? No. In fact, *not* writing religious jargon will probably be a plus in your novel. But you do need to respect scripture and have some experience with seeing it applied to your own life for positive change. Whatever your personal beliefs on the authority of scripture or its interpretation, you need to be aware that the conservative Christian market is likely to take the Bible quite literally and very seriously.

One of the best examples I have come across recently is the way Jan Karon handles issues of personal faith in her Mitford series, originally published by Lion (the British division of Cook), and picked up by Penguin for distribution in the general market. I do not know Karon personally, nor do I have any knowledge of her own faith journey or religious background. But in the Mitford books, her central character is an Episcopal priest who ministers to a small-town parish. Not the scenario most people would cite for success in the evangelical market. Karon, however, develops the situation masterfully: Father Tim is a self-effacing man, well loved by his congregants, who lives a simple, grace-filled life informed by his personal faith in Christ. Karon downplays the liturgical aspects of Episcopal life and even has Father Tim leading a traveling salesman to Christ when the stranger comes into the church to pray.

Karon's books are not evangelical in setting, but certainly are conservative in nature. She does not draw denominational lines in terms of controversial issues, or even in her handling of scripture. In fact, Father Tim rarely quotes scripture except to comment on his own life or to get his dog, Barnabas, under control. The result is a charming, inoffensive, uplifting novel that is accessible to all kinds of people, both non-Christians and Christians from almost any doctrinal persuasion.

No, you don't have to be a conservative evangelical to write fiction for a Christian publisher. But you do have to understand the ground rules and the faith basis for Christian fiction. And you do need to choose carefully what battles are important enough to fight—whether you can, in good conscience, make the compromises necessary to succeed in the market.

WHAT ARE THE LIMITS AND STANDARDS OF CHRISTIAN FICTION?

Writers who hope to succeed as novelists in the Christian market need to understand how the Christian Booksellers Association market works, and to take into account a number of primary considerations before attempting to sell a proposal.

Like any other marketplace, the Christian publishing market has its benefits and its limitations. For the Christian who wants to write high-quality moral fiction, CBA publishers offer the opportunity to publish in an environment open to spiritual truth, and to reach an audience hungry for that truth. In most cases a writer does not need to have an agent to get a reading from a CBA editor, although many Christian writers these days are opting to ally themselves with literary agents who specialize in marketing to CBA publishers. Many Christian publishers are smaller than the New York megahouses; thus, a writer may find that the atmosphere in a Christian publishing company is warmer and more intimate, and that Christian companies tend to give more attention to their writers. In general, Christian publishers are a bit more open to untested writers and more willing to take a chance on a new writer if the author's work shows promise.

The limitations of publishing with a CBA house relate primarily to theological and financial issues. Theologically, the more conservative publishers expect fiction to have a strong evangelical content and an overt moral lesson or spiritual "take-away value." Other less conservative companies emphasize quality of writing and development of plot and character, but still demand a certain level of theological rectitude: characters who are identifiably Christian (or who come to Christian faith during the course of the story), a biblically based representation of God and a worldview that reflects the justice and mercy of God, where the good get rewarded and the evil get punished.

In financial terms, many of the smaller evangelical publishers do not have sufficient working capital to invest enormous amounts of money in marketing and advertising. Advances, particularly for new writers, are generally minimal, and first print runs tend to be small. But the larger, more profitable "big-name" companies in the CBA are beginning to match some of the New York houses, offering substantial advances, good royalty schedules and excellent marketing.

Distinctive Features of Christian Fiction

A writer who wants to publish novels in the religious marketplace needs to have a clear idea of the distinctive features that separate Christian or evangelical fiction from general-market fiction. In general, the Christian market is geared toward the conservative end of the evangelical spectrum. Readers, booksellers, editors and publishers expect a certain level of conservative Christian theology. This perspective does not always have to appear in the form of decisions for Christ, sermons or prayers, but it must be visible in some form.

Some Christian publishers provide a detailed doctrinal perspective for potential writers in their writers guidelines; others require the use of specific Bible translations for any scripture passages that may be used. And almost all publishers are looking for particular kinds of books that fit into their publishing grid. In addition to genres that fit the specific niche of each evangelical publisher, most CBA publishing houses will be looking for the following issues in the novels they acquire.

A clearly articulated Christian worldview. A Christian worldview is based on the assumption that God is in control of the universe, and that true meaning and fulfillment in life are based on a relationship with the Almighty. This does not mean that bad things never happen, but that evil will be punished in the end, and good will prevail—either in this world or in the world to come. A Christian worldview offers a perspective of a universe that includes spiritual vision, order and moral resolution. Christian writers do not have to blind themselves to reality, but their writing must hold out the possibility of *hope*.

A familiar but intriguing setting and/or time frame. According to a survey conducted by a major CBA publisher, readers are most often drawn to settings they feel comfortable with or that are familiar: American rural/small-town environments (as in Janette Oke's nostalgia novels), and well-known historical time frames such as World War II, the Civil War or Victorian England. These settings and time frames attract audiences because readers feel they already know something about the era and the environment.

Universal themes and subject matter. Novels usually work best in the CBA market when they connect with some issue of current interest or universal appeal: love, suffering, injustice, moral challenges or family relationships. Contemporary novels often approach controversial issues directly (abortion, for example), but these issues must also be approached carefully lest they become extended sermons.

Action orientation. Action-oriented books that include intrigue, movement, suspense, danger and ultimate resolution usually work best in the CBA market. This general principle does not eliminate the value of character-oriented books, but it's a good idea to steer clear of psychological novels comprised mostly of self-awareness, internal insights or relationships. Something has to *happen* for a book to be successful in the Christian market.

Viable Christian characters. Conservative Christian readers look for characters they can relate to: "good Christian people." Characters do not have to be perfect (who is, after all?), but main characters—heroes and heroines—are generally most acceptable when they have a clearly identifiable evangelical faith, along with some kind of memorable "conversion" in their history. Most Christian readers are looking for a conflict of "good vs. evil"—one of the universal themes described previously. At the very least, the central character must have redeeming faith values, an intrinsic goodness or nobility . . . perhaps a "lapsed Christian" with a background of faith that ultimately leads to recommitment. Some of the more conservative Christian publishers tend to be wary of characters who are too catholic in their expressions of faith.

Series plans or potential. Although some companies are now successfully publishing stand-alone novels, many publishers have found that a series is more marketable than a single novel, particularly with historical fiction. Compelling characters or intriguing plotlines lead the reader to anticipate the next book, and the series creates its own natural marketing momentum. Plans for a trilogy, a four- or five-book series, or even a single sequel can be a major selling point for a proposal.

Strong evangelical perspectives. Certain Christian publishers insist on a strong conservative perspective that goes beyond a basic Christian worldview. These publishers will respond positively to characters who pray and see obvious answers to their prayers, who make decisions based on Scripture and who have significant changes wrought in their lives and attitudes by the power of God working in difficult circumstances. Most CBA publishers expect their authors to refrain from writing scenes that include gratuitous sex or overt sensuality, obscenity and profanity, humanistic philosophy or excessive violence (particularly toward women).

Acceptable Compromises

Some of these limitations present significant problems for novelists in the Christian market. Since real life contains violence, sex and profanity, how do you write "real" fiction and create "real" characters under such constraints? Perhaps the key to that dilemma lies in the Christian novelist's perceptions—that Christian worldview. The fact is, spiritual growth and the search for truth are also integral issues in human life, issues that are sometimes ignored altogether in general-market fiction.

When personal religious compromises are necessary, they should be evaluated on the basis of the author's own belief system. Some issues can simply be soft-pedaled, as Jan Karon has done so well in the Mitford books; others can be addressed head-on through characters who exhibit growth and change as the novel progresses. I would never advise authors to try to write something that is in direct contradiction to their personal values, but I often encourage authors to find the common ground between their own beliefs and the perspectives of their readers.

The challenge to the Christian writer, then, is to create fascinating, memorable characters and gripping plotlines, and still represent the validity of Christian faith in human life. This book, in fact, is based on the premise that writers who employ sound principles of good fiction can find ways to communicate a clear Christian worldview without compromising the artistic and literary demands of high-quality fiction.

Jesus was "God who told stories." And we, as writers who bear Christ's name, have the same calling: to tell our stories with skill and craft and passion, and to allow God to use our words in the lives of others.

It is a gift and a calling. But it is also a job.

Work hard. Listen. Learn. Grow.

God is in charge of the outcome.

Chapter Two

God and the Genre Dilemma

Discovering Your Niche

A friend and I were browsing in a large bookstore—a dangerously expensive pastime for a writer, to be sure—when she stopped in front of a rack of potboiler romances. They all looked alike: gaudy cover art showing a bare-chested macho man with bulging biceps leaning against a raven-haired beauty (or golden-locked or sable-tressed, take your pick) whose bodice could have done with a bit more fabric. "I don't get it," my friend muttered. "Genre fiction all looks alike to me."

I understood what she meant. She was using the word "genre" in its modern connotation: pulp fiction. In contemporary terms, the word "genre" has taken on a pejorative meaning. Genre fiction is formulaic fiction: the predictable romance, the one-plot western or the seamy detective novel.

In literary terms, however, a genre is simply a type of writing. Poetry and drama are genres, as are the short story, the novel and the essay. For our purposes, "genre" will be used in its original meaning to define the various types of fiction available to the would-be novelist.

Once you have determined that the CBA market is the best fit for your novels, do some rudimentary market research and give serious consideration to your choice of genres. As you begin to research possible publishers, you'll discover rather quickly that most houses have a particular "niche" in the market. One or two publishers will seem to lead the market in historical fiction; others will specialize in fantasy or intrigue; still others will do a number of westerns, nostalgic novels, adventures, or romances.

This is not to say that publishing houses never expand beyond their niches. Someone, after all, had to begin the trend—someone had to write the first biblical novel, the first historical fiction series, the first prairie romance or the first supernatural block-buster. We hear names such as Oke and Thoene and Peretti, see their sales figures and long for that kind of recognition. But Oke and Thoene and Peretti were unknowns at one time—until some perceptive editor took a chance on a new writer with a new idea. Breaking ground in a new genre can be accomplished by a single capable writer who produces an excellent manuscript.

Still, publishers have found that if they become known for producing quality historical fiction, for example, they tend to attract more of the same. They establish a reputation for the genre among booksellers, and their authors develop a following. Thus, it is important for you as a writer to understand different genres and to get a feel for which publishing houses might be open to the kind of book you want to write.

RESEARCHING THE MARKETS

If you intend to publish Christian-oriented fiction with an evangelical publisher, you should first determine the possible markets for your novel. Sally Stuart's *Christian Writers' Market Guide* is a good place to begin. Published annually, the guide offers listings of hundreds of Christian publishers, with details about the kinds of writing each house is seeking. The guide provides names of editors to contact, information on how to present an idea, whether the publisher is accepting new material and whether you should send a query letter, a proposal, sample chapters or a full manuscript.

It's also helpful to familiarize yourself with what is presently on the market—a publisher who is already doing two Civil War series, for example, would probably not be open to a third. A few hours in a large Christian bookstore can give you a good basic education about publishers: which publishers are doing what kind of fiction, what kind of cover art they choose, what kind of marketing their writers are likely to get—in short, which houses seem to fit with your vision of what you want your book to be.

A third approach to educating yourself about the market is to attend a writing conference or two. There are a number of good conferences to choose from every year—on the West Coast, the East Coast, in Colorado, Chicago or Philadelphia. The speakers, workshops and hands-on classes usually offer high-quality instruction for writers at various levels, as well as the opportunity to meet other writers, to network and to exchange ideas. But for a writer seeking a publisher, the greatest benefit of attending a writing conference is the chance to meet and talk with editors. Almost all these conferences bring in a wide variety of editors from various publishing houses, and most offer conferees time to make appointments to discuss book plans or to have manuscripts critiqued. Although you are ultimately judged on the quality of manuscript you can produce, meeting personally with editors gives them a chance to attach a face and a personality to the words on the page, which can sometimes mean the difference between acceptance and rejection of a book.

Too many writers jump into the process of attempting to sell a novel before they truly understand what is involved in becoming a published author in the CBA system. You'll save yourself a lot of time, effort and emotional stress if you determine a few things before you begin.

- Is the CBA the right market for my book?
- Do I have a strong story line, compelling characters and a firm spiritual foundation?
- Does my story lend itself to a series, or at the very least to a possible sequel? What might that sequel be?
- Am I willing and able to make compromises in order to accommodate the expectations of the market?
- Am I ready to listen to an editor's advice?
- Have I done my homework? Do I have a clear understanding of which publishers might be interested in my project?

Once you've determined the answers to these questions, you're ready to take the plunge—to begin crafting a Christian novel that will usher your readers into a world of spiritual, emotional and physical reality that you have created.

AN OVERVIEW OF GENRES

The consideration of genre is, at best, muddy water. Most novels, except those that follow the strict codes of their forms (such as formulaic westerns and romances), do not fall neatly into a single category. In fact, because women are the primary buyers and readers of CBA fiction (as high as 89 percent, according to some sources), most genres overlap with the general category known as "romance." Historical fiction, suspense, westerns, intrigue novels and nostalgia all include, to one degree or another, a love story.

The following list is not exhaustive, and therefore the categories are not set in stone, but at least it will give you an idea of some of the possibilities.

Historical Fiction

Historical fiction is a kind of catchall term that is often used for any novel set within a noncontemporary time frame. Strictly speaking, *true historical fiction* is set within a specific period of history. The plot is integrally interwoven with actual historical events, and some of the characters are actual historical figures. True historical fiction depends heavily on accurate research and a thorough knowledge of the significance of the historical events contained in the book. This contrasts sharply with *historical romance*, which sets fictional characters against a backdrop of a historical time frame, but does not directly involve them with the actual events of the period. History simply texturizes the novel and gives it a sense of place, time and setting. In between the two lies the *historical-frame novel*, which incorporates fictional characters into actual historical events, but involves real-life people from the time period only as minor characters. A fourth category of historical fiction is *biblical fiction*, which ironically had lapsed in the CBA market in recent years, until its resurgence with Francine Rivers' novels from Tyndale. A well-crafted biblical novel is not simply a retelling of a Bible story, but a deeply-researched and vibrant rendition of biblical characters, as in *Ben-Hur* and in the novels of Taylor Caldwell and Thomas B. Costain.

If you want to write true historical fiction, count on spending a great deal of time in intensive research and in producing a long, complex, multiplot manuscript.

Romance

In earlier times, the term "romance" referred to action and adventure: the swashbuckling pirate, the noble knight crusading for the truth or the rebel who fights for his people's freedom— *Robin Hood*, *Ivanhoe* and *The Scarlet Pimpernel*, for example.

In modern parlance, "romance" refers almost exclusively to love stories, and the term applies to everything from formulaic dime-store romances to the best-seller *Bridges of Madison County*. Most Christian publishers produce some kind of romance line, although until recently they rarely used the term. For some reason (perhaps the incredible success of the less-than-upright romance novels of the general market), CBA publishers were reluctant to apply the term "romance" to their books. Years ago, one publisher actually advertised their novels as "Romance without the blush!"

Recently, many publishers have returned to the term and now advertise their new "romance lines." Tyndale has just launched a new romance line with Catherine Palmer's Treasure series; the line includes both historical and contemporary series and novella anthologies. Palisades and Harvest House have a strong line of romance novels, and Bethany House has been producing historical romances for years.

But whether it is called "romance" or not, the element of the love story is an essential ingredient in almost every Christian novel, and produces such cross-genres as *historical romance*, *romantic suspense*, *prairie romance* and *romantic intrigue*.

Because the majority of readers are women, most evangelical publishers look for some element of romance in all the books they acquire. There are exceptions, of course, but nearly all the genres listed here include some romantic interest—some he/she conflict that ends in romantic love. The romance element may not be the primary factor in the plot, but it is there nonetheless.

Fantasy, Science Fiction and Spiritual Warfare

A few Christian publishers have had success in this genre—notably Crossway, with Frank Peretti's *This Present Darkness* and its sequels; and Lion, with Steven Lawhead's fantasies. Publishers who look for this kind of novel do not seem to be interested in science fiction per se—knockoffs of *Star Trek*, for example—but rather in futuristic fantasy that relates specifically to the Christian market and Christian concerns.

The coming millennium, the fulfillment of biblical prophecies, end times and battling the forces of spiritual darkness are more likely to be the focus of this genre in the Christian market than are alien invaders from outer space.

Nostalgia

The obvious example of success in this genre within the CBA is Bethany House's phenomenon with Janette Oke's books. The Oke series is a good example of combined genres—strictly speaking, they are romances, but they draw on the kind of nostalgia evident in the Little House on the Prairie series and the TV series *The Waltons*.

Nostalgia comes in all shapes and sizes, from life on the prairie to life in Lake Wobegon. The common denominator here is a wistful return to yesteryear, when life was simpler and morality was clearer, when people held strong values and lived by them.

Westerns

The western novel represents a specific kind of nostalgia, based in a particular time and place. This genre presents several different options: the standard western, based on real men making a stand in a lawless land; the romantic western, which includes the dynamic of "cowboy meets cowgirl"; and the female-oriented western, which places a young girl or woman in a man's world, fighting against the odds to make a life for herself. Most CBA novels in this genre include a romantic angle, as in Brock and Bodie Thoene's Shiloh series and Michael Phillips' *Journals of Corrie Belle Hollister*.

Coming-of-Age Novels

This type of fiction, often written from a first-person perspective, chronicles the maturation of a young central character on the brink of adulthood. The character encounters various rites of passage into the adult world—facing death, disillusionment or spiritual challenge. Most coming-of-age novels are set in a contemporary time frame rather than against a historical backdrop, pitting the central character against modern problems of morality, decision-making and religious transformation. Because few publishers in the CBA acquire contemporary novels, finding a home for such a book may be difficult, but the genre has a history of success in the general market. One example in the American Booksellers Association (ABA) is Gail Godwin's *The Finishing School*; among CBA publishers, perhaps the best example is *Saint Ben*, from Bethany House.

Mysteries

Although mystery novels account for an enormous percentage of sales in the general market, true mystery has yet to find its place in the Christian market. Some Young Adult titles, such as Lois Walfrid Johnson's Northwoods series from Bethany, have been successful. Angela Elwell Hunt's *The Proposal* (Tyndale House) might fall into this category, but suspense and intrigue novels are much more common in the CBA.

Mysteries center on crime: whodunit, how (or why) did they do it, and what are they going to do next? This genre includes a number of different subcategories.

- The *police procedural*, in which the investigation and collection of evidence is an integral part of the plot.
- The *whodunit*, which generally begins with a murder or other crime and builds a plot around finding the identity of the perpetrator.
- The *locked-room mystery*, a familiar subcategory for Agatha Christie fans, in which the plot turns not only on whodunit, but on how he did it.
- The *Victorian mystery*, which sets a mystery plot against the particular social mores of the Victorian era.

Suspense Novels

Suspense novels differ somewhat from mysteries in that the drama of the plot centers not so much on the crime that has already been committed, but on the one that is about to be committed. Usually the suspense novel has a character (almost always a woman) in jeopardy, and the plot develops around the danger the character is in and finding a way out of it. Mary Higgins Clark is a master of the mainstream suspense novel, and probably the best example to emulate. Without resorting to gratuitous sex, violence or profanity, Clark, who is called the "reigning queen of suspense," has built an empire on fine plotting, interesting characters and spine-chilling tension.

Like the mystery, the suspense novel has a number of subcategories—many of which have been invented (or re-invented) by the authors who made them famous: the *medical thriller*, such as Robin Cook's *Coma*; the *legal thriller*, such as John Grisham's *The Client* and *The Pelican Brief*; and the *romantic suspense*, in which a love story is combined with the jeopardy of the main character. More recently, the religious thriller has made a comeback with the publication of "end-times" novels such as *Left Behind* and *Tribulation Force* by Jenkins/LaHaye (Tyndale), and *Millennium's Eve* by Ed Stewart (Victor/Chariot), but these titles could be also be categorized as "prophecy" novels.

International Intrigue

Popularized by writers such as Tom Clancy and Robert Ludlum, international intrigue is the "spy" novel, set in exotic locations and filled with danger, adventure and espionage. International intrigue primarily attracts a male readership, and the CBA has attempted it a few times. Perhaps the best example is Jon Henderson's Tourmaline series (Tyndale).

Gothic

The Gothic, marked by dark, brooding, suspenseful isolation with a touch of the supernatural (which is resolved naturally at the end of the book), has been popular in the general market since the publication of *Jane Eyre* and *Wuthering Heights*. Gothics are often historical in setting, but can also be contemporary if the setting is isolated enough. In today's general market, Victoria Holt's writing offers good examples of this genre. In the CBA, B.J. Hoff's St. Clare Trilogy (Bethany) provides the best example of Christian Gothic.

Contemporary Character Novel

These novels, placed in a modern setting with modern events, center around the experiences of a character or group of characters. Such novels are essentially character driven; the characters, their struggles and joys, their growth or degeneration are more important to the book than what happens in the plot. In today's general market, some of the best examples come from authors Maeve Binchy (*The Copper Beech, Silver Wedding, Circle of Friends*), Rosamund Pilcher (*The Shell Seekers*), Jon Hassler (*The Green Journey, Staggerford*), John Irving (*A Prayer for Owen Meany*) and Gail Godwin (*A Mother and Two Daughters, Father Melancholy's Daughter, The Good Husband*). Jan Karon's Mitford series (*At Home in Mitford*, etc.), originally published by Lion and picked up by Penguin for general-market distribution, is a good example in our market.

Short Stories

The short story (frequently written by already-established novelists who have a following) has enjoyed a long and profitable life in the general market, but it has yet to come into its own among Christian publishers. A few houses have produced short stories: Harold Shaw's *Northcote Anthology of Short Fiction*; *Turner's Crossroads* (LifeJourney/David C. Cook); and *Good News From North Haven*, a spiritually oriented collection from New York publisher Doubleday. Short stories can be as varied in content as longer works of fiction, but successful publishing in the CBA depends upon a strong hook—a connecting link, through characters or locale, that enables the book to find the kind of marketing niche used for easily categorized novels.

Characterizing a novel as belonging to one genre or another is helpful to both writer and publisher, particularly when presenting a proposal, but many novels combine elements of several genres. My own Faith on the Home Front trilogy (Tyndale) is categorized as historical romance—it is a World War II story with several interwoven-relationship plots, but in essence the books are character novels about the spiritual battles and victories of three couples trying to find God's direction during a tumultuous and confusing era.

THE LEGITIMIZATION OF CHRISTIAN FICTION

The surge of interest in fiction among Christian publishers is a relatively recent phenomenon. Twenty years ago, only a few biblical novels and prophecy novels were being done, and fiction generally had a bad reputation among evangelicals. The success of authors such as Janette Oke, Bodie Thoene, Frank Peretti and other ground-breaking writers opened the floodgates and made a way for the legitimization of fiction in the Christian market.

But why did Christian fiction need to be "legitimized" in the first place?

For years, many conservative Christian denominations decried external "worldliness" and sought to maintain a separation from the world, particularly in regard to secular entertainments. Some groups prohibited movies, television, dancing, the use of cosmetics and "mixed bathing" (i.e., coed swimming). Some of these traditions hark back to the strict standards of the Puritans; some were merely attempts to keep the church untainted by the world. For some groups, fiction fell into the category of "unwholesome entertainment." Christians are called to truth, after all, and fiction is a fabrication, an escape.

Fortunately for novelists who also happen to be Christian, times change and attitudes change. Gradually, standards began to loosen a bit, allowing for Christian fiction that was biblically based (novels about Biblical characters, or religious romances, or stories that demonstrated God's miraculous work in the world).

As fiction came into its own, the story took precedence and religious publishers began clamoring for fiction that would present a Christian point of view. But for a long time, religious fiction was considered to be somewhat second-rate—at best, a nice story with a happy ending; at worst, absolute propaganda.

In recent years, however, the quality of Christian fiction has improved remarkably, and the reputation of Christian fiction has improved among general distributors. We now see the work of novelists such as Bodie Thoene, Frank Peretti, Janette Oke and B.J. Hoff on the shelves of big chain stores like WaldenBooks and Barnes & Noble—albeit in the "religion" section and not on the general-fiction shelves. But the general market cannot deny the power of sales, and its representatives are beginning to realize that Christian fiction does have its place in publishing.

The battle for the legitimization of Christian fiction has been a long and difficult one—both on the home front, to overcome the resistance of conservative consumers, and in the general market, against prejudicial attitudes. But the war has been worth it. Successful Christian novelists now enjoy an unprecedented level of respect, and sales from fiction provide the majority of income for many Christian publishing houses.

Certainly, Christian fiction has come a long way. But there are still a number of genres that enjoy tremendous success in the general market that have yet to be tried, or have been tried very tentatively, in religious publishing.

In general, the most successful and therefore most often-acquired genres among CBA publishers seem to be *historical fiction, spiritual warfare/prophecy, nostalgia, westerns, romance*, and more recently, *suspense*. Some inroads have been carved out for *international intrigue, coming-of-age novels* and *gothic*, but the markets are minimal and still difficult to find. The hardest sells among CBA offerings seem to be *contemporary character novels* and *short stories*.

SERIES OR A SINGLE NOVEL?

Once you have an idea of the *kind* of novel you want to write, consider the possibility of turning your idea into a series of books rather than a single novel. Many CBA publishers specifically look for series, or for book ideas that could be developed into a series, and the reason is fairly obvious. A series of novels creates a following; readers get involved in the lives of the characters and want to continue with their stories. From a marketing standpoint, the series tends to sell itself—once the first couple of books find some measure of success, the rest of the series takes off and stimulates increased sales of the earlier books.

A series can be developed in several ways. The most common is to have a set of characters whose experiences span several books, perhaps focusing on a different character or couple in each book. With historical novels, an author will often set characters in an active historical environment and build each book around some significant event in history. The "generational saga" creates a stable of fascinating characters whose stories span several generations. Readers can vicariously experience the birth of children and their upbringing, and then follow their lives into adulthood . . . and perhaps into the following generation as well. Another approach is to include minor characters in the first book that will become major players in the next. If the characters are appealing and interesting, they can carry the momentum from one book to the next. A less obvious option is to link the series together with a common locale or premise: the stories of the characters of one town, the interlocking stories of a group of people connected by a shared heritage, or the tales of different people brought together by a mutual struggle.

The possibilities for connecting stories together as a series are many and varied; the common denominator in successful series writing is establishing a viable connection that builds reader interest from one book to the next.

IDENTIFYING READERSHIP

One of the puzzling aspects of Christian publishing is the question *What makes for a best-seller?* If editors could predict the answer, of course, their jobs would be infinitely easier, and the process of acquisition would be much simplified.

But no simple answer exists. Part of the answer, however, may lie in an understanding of the *readership base*—the potential audience to which a book appeals or fails to appeal. A discussion of readership base in no way implies a value judgment about the relative excellence or mediocrity of the work. The fact is, certain kinds of books appeal to certain kinds of readers, and frankly, simpler stories—romances, westerns and nostalgia books—begin with a broader potential readership base.

We might think of potential readership as a pyramid. The lower you go on the pyramid, the wider your scope of potential readers. At the top of the pyramid is erudite, often "elitist," literature—T.S. Eliot's poetry is a good example. Directly below the peak of the pyramid come what are often called "literary novels"—Faulkner, perhaps, or Tolstoy. Still further down we move into the range of "sophisticated fiction," a category that ranges from psychological fiction to contemporary character novels. This category usually appeals to readers with a higher educational level. Below that lies "mainstream fiction," a wide range of genres that, depending upon a book's style, complexity and character development, may appeal both to sophisticated, educated readers and to the broader base of average readers. At the bottom of the pyramid, with the widest potential readership, is "popular fiction"—books designed primarily for entertainment, not for lasting literary acclaim.

Consider the pyramid illustration on the following page. You can see why books on the bottom of the pyramid naturally have a larger readership base from which to draw.

"Popular fiction" in the CBA might include romances, westerns and nostalgia novels. In the general market, popular fiction is often perceived as "escapist literature" and enjoys a wide readership, especially among women.

"Mainstream fiction" covers a broad base of genres as well as a wide range of potential readers. Mainstream novels are usually longer and more complex and include historical fiction, supernatural/prophecy novels and romantic intrigue.

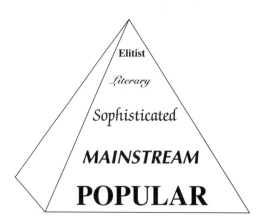

WHO CARES ABOUT GENRES, ANYWAY?

"I just want to write a good mainstream novel that will appeal to everybody," a would-be writer tells me at a writing conference. "I don't want to be labeled as a romance writer, a supernatural writer or a nostalgia writer. Who cares about genres, anyway?"

Publishers care. They know what succeeds and how to market it. They know their readership. They keep abreast of trends. And when they get a promising new author under contract, they have to be able to market a book that will be recognizable to consumers.

Booksellers care. Their sales depend on name recognition and genre recognition. Their stores are organized around genres, and if there isn't a niche for a new novel, the book won't sell, no matter how good it is.

And novelists should care. According to Donald Maass, author of *The Career Novelist*, genre identification is the author's most valuable tool for building a successful career. He likens building a readership in fiction to opening a store:

> Publishing a first novel is like opening a store. In that store, you are selling certain goods. Customers come in. They like what they find. They come back. They tell their friends. Eventually you are making a nice living. . . .
>
> Take my analogy a step further. You have opened a store. Suddenly you decide to replace your merchandise. One day you are selling fruit; the next day, auto parts. Will business

continue as before? Certainly not. Old customers will vanish. New customers must be won over. . . .

The nimble and talented may get by that way. What they will fail to do is build an audience . . . readership will not grow to the numbers that make success real and lasting. For that one must be mindful of one's audience, a consistent storyteller.

I think Maass's advice is sound counsel for any author who wants to make a career of fiction writing. Maass estimates that it takes five books (in print and selling) to establish a readership. If you switch genres—in his analogy, if you're selling fruit one day and auto parts the next—you are starting over, trying to build a new readership with every new book.

This is not to say that as writers we must get into a rut and stay there, writing the same book over and over again. Some authors I know of have built their careers on this pattern, and although they are financially stable, I wonder if they're not deathly bored. We can effectively expand the boundaries of a particular genre by doing it better, deeper, and with a greater commitment to excellence than others have before us. We can push our way into combined genres—adding suspense to romance or moving from simple romance into the larger, more complex historical romance. But if we want to build a readership and have "repeat customers" for our novels, we need to gain a healthy respect for the value of being labeled.

On the readership pyramid, there is a good deal of overlap in the readership of popular and mainstream novels. Readers on the upper or lower fringes of any given category often move freely between them: A reader who normally buys historical fiction, for example, may also read prairie romances. But it is less likely that a reader who enjoys the complexity and depth of literary novels or sophisticated character novels would also read entertainment-oriented westerns. In other words, readers often move back and forth between adjoining categories, but rarely drop or rise more than two categories. If Maass's "store" image is accurate (and I believe it is), those readers are not likely to follow us if we move into a radically different category with our work.

As we consider the demographics of the pyramid, we can easily see why popular and mainstream fiction may end up on the best-seller list, while more sophisticated or literary fiction records rather modest sales: On the bottom of the pyramid, there is simply a larger audience base from which to draw.

By the same token, books that fall on the upper ranges of the pyramid are more likely to be considered "serious literature," with the potential for enduring value. I don't remember a nostalgic romance in recent years that has been nominated for a Pulitzer, but then again, I expect a lot of Pulitzer nominees don't make an annual income of six figures with their writing. The lower a book falls on the readership pyramid, the more likely it is to sell well in its own time; the higher it rises, the more likely it is to be considered a "classic" in future generations.

For the writer of fiction, this dichotomy presents a dilemma: Do I write for the "throwaway market" of the present, or for the "enduring market" of the future? The answer is fairly simple: *Write the best book you are capable of writing, keep growing as a writer and let the future take care of itself.* But do guard against becoming so self-absorbed and elitist that you rise right out of the range of your market.

Dickens, Twain and Shakespeare, after all, were derided by the critics of their day for writing "commercial" fiction and drama designed to appeal to the masses. Most of Dickens' novels, the ones studied in literature classes, were serialized in popular magazines. Shakespeare, by his own admission, wrote for "the people in the pit." Good writing will endure; mediocre writing will die a natural death.

PRESENTING YOUR IDEA TO A PUBLISHER

Once you have an idea of what kind of novel you want to write, what kind of readership you're aiming for and which publishers are most likely to accept your book, how do you present your project in a way that will capture and hold an editor's attention?

Editors, after all, are often overworked, underpaid, stressed-out people. They get thousands of unsolicited manuscripts and proposals every year, only a fraction of which are appropriate for their publication needs. If your manuscript is going to be one of the favored few, what the editor initially sees of your work must be clear, creative and captivating.

Because they are inundated by a tidal wave of paper, many publishers no longer accept unsolicited material—certainly not full manuscripts, and for many publishers not even unsolicited proposals.

If you don't have an agent, your first line of offense is the *query letter*. Most writers workshops and books about writing can give you examples of effective query letters. Sally Stuart's *Christian Writers' Market Guide* contains an excellent article, entitled "Getting Your Manuscript Published," by Carol Johnson of Bethany House Publishers. The article offers a clear step-by-step guide to writing a good query letter.

The query letter should be addressed to the *acquisitions editor*, by name, or to the specific editor who has expressed interest in your project. If you don't know the acquisition editor's name, you haven't done enough homework. Find out—call the publisher and ask, and make sure you get the spelling right. *Christian Writers' Market Guide* can help, but be sure to double-check it—there is a good deal of turnover in publishing houses, and sending a proposal to an editor who is now working for the competition doesn't make a good impression.

A brief aside here about good impressions: Appearance *does* make a difference. Invest a little money to present your query letters on an understated but classy letterhead—a quality bond in a neutral color or a subdued pastel. Pink neon stationery annoys an editor even after she's had her morning coffee. Include a business card that has your phone and fax numbers and e-mail address. And restrain yourself from decorating your letterhead with cutesy sunflowers, smiley faces or "Jesus is everything to me" calligraphy. If you want to be regarded as a professional writer, take pains to look professional.

If you're still using that old dot-matrix printer, donate it to charity and replace it with a laser or high-quality inkjet. Print your query letter on 20-lb white paper; don't use photocopies unless they're really good quality. Send your letter flat and unstapled in a manila envelope. It's a good idea to have a header with your name and the book title on each page: Papers get shuffled sometimes, or routed around the office in sections. And don't forget to include a self-addressed stamped envelope (SASE).

Once an editor responds positively to your idea and asks to see more—or if you've met an editor at a writing conference and the editor has asked to see your work—be prepared to present a full proposal. Mark your proposal "Requested Material" on the outside of the envelope; it's less likely to get buried in the slush pile.

Novice writers often ask if they can sell a first novel before it's written. The answer depends entirely upon the publisher. If the author has previous publishing credits and a track record, and if the writing samples are impressive enough, a publisher may take a chance. A finished novel (preferably the first in a series) is certainly less of a gamble for the publisher, because the buyer can see exactly what is being offered. Many publishers have taken a beating on authors who were charming and convincing but could not produce the quality that was promised.

In the general market, selling a first novel without a finished manuscript is nearly impossible, as most New York agents will confirm. But in the Christian market, where authors often represent themselves, and editors may be a bit more willing to listen, a proposal and a few sample chapters may generate the contract you've longed for.

One important factor you should keep in mind when an editor asks for a proposal: This is your first (and perhaps only) chance to show what you're capable of doing. Don't undermine your odds by presenting slipshod work on the proposal, and don't shortchange yourself by skimping on the synopsis. Spend time and effort to put together a winning proposal—the results will be worth it in the long run.

The *proposal* is a detailed outline, usually accompanied by two or three sample chapters, that will give the editor enough exposure to your writing to decide whether or not to issue a contract for your book. Most publishers are not opposed to accepting simultaneous submissions (submitting a book to more than one publisher at a time) as long as the proposal is clearly marked "Simultaneous Submission." Some publishers in the New York houses don't like to get simultaneous submissions, but most CBA publishers understand that the process of evaluating and accepting a manuscript can often take several months, and waiting for an answer before submitting the proposal to another company can put the writer at a distinct disadvantage. As long as you are honest with the publisher about submitting the proposal to more than one company, you shouldn't encounter any serious problems.

Your proposal should include:

- a detailed plot synopsis
- a chapter-by-chapter outline (if you have one)
- a summary of possible sequel ideas
- an identification of your genre and target audience
- a marketing comparison (how this book is similar to or different from others in the same genre)
- a brief biographical note that includes your publishing credits
- two or three sample chapters (for a novel, usually the opening chapters)
- a projected completion date

If the proposal generates interest among the editors in a publishing house, it will probably go before an editorial committee, where a number of possible results may occur.

- The editor may ask to see a completed manuscript.
- The editor may ask for changes or alterations that involve rewriting.
- The proposal may be routed to other editors or objective readers for evaluation.
- A contract may be offered on the strength of the proposal and sample chapters.

Many young writers become discouraged when a proposal is not accepted, and in their discouragement fail to see the positive in their so-called "rejection." If an editor sends you a personalized rejection letter rather than a prefabricated "this-does-not-meet-our-present-needs" card, your manuscript held some interest for the publisher. If the editor says, "Make these changes and let me see it when you're done," your project has real potential of being accepted—if you make the changes and get back to him. If she says, "This won't work for us, but do you have other writing we can see?" or "We're overscheduled right now; come back to us later," don't write her off your list.

Editors don't have time to train writers, to rewrite manuscripts or to waste precious hours giving spurious advice. Accept any suggestion or individual response as a sign of serious interest, and be equally serious about following up, making changes or contacting the editor at a later date. If you're willing to make adjustments and have a quick turnaround time in getting your project back to the editor, you will earn respect as an author who can do the job.

Because the proposal is so important to the acceptance or rejection of your manuscript, it should represent your writing at its best and brightest. You want to be clear and direct, but not mundane, in expressing your idea. The editor, after all, is not only looking for content, but for style—she wants to see *how* you do it as well as what you do. If your novel has a humorous bent, let your humor show in the proposal; if your plot is dramatic and heartrending, your proposal should reflect the drama. But beware of being too "cute" in your synopsis—if you're writing a suspense novel, don't leave an editor with a cliffhanger. She will probably not be amused.

Consider the following excerpts from an actual proposal for a manuscript that was ultimately accepted for publication. Proposal 1 is simply a direct, nuts-and-bolts description of the project; Proposal 2 allows the creativity of the writer to come through. If you were an editor, which one would you accept?

Proposal 1

Turner's Crossroads is a collection of short stories about the inhabitants of a small Midwestern town. The time is the early 1980s. The people are extremely conservative, as most Midwesterners tend to be. Each story contains the experiences of one of the townspeople, demonstrating how God works in the crisis points of their lives to bring them to a deeper level of spiritual understanding. The farmers, the waitress in the cafe and the local pastor all discover God's hand in places they never expected.

Proposal 2

In a small town in the center of the Grain Belt, something very strange is happening . . . people are beginning to change. *Turner's Crossroads* is the chronicle of that change.

When the Four Korners Kafe opens and the people of Turner's Crossroads gather for morning coffee, the whole world seems to lurch backward fifty years, and the lines of demarcation are clearly drawn.

The farmers sit on stools at the counter like ancient crows on a power line, craning their necks to try to hear the conversation at the other end of the row. The guys from American Home Insurance fill one of the booths, while the office workers from Tri-County Electric hover over a table near the window. The loan officer from First Farmers Bank sits in a booth by himself, his back to the wall. And sometimes at the center table, within earshot of all the local gossip, a lone professor from Crossroads Christian College will sit quietly sipping his tea, monitoring the moral standing of the community.

Yet for all their diversity, the citizens of Turner's Crossroads get along remarkably well. Through the unshakable power of memory, they defend against unwelcome change.

Most of the time.

But when Mansfield Fisher moves to town, change comes whether they want it or not. . . .

In the case of this particular book, the creative work of the proposal served several purposes. It caught the editor's attention and ultimately resulted in a contract; it gave the editorial committee a clear idea of the author's style, and it was ultimately incorporated into the author's introduction to the finished work. In addition, it generated interest among several editors who rejected this specific project, and stimulated several offers for completely different writing assignments.

Whether the actual words of your proposal make it into print or not, proposal writing is not "lost work." It is your opportunity to shine, to make your book irresistible to the editor who first sees it. You must hook an editor with your proposal before you'll ever have the chance to hook a reader with your first chapter.

PASSION, PRIDE AND PREJUDICE

It's one thing to have a great idea, a contact at a wonderful publishing house and a brilliant proposal. But for the Christian fiction writer, other elements are equally important to your success as an author.

Passion

If you attend writing conferences, you will inevitably hear some writing teacher emphasize the importance of "writing out of your passion." I've said it myself, and as I look out and see the expressions on the students' faces, I can almost predict which ones of them will have a chance of succeeding. Some of them don't have a clue what "passion" means. Others mistake passion for their personal agendas: They ride their religious hobbyhorses with a vengeance, never mind what anyone—even the possible publisher of their dreams—tells them. But a few have that gleam in their eyes and the understanding that good Christian fiction rises up from a deep reservoir of spiritual reality within the human soul.

You can't fake passion. If you're writing what you think the market wants, or what will sell, and you have no inner commitment to the project, your lack of passion will inevitably show in your work. You have to believe in your idea, have faith in yourself and in God and trust your calling. But you also need to listen to those who have been around longer (sometimes a lot longer) than you have.

It's a delicate balance to strike. Some writers are doormats, poor codependent souls who, instead of discerning what they have a passion for, respond like Odo the Shapeshifter on *Star Trek: Deep Space Nine*, conforming themselves to whatever shape an editor seems to want. Others are so headstrong and bullish that they refuse to budge an inch from their original plan. If the editor is so stupid that she can't see how brilliant this idea is, then, by golly, that writer will keep looking until she finds a publisher worthy of her efforts.

The more professional choice—and the wiser, if you want to be published—is to look deep into your heart and know what you want to write, and then be prepared to adjust your idea to a publisher's concept. Good writing is co-creation, and your editor is part of that process.

Pride

Christians are often conditioned by religious society to avoid any sort of pride, in the same way we'd avoid a snake pit. If we do something good and others praise us, we humbly lower our eyes, shake our heads and push the affirmation aside with, "Oh, don't thank me, just give the glory to Jesus." That may seem like a noble response, but a certain amount of ego is essential to a writer. After all, if you don't think you have anything worthwhile to say, why are you writing in the first place? If you don't take pride in your work, you will end up with slipshod writing.

As with passion, balance is the key. An excess of pride can lead to stubbornness and self-destructive attitudes—as I heard an editor once say about a writer, "I'm afraid her ambition exceeds her abilities." On the other side of the coin, insufficient trust in oneself can result in creative paralysis.

Believe that you can do it. Then learn all you can to do it better.

Prejudice

For good or ill, passion shows in your work, and so does pride. But for the Christian writer, one of the most insidious problems that can mar a work of fiction is prejudice.

I'm sorry to say, I've encountered prejudice countless times in my years of editing—bigotry that rears its ugly head in the form of stereotyped characters or not-so-subtle author intrusions. Racial prejudice, class prejudice and even religious prejudice; despite the fact that most Christians would decry intolerance as a distinctly un-Christlike attribute, it still appears far more often than we'd like to believe. And most of the time the author is completely oblivious to the deep-seated anger, even hatred, that is evidenced in the work.

Prejudice, by definition, is the predisposition to judge another person, group of people or system of beliefs on the basis of preconceived notions. Sometimes prejudice is easy enough to spot— the stereotype of the ignorant Southerner, the lazy sharecropper, or the savage and bloodthirsty native. But often it is much more subtle—the ingrained belief that somehow we, as Christians, have a handle on the whole truth, and the rest of the world is languishing in darkness.

Jesus didn't perceive people that way. He surrounded himself with uneducated fishermen, women of the night and cheating tax collectors, and with gentleness and love he uncovered and nurtured the good in all of them.

As Christian writers, if our goal is to portray the story of human life and struggle in all its rich diversity, we need to set aside our prejudices, to humble ourselves and to admit that we have neither all the answers nor the right to impose them upon our readers. Later, in chapter eight, we will discuss techniques for writing balanced characterization. But before we even begin, we need to understand the role of humility and grace in the writer's life.

If you want to be a writer, rid yourself once and for all of any notion that you are holier than your neighbor. Get out among the people, saved and unsaved alike, and find out what makes them tick. Share their doubts and fears and failures. Strive to understand their loves and hopes and dreams. You will be a better writer—and probably a better person—for the effort.

A successful career as a Christian fiction writer is inextricably linked with the writer's own spiritual life and vision. If we hope to become writers of depth and substance, we need to find that sense of calling, to identify the readers we hope to reach and to discern which publishers might best share that vision and help us accomplish it. And we need to learn and keep growing—not just as writers, but as people chosen of God and created in the Divine image. Wonderful opportunities are available to writers who are willing to be taught, to work, to compromise when necessary and appropriate, and to make the most of the gifts and abilities God has given them.

Chapter Three

Spiritual Disciplines for the Aspiring Novelist

emember the movie *Chariots of Fire*? As Eric Liddell prepares to go back into training and to leave his sister in charge of the mission they have established, he struggles with God's direction in his life. It seems selfish to leave the "work of God" for the Olympics and to attain glory for himself. And yet that is not Liddell's motivation. He concludes, with fire and passion in his eyes, "I feel God's pleasure in me when I run."

Only a few writers I know "feel God's pleasure in them when they write." Lots of people want to be writers. They long to be published, to see their name on the cover of a book, to hold it in their hands and touch the pages, to inhale the scent of fresh ink and glory in the accomplishment. They want to *have written a book*. But they're not particularly crazy about the work involved in the *process* of writing.

Writing is a gift and a calling. But it is also hard work. Not just the physical labor that results in back strain, headaches, bifocals and terminal carpal tunnel syndrome—it's emotional and spiritual work, too. As Red Smith says in *The Writer's Quotation Book*, "There's nothing to writing. All you do is sit down at a typewriter and open a vein."

Some of my friends envy me for being a writer. I get to stay home, sleep as long as I need to, go to the office in jeans and never have a bureaucratic supervisor breathing down my neck. Most days I work from nine (or later) to four (or earlier), sometimes meeting a friend for lunch or making a run to the grocery, with half an hour set aside in the afternoon to watch *Jeopardy!* (I call it research).

What they don't understand, and can never understand unless

they give up their regular paychecks to follow a similar dream, is that five hours of writing can be equivalent to fourteen hours on a "real" job. Writing is tedious, exhausting work that drains not only the mind, but also the heart and soul. It can also be fulfilling and exhilarating, of course (otherwise, who would do this for a living?), but in the process, it demands a total concentration of the whole person. And we as Christian writers have the added awareness that we are accountable to God, as well as to our readers, for the influence our words may have for good or evil.

For the Christian, writing is a career of eternal proportions, so it's important not only to be skilled and ready, to be organized and professional, and to be mentally sharp, but to be spiritually equipped for the task as well.

On the whole, this book is about developing skills, learning the trade and finding your niche in the CBA. But Christian writing is more than simply doing the job well. It is about being the person God has called you to be—exemplifying Christlikeness in action and attitude, and exercising a spiritual life that seeps into your work as water and nutrients seep into the roots of a tree to make it strong.

PUTTING DOWN ROOTS

As a young Christian in college, trying to find my way to a deeper spiritual life, I became involved with a campus group that stressed **DISCIPLINE**—in bold black capital letters. A true disciple of Jesus Christ, I was taught, lived a disciplined life marked by an unfailing commitment to daily devotions, prayer, Bible study, worship and evangelical outreach. It was a little like boot camp: 6 A.M., forty-five minutes of devotions . . . 6:45, shower and dress . . . 7:30, meet with others for prayer before breakfast . . . 8:00, breakfast . . . noon prayer time . . . afternoon Bible study . . . evening worship. For more than four years of my life, I spent a minimum of three hours a day in prayer and study, and to this day I count it nothing short of a miracle that I ever finished my graduate degrees.

It was great discipline, certainly, and I've never regretted it. It provided me with a solid foundation in the scriptures and a respect for prayer and worship. But it's not the kind of life schedule most of us can maintain on a long-term basis.

Most Christians acknowledge (at least theoretically) the value and importance of regular times of prayer, Bible study and devotion to continue to deepen in our spiritual lives. These are important disciplines for the Christian writer, to be sure, but in addition, we need to look beyond what we *do* to who we *are*. Deeply rooted spirituality is not a matter of marking religious tasks off a checklist, but of immersing ourselves in the love and grace of God in order for that love and grace to come out in our writing.

What attitudes, then, do we as Christian writers need to maintain to fulfill the Lord's calling upon our lives and work? First and foremost, we need to remember that we are not masters, but servants; not celebrities, but crafters.

Perhaps it's an assumption that needs no discussion, but in my years of editing and writing I have known many authors who seem to forget this important principle. They become so caught up in building a career and creating a public image that they lose sight of the fact that God, as Creator and Redeemer, is the source of the gift and the director of the vocation.

In practical terms, serving God means that all we do, from initial concept to final revisions on a manuscript, ought to be done with a commitment to excellence. It means not getting by with writing that is "good enough." Good enough to get published, even good enough to make the best-seller list, is not good enough if it does not represent our best, our most dedicated effort—the highest fulfillment of our gifts that we are able to produce at any given time.

It's not my purpose here, of course, to create a race of monsters—perfectionists who never finish what they begin, or who never meet deadlines because they are never satisfied with the outcome. At some point, either with reluctance or relief, you will turn your novel over to an editor to be fine-tuned, polished and prepared for publication. If you present your book to the publisher as if you were presenting it to your Lord, you will earn the respect of the publishing house, as well as the satisfaction of knowing you've served the Lord with integrity.

Publishers, because of the time constraints involved in producing a novel, and perhaps because they don't often get the kind of excellence they dream about, often accept manuscripts that do not reflect the author's awareness of service to God. Maybe the writer has a big enough name that the book will sell no matter what shape it's in. Maybe the publisher doesn't want to battle with the author over revisions. And so the manuscript goes to editing half-baked and full of holes, and the editor is expected to fix it, perhaps even to rewrite it, to make a salable novel out of it.

But whether you're a plumber, a carpenter, a teacher or a writer, an attitude of servanthood toward God should result in a commitment to doing your job right. If, when the job is done, the pipes leak or the roof sags, the work does not give glory to God, no matter how much time the plumber and the carpenter have spent in prayer. While you have the manuscript in your possession, while your deadline still looms somewhere in the future, your job is to make it the best it can possibly be—to rewrite and revise, to check and double-check your logic, facts, timing and plot development, and to present as an offering both to God and to your publisher the best book you are capable of writing.

THE DISCIPLINED LIFE

Rootedness in God, in a meaningful spiritual life and in a commitment to excellence, provides the writer with a strong foundation for a career as an author of Christian fiction. But the process does not end there. The root system of a tree not only anchors it firmly in place, it also provides the nourishment necessary for the tree to grow, to fulfill its destiny and to reproduce itself through its fruit.

Just as a tree must be pruned and trained in order to maximize its potential, we as writers must commit ourselves to certain self-disciplines if we intend to succeed—and to glorify God by our success.

The practical work of our servanthood to God in the way we do our jobs and give ourselves to the work is not, as some might argue, separate from our spiritual lives. In *The Practice of the Presence of God*, that classic testament of everyday spirituality, Brother Lawrence prays:

> Lord of all pots and pans and things . . .
> Make me a saint by getting meals
> And washing up the plates!

Brother Lawrence knew—and we might do well to remind ourselves from time to time—that, as Christians, *everything* in our lives is spiritual. Making dinner, washing the dog or rewriting the epilogue for the fifth time are no less holy exercises than worship, prayer and Bible study.

Attitude is everything.

When I talk about self-discipline, I'm not referring to wearing a hair shirt, getting up at four in the morning, or sitting at the computer continuing to crank out text three hours after your brain has quit for the day. True self-discipline is a matter of the heart, of self-perception and of determination. As Robert Browning says of art and artists in the poem "Andrea del Sarto":

> In this world, who can do a thing, will not;
> And who would do it, cannot . . .
> And thus we half-men struggle.

In other words, some of us have the gift, but not the incentive, to create; others have the desire, but not the ability—"and thus we half-men struggle."

It matters not how gifted we are if we do not discipline ourselves to do the work and do it well. In addition, certain attitudes about ourselves and our writing often mean the difference between excellence and mediocrity.

Professionalism

In chapter two, we touched on a few practicalities of professionalism in regard to presenting a proposal—image issues such as letterhead and business cards, manuscript preparation, and the like. But professionalism for a writer goes deeper than image—it goes to the heart of how we see ourselves and, thus, how we do our work.

Whether you're a housewife with three preteens, writing at your kitchen table while the kids are at school and dropping your work midsentence to take your son to baseball practice when the clock chimes three, or a construction worker devoting Saturday mornings to working on your novel, for those hours you sit at the computer, you are a professional writer. Think of yourself as such.

Create an office for yourself in the spare bedroom, the attic or the back corner of the basement—any place where you can devote yourself to writing undisturbed. Agree with your family on specific writing times, if necessary, when you won't be interrupted unless there's blood or a broken bone involved. Organize your office so that your files, address lists, research materials, phone, and fax are within reach, even if you have to arrange file folders in a plastic crate and set them on the floor at your feet.

Fancy office furniture may be a luxury you can't afford, but certain equipment should take priority: a reliable computer with an updated word processing program; online capabilities and an e-mail address; a laser or inkjet printer; a telephone and fax machine; and a comfortable office chair that supports your back.

Some writers organize their writing time religiously, setting daily or weekly goals. There's no "right" way to begin working in a professional manner, of course, but for many beginning writers such goals are extremely helpful in establishing a pattern of productivity. Say you're working on an idea for a novel, and you set yourself a goal of finishing it in a year. Impossible, with your schedule, you say? Can you write two and a half pages a day? Twelve and a half pages a week?

There are fifty-two weeks in a year. Take two weeks up front to create a good proposal, and four at the end for revisions and rewriting. Take a week off for vacation, another week for Christmas and three days for Thanksgiving. Figuring a five-day work week, you still have 217 days. Averaging just two and a half pages a day, you can produce a 540-page manuscript—with a whole day to spare.

Reality rarely works as well as statistics, of course, but the principle stands—*if* you commit yourself to a professional attitude.

Teachableness

The second attitude a writer needs to succeed—in spiritual terms, at least, if not in the practical sense—is teachableness. You'd think most beginning writers would be blessed with the awareness of how little they know, but my experience (both in editing and in teaching writing) convinces me otherwise. We learn to write at age five or six. But the ability to put a coherent sentence on paper and spell the words correctly doesn't make a writer. Just because I know which end of the scalpel is sharp doesn't qualify me to perform open-heart surgery.

Far too many writers in our market, and in the general market as well, lose their desire to learn somewhere along the way. But writers who think they know it all stop growing. Their creativity atrophies, and they find themselves reproducing the same book over and over again. Even if they hit the best-seller list with every new release, they are no longer fulfilling the promise of their gift.

The wise writer—the one who wants more than just material success—commits from the beginning never to stop developing, learning, expanding and listening.

When I was in graduate school, I played tennis two or three times a week with my friend Kim. Kim, ten years younger than I and a state singles champion, had me beat before we ever walked onto the court. She was thinner, faster, and smarter, with better form, more experience, and a forehand volley that rattled my teeth. I was good enough (barely!) to give her a workout and keep her in shape, but I never won. I did, however, improve my own game. The challenge, even in defeat, made me a better player in the long run.

So it is with writing. We grow by exposing ourselves to those who know more than we do, and who will be honest with us about our shortcomings. That means investing time and money to attend writers conferences, reading voraciously, writing consistently and, most importantly, paying attention to those people in our writing lives who know what they're talking about.

Your editor, for example. Too many writers perceive the editor as the enemy, the meddling monster on the other end of the manuscript who has a compulsion to "mess with my work." But your editor, if he or she is a good one, has no desire to take over your book—only to make it the best it can possibly be. And that editor is your best source of information about what areas of weakness you need to work on, how your manuscript can be adjusted to fit the needs of the market, and whether or not your book contains material that will be inappropriate or offensive to your readers. You may not always agree with editors, but if you listen to them, you'll learn—and you'll be warmly regarded as one of those rare authors who is willing to take instruction.

Many young writers ask me, "Do I need an agent?" If you are just starting out in the world of CBA fiction, the answer is generally "No." Most CBA publishers are more than willing to work with new and promising authors, and many actually prefer working directly with writers rather than going through an agent.

In the general market, literary agents are a necessity—in part, because they serve as a built-in "rejection editor" for the New York houses. Good agents won't take chances with your reputation by presenting an inappropriate manuscript to a publisher, and they make it their business to know what kind of books are selling and with whom. In the CBA market, however, you can usually get by just fine without an agent, as long as you are willing to do your homework and spend time in market research.

A writer friend of mine was recently working on an article for *Publisher's Weekly* and called to ask about my experience with agents. "They're like computer systems," I told her. "When they work right, they're a blessing; when they don't, they're a curse."

A good literary agent, however, can be one of your best sources for information, encouragement and direction. I personally am represented by an agent in the general market, and represent myself in the CBA. My agent does a lot more for me than place manuscripts. She evaluates my writing, advises me about redirecting certain ideas, serves as a career manager for long-term decisions and encourages me to keep going when I'm ready to throw in the towel.

The problem is, getting a good agent to represent you is a lot like finding that first job right after graduation: You can't get hired without experience, but how are you supposed to get experience if you can't get hired? Agents make their living by representing writers who sell manuscripts. Even if you decide you want to work through an agent in the CBA, you'll probably have to do your own legwork, sell the first few books yourself and get some sales figures under your belt before you can attract the interest of a literary agent.

Your best source of continued instruction and growth, whether you're just beginning or have been writing for a long time, will most likely be the contacts you make when you rub elbows with other writers and editors. Go to conferences, meet people, and develop a network of other writers who understand your struggles and editors who see promise in your work. Listen. Learn. Stay teachable. Keep stretching. The rest of it—agents, contracts and published books—will fall into place in due time.

Priorities

The final commitment we, as writers, need to make in order to fulfill the potential of our God-given abilities is the determination to keep our priorities in order. Setting aside time to write is vital, of course, but writing is not the only priority in life. Most of us have families, church commitments and personal needs that demand our time and attention. But like junk that mysteriously multiplies in the darkness of a closet, the demands of our lives will somehow expand to take up every available inch of space—unless we take control first.

Years ago the Navigators Ministry published a little booklet entitled "The Tyranny of the Urgent," describing how the "urgent" things in life often usurp the rightful place of the really important things such as our relationships with God, our families and our calling. And it's true. If we don't prioritize our lives, we can spend so much time putting out brush fires that we deny ourselves any opportunity to accomplish something really worthwhile.

My mother used to prod me into cleaning my room with maxims like "Anything worth doing is worth doing well." Your mother undoubtedly said the same thing; all mothers read the same book. But as I grew up, I realized the subtle deception of such a proverb. The fact is, there are lots of things in our lives that have to be done that don't really need to be obsessed over. The dishes will wait, if we're not too compulsive to let them sit in the sink for an hour. My kitchen floor is clean enough to eat off of—the dog does it all the time!

Everyone's priority list is different, of course, depending on the demands and needs of the individual's life. But for a Christian writer, some general principles apply.

God comes first. This concept is not as simple as it sounds, because putting God first means discerning what is (and is not) God's priority in our lives. Sometimes we get caught up in "doing good"—in religious activities and responsibilities—and mistakenly think we are doing God's will, when what we actually need is to be saying "no" instead of "yes" all the time. My personal relationship with God is a priority in my life, so I set aside time for worship, for prayer and for centering myself in a sense of God's presence. Sometimes that happens in church, in the privacy of my office, in a group of friends or when I'm sitting at my computer writing. At certain times in my life, putting God first has meant making the effort to engage in personal counseling or setting aside two days a month for spiritual direction or retreat. Whatever you need to do to put God first in your life, go ahead and do it. But remember that Christ-centeredness is essentially an attitude of the heart—"becoming a saint," in Brother Lawrence's words, "by getting meals and washing up the plates."

People are more important than things. I once heard a successful writer boast about his commitment to his writing. When he was at work, his family knew he was not to be disturbed for any reason. His children tiptoed past his locked door so as not to annoy him, and his wife brought his dinner on a tray and left it in the hallway for him. Everyone applauded his dedication to his work, but I secretly wondered how his wife felt about his writing. A few years later I heard by the grapevine that he was divorced and living alone while his wife had custody of the children.

He got his wish for privacy, but at what cost?

The importance of family in our lives—spouse, children, parents and close friends—cannot be overestimated. We need people. We need the support of those who love us. And there is a vast difference between negotiating with our significant others to give us the time we need to write and selfishly putting our own desires ahead of those of everyone else.

Again, it's a balancing act. Those of us who are intrinsically self-consumed and have no problem shutting people out probably need to discipline ourselves not to work all the time. Those of us who tend to be codependent and always cater to the needs of others might need to generate a little backbone and learn to say "no" once in a while.

Each of us must determine what our individual "people priorities" are going to be. But if we intend to live a balanced, healthy life, boundaries are essential. Without them, we'll burn out, run ourselves ragged taking care of the urgencies of life and never get around to what's really important.

It's not selfish to take care of yourself. This means not only taking time for yourself, for your relationship with God and for your writing, but also taking time for relaxation and rejuvenation. Time when you lay the manuscript aside and play fetch with the dog. Time for a game of miniature golf with the kids. Time for a long soak in the bathtub or a weekend at a cabin in the mountains.

Time for yourself also includes the hours you spend organizing, planning and goal-setting, both for your spiritual life and for your career. I always take a few days off—sometimes even a week or two—between book projects. I plan my schedule to avoid working on weekends or at night. I give myself three days at Thanksgiving and a week off at Christmas, even if I'm facing a December 30 deadline. The first of January and the first of September are times set aside for planning, dreaming and evaluating. On my birthday I spend a few hours chronicling the accomplishments and failures of the previous year, and determining changes and directions for the next.

I believe that God wants us, as Christians and as writers, to be whole, healthy, integrated, Christ-centered people. And we can only realize that purpose as we come to know ourselves, our priorities, our gifts and our calling.

We don't have to be fragmented, frazzled people. If we approach our work with professionalism and our lives with balance, we can become writers whose words are infused with a power and anointing that comes from the deepest recesses of our souls. We can enter into the fulfillment of our gifts with a humble spirit, with a servant heart, and with the assurance that God has led us, is directing us and will honor our efforts.

We can "feel God's pleasure in us as we write."

PART TWO

Stories, Sermons and Sunday School

Chapter Four

I Love to Tell the Story
Planning and Plotting

Not all storytellers are novelists, but all good novelists are, at heart, storytellers.

Years ago I heard Philip Yancey deliver a plenary session at a writers conference, and his words made an indelible imprint upon my life and writing. He spoke of the tendency among Christian writers to be guilty of "content idolatry"—to be so concerned about the message of our writing that we neglect to give sufficient attention to the medium.

For many Christian writers, telling a good story doesn't seem to be enough. They want to evangelize, to teach and to fill their fiction with high moral purport, doctrine and direction. This all sounds quite noble, of course, except that the purpose of fiction is not propaganda. The proper place for preaching is the pulpit, the evangelistic crusade or even the pages of the nonfiction book. Fiction is different. Fiction is story.

It's a grave temptation for a Christian novelist to begin by trying to establish a religious theme for the work: the adverse effects of abortion, for example, or the changes conversion brings to the sinner's life. But when we start with a theme, we often end up with one-dimensional characters and a mundane plotline, and then simply follow the idea through to its preconceived (and often sleep-inducing) conclusion.

John Gardner, one of the finest writing teachers of this century and a Christian committed to spiritual integrity in his writing, in *On Becoming a Novelist* described fiction as "a vivid, continuous dream" that sweeps readers into the author's world and keeps them firmly entrenched there until the last sentence of the book. Samuel Taylor Coleridge described this vivid, continuous dream as the "willing suspension of disbelief."

For a writer to succeed in captivating readers, all the elements of the story—plot, characters, setting, language, motivation and point of view—must work together to weave a seamless fabric that surrounds readers and draws them into the writer's imaginative world. It's easier said than done.

Where do you begin if you want to create a book that is story rather than sermon? A true novel begins in one of two places: with a compelling plot or with fascinating characters.

THE CHARACTER-DRIVEN STORY VS. THE PLOT-DRIVEN STORY

An inexperienced writer once approached me at a writers conference to ask for advice and input. "It's a historical fiction series," she explained. "Long, complex and full of research. I have about six hundred pages of the first book done, and I wondered if you could give me some tips on plotting."

Obviously, six hundred pages into your masterpiece is no time to *begin* thinking about plot. Long before you begin to write the first paragraph of the first chapter, you need to have a clear idea of where your work is going, who your characters are and how your novel is likely to develop.

One of the first decisions you will face as you begin planning your novel is whether you want to write a plot-driven story or a character-driven one. If your idea centers around action, intrigue and plot twists, you will probably end up with a plot-driven novel. If your idea hinges on a fascinating character or set of characters, you will likely write a character-driven story.

We often see the character-driven story in contemporary novels (such as the coming-of-age story) where the personal growth of the characters is of primary importance. *What* happens is important primarily in relation to *why* it happens and what the results are for the characters. In the plot-driven novel (such as a detective mystery), the events of the story take precedence: What happens is of first importance.

Sadly, many teachers of writing (or writers who want to teach others) deal with plot as if it were the sole source of direction for a story. They instruct their students to plot carefully—to outline, to summarize chapters and to have significant plot turns at points A, B and C. In short, they treat all novels as if they are (or should be) plot-driven, and ignore the possibility of a character-driven story. But many fine novels are not plot-driven at all; they are character stories, and they appeal to many readers.

In part three, we will deal directly and specifically with characterization—the connection between plot and character, creating memorable characters and making characters come alive to the reader. For now, we'll simply explore the difference between the plot-driven and the character-driven novel.

The plot-driven novel centers on the action of the story—what happens, the complications that arise and how the characters work their way out of difficult circumstances. John Grisham's legal thrillers (*The Client, The Pelican Brief, The Firm*) are examples of the plot-driven story, as are the best-sellers *The Hunt for Red October* by Tom Clancy and Scott Turow's *Presumed Innocent*. On the silver screen, the plot-driven story might be represented by the James Bond movies, in which the action centers around Bond's espionage, the complications and dangers that come to him, and how he works his way out of those dangers to fulfill his mission. The plot-driven story has been described by one editor as the "galloping-horse novel," in which the reader is placed on a "galloping horse" on page 1 and not let off until the end of the book on page 425.

The character-driven story, on the other hand, appears in best-sellers such as Gail Godwin's *Father Melancholy's Daughter*, Anne Tyler's *The Accidental Tourist*, Fanny Flagg's *Fried Green Tomatoes at the Whistle Stop Cafe*, Pat Conroy's *Prince of Tides*, Jon Hassler's *Staggerford* and *The Green Journey*, and Chaim Potok's *The Chosen*. Hollywood's version of the character-driven story appears in films such as Barbra Streisand's *Yentl* and *The Way We Were* (as well as several of the above-mentioned novels made into movies). The action that takes place in these novels is integral to the story, but the primary significance lies in the motives, changes and growth of the characters.

This is not to say that characterization is unimportant in a plot-driven story, or that plotting is dispensable to a character-driven book. The difference lies in the source of the momentum of the story—whether it derives primarily from plot or from character.

In the plot-driven story, the reader cares most about *what happens*; in the character-driven story, the reader cares most about the *people*. We don't normally cry over a plot-driven book; instead, we are gripped by the action and suspense, and we want to finish the book (if it's a good one) to find out what is going to happen. A good character-driven novel often has the opposite effect: We don't want it to end, and when it's finished, we find ourselves wondering what the characters are doing, as if they are carrying on life without us, outside the scope of the novel.

Both arenas hold certain kinds of pitfalls for an inexperienced or careless author. A writer who focuses on character development may load readers down with long and involved inner dialogue and philosophizing at the expense of the movement of the book, and the reader's response is, "Get on with it!" The author who concentrates on plot may skim over motivation and leave readers scratching their heads, wondering why on earth the character did *that*.

In my years of editing, I have seen weaknesses on both sides. I know gifted writers, some of whom regularly appear on the best-seller list, whose work still does not demonstrate the kind of balance editors long for. The plot may be fast-paced and gripping, but the characters are sketchy and underdeveloped. Or the characters may be fascinating, memorable people, but the plot is riddled with logic flaws and loopholes.

Whether your novel is essentially plot-driven or character-driven, both elements are important for a well-written story. An action writer must give attention to characters and motivation; a character novelist must attend to the development of plot.

WRITE WHAT YOU READ

How do you decide whether the story simmering in your brain is a plot-driven novel or a character-driven book? What determines the kind of novel you will write?

For generations, writing teachers have been giving the same sage piece of advice to aspiring novelists: *Write what you know*. To this maxim I will add a second commandment: *Write what you read*.

For twelve years, before God pushed me off the cliff into the dangerous headwinds of the freelance life, I taught writing and literature at the college level. One afternoon a creative writing student appeared at my office door, wanting to discuss her grade on a poem she had written. It was, frankly, a terrible poem, littered with unworkable imagery and bogged down by unnatural rhythms. Not wanting to crush her fragile ego, I began to probe into the background of this pathetic effort. "What kind of poetry do you read?" I asked with all the gentleness I could muster.

"Oh, I don't *read* poetry," she said brightly. "I just *write* it."

Chuckle if you like, but the woods are full of aspiring novelists with exactly the same perspective. "I don't read action adventures, but that's what I want to write because it's popular." "I made D's in history and never cracked the pages of a historical novel, but that's what the publisher is looking for, and that's what I'm going to write."

It won't work, at least not over the long haul. Reading is not merely an intellectual exercise, but a subliminal assimilation of thought, perspective, expression, vocabulary, structure and a thousand other intangibles that play a part in affecting a writer's individual style. As writers, we are what we read. And then, by extension, we write it—filtered through the sieve of our own experiences, beliefs and imagination.

Make no mistake: I'm not talking about imitation of another author, the kind of mindset that says, "I want to be as successful as John Grisham, so I'll do it exactly the way he does it." A photocopy never has the crisp, clear quality of the original. Good writers don't read widely in a certain genre so that they will be able to reproduce the techniques in their manuscripts. They write what they know, and they write what they like to read.

Flannery O'Connor, in *Mystery and Manners*, put it this way: "The great novels we get in the future are not going to be those the public thinks it wants. . . . They are going to be the kind of novels that interest the novelist."

It's an issue of passion. Oh, if you're good enough, you can pull it off—you can write a particular kind of book just because you know it will sell—but the lack of passion will show in your work. And passionless writing will not endure, nor will it be fulfilling and satisfying to the writer, except perhaps in the wallet. An author who produces only what the market demands is known by the nastiest of four letter words: *hack*.

On the other hand, we do have to make certain concessions to the practical issues of publishing. The writer of CBA novels must be aware of what CBA readers, and therefore CBA publishers, expect in a Christian novel. You will probably not have a great deal of success in the CBA, for example, producing deeply introverted psychological novels in the manner of James Joyce, and you won't make a living on erudite poetry like that of T.S. Eliot.

But there is a balance. You study the markets and learn what publishers are looking for, and then try to discern how what you want to write might fit into that grid. You might find, as I did with my first fiction series, that what you had originally envisioned as a stand-alone novel could be developed into a trilogy or a five-book series. You make plans, adjust and reevaluate—as long as compromising your plans doesn't compromise your integrity as a writer.

CROSSING OVER

In recent years a lot of discussion, some of it rather heated, has arisen in publishing houses, at writers conferences and in chat rooms on the Internet about the possibility of what is popularly termed "crossover fiction."

Crossover fiction is the phenomenon that occurs when a book written for the CBA market finds success in the general market, or vice versa. I often hear young writers talking about their desire to write a crossover novel; that is, to be wildly successful in both markets simultaneously.

My discussions with writers and editors demonstrate varied attitudes toward the so-called "crossover" novel. Sally Stuart, author of *The Christian Writers' Market Guide*, cites Jan Karon's Mitford books (initially published by Lion and then acquired by Penguin for general-market distribution) as the best recent success story where a crossover novel is concerned. "I asked the bookstore manager why she liked them," Stuart says, "and her response was that they were real."

Karon's success, however, is the exception rather than the rule: It worked for the Mitford books not because the CBA publisher was able to market the novel in the general bookstores, but because Penguin, a New York publishing house, picked it up and distributed it. This in no way diminishes Karon's capabilities as a writer; it simply shows that crossing over is a difficult process, not the glamorous success story that most writers envision.

Judith Markham of Blue Water Ink gives a realistic, if not extremely optimistic, opinion concerning crossovers:

> I am truly gun-shy when it comes to the term "crossover," because over and over again I have seen it set everyone up for disappointment. As long as the misconception is out there that no serious fiction is being done in CBA, crossing from CBA to ABA will be difficult, if not impossible. . . . In order for any "crossing" to be done, the novels have to be in ABA stores—at least until serious fiction readers begin to darken CBA stores, which because of their "trinket shop" nature is not a likely scenario. . . .

Lisa Bergren, Executive Editor for WaterBrook Press, the new CBA offshoot of Doubleday, might be expected to tout the feasibility of the crossover novel. But Bergren says, "Crossover novels are rare. Write the novel you're inspired to write, and if it's excellent, and God smiles, it will happen. Until that day, concentrate on your target audience."

I tend to agree with Bergren and Markham. A successful crossover novel is very difficult to accomplish. It's a case of trying to please all the people all the time. If a book has sufficient evangelical content to satisfy a CBA publisher—and, by extension, CBA booksellers and consumers—it is likely to be far too "Christian" for the general market. If it is subtle enough in its portrayal of spiritual issues to find placement in the general market, it will probably be "too generic" for CBA.

I think we need to be realistic in our expectations as we set out to write. We need to determine whether a particular project, by virtue of its subject matter and execution, is appropriate for the CBA market or the general market, and then—as Lisa Bergren advises—write specifically to that audience. Rather than taking a scattergun approach ("I'm writing for all people everywhere"), we will probably be more successful if we target a particular group of readers and a specific publishing market.

When I began work on *Home Fires Burning*, which ultimately became the first in a trilogy of World War II home-front novels for the CBA, I had planned the book as a single novel for the general market. I soon came to realize, however, that the spiritual dimension of the book—the individual faith journeys of my characters—was a vital issue that could neither be eliminated nor underplayed in the development of the book. I went back and redesigned the first hundred pages or so, focusing the novel specifically for the CBA market—and one publisher in particular. I developed plans for two sequels, presented the proposal as a CBA trilogy and was rewarded with a contract. Even more important than the acceptance, however, was the realization that I had found the right niche for this particular story.

Had I written the book with the general market in mind—or if I were to go back now and rewrite it for that market—it would be an entirely different novel. The same characters, perhaps, and the same general plotline, but not the same book.

Time and time again, I've heard the argument that "a good book should be able to stand in either market." Perhaps that's true theoretically, but in real life it almost never works out that way—at least not in the sense that a novel published under a CBA imprint can go into B. Dalton's or Books-A-Million and end up as a best-seller on the *New York Times* list. Of course, we can always cite a few aberrations—the success of Frank Peretti and Bodie Thoene, for example. Their books made it into the general bookstores, but they were usually displayed in the religion section—not the fiction section. In general, New York publishers sell to general bookstores; Christian publishers sell to CBA bookstores. Rarely do publishers have success crossing into one another's territory—and usually only when a CBA book is picked up by a general publisher and distributed under a different imprint, as happened with Jan Karon's Mitford series.

Well-meaning authors often bewail this division of markets: "I want to minister to the unsaved!" they say. "I want to bring the truth to the world, to light a candle in the darkness." And so do we all. But the fact of the matter is that the majority of Christian writers will be read by Christian readers. Even if your books end up on the shelf in Borders or Barnes & Noble, unless there is a compelling general salability to your product, such as with Madeleine L'Engle's books, your novel will most likely be dubbed "Christian fiction" and consigned to the religion section, where most browsers are already looking for a "religious" book.

I know that's not comforting for an author who truly does want to minister to the world at large. But it is the reality of publishing. People don't read fiction primarily to have their values challenged or to seek out new directions in their lives. They read fiction that makes them comfortable, that entertains them or that relates in some way to their own life experiences. Thus, Christian fiction has a viable ministry, but it is typically a ministry to those who already accept its underlying premise. Your fiction may reach a seeker looking for something different, deeper or better in his spiritual life, or may bring new insight or a different perception of God to a struggling new Christian. Your fiction may even lead to an occasional conversion. But if you are writing evangelical fiction and publishing with an evangelical publishing company, the impact of your novel will probably be limited primarily to readers who deliberately seek out a story with Christian values and a Christian worldview.

Occasionally we do see efforts being made to bridge the gap—a big promotion for the new Frank Peretti book in *Publisher's Weekly*, or a drive in the general market for some other big-name author. But we need to remember that the publishing industry operates on the Jerry Maguire principle: "Show me the money!" If a CBA publisher can generate big enough sales for a Christian author, the general publishing world will take notice. Secular bookstores are beginning to acknowledge Christian fiction as a slice of the pie—but it is still a fairly small slice and still labeled "religious" publishing.

And let's get one issue out of the way: There is absolutely nothing wrong or second-rate about being a "religious" or "Christian" writer. It is a high and holy calling, and if we keep our wits about us and our egos in check, it can be a fulfilling and fruitful ministry—and sometimes even a fiscally sound business venture.

But we need to be realistic about who we are ministering to and what the purpose of our fiction writing is. Some authors who pine for crossover success genuinely want to save the lost and give sight to the blind. Others simply want to be successful, and although success is not a sin, greed almost always results in negative consequences.

Saving the lost is a noble sentiment and a valid ministry, but it is not the venue of fiction. Writers who have as their primary motive smuggling the truth of God's word into an unsuspecting reader's heart may unwittingly fall prey to deception and manipulation. Think about Donald Maass's "store" image. If you're selling fruit, advertise it as fruit, and don't try to pull the wool over your customer's eyes by slipping fruit-flavored auto parts into his bag. If you want to preach or proselytize, get a pulpit or write nonfiction. If you want to tell a story, tell it faithfully and trust that the readers who follow your work will be blessed and uplifted by your writing.

Can crossover success happen? Of course it can. But it doesn't happen often, and I believe a wise writer does better to choose a market up front and write specifically for that readership, rather than trying to be all things to all people. With any given book, success in either market is difficult enough: Success in both is a long shot.

COMPLEXITY VS. SIMPLICITY

You've decided that the book you want to write is most appropriate for the CBA market. You've looked around and have a list of potential publishers in the back of your mind. Where do you start in plotting a story that will grip your readers and not let go?

You may, as many authors do, begin your novel with a single plot thread: Joe falls in love with Mary, but she won't have anything to do with him because he isn't part of her social class. Joe goes to college and becomes Dr. Joe, solving the problem, and they ride off into the sunset toward eternal happiness.

For a short romance, that may well be enough—but it is not sufficient to sustain a longer work. You can't build four hundred pages on details of Joe going to medical school and Mary changing her mind about his suitability as a husband.

Most longer, more complex novels are built not on one plotline, but on several. This process is called "texturizing," and it results in the difference between looking at a photograph and seeing a three-dimensional hologram.

Building texture into your novel can often be accomplished by the use of multiple plotlines, or a single primary plotline supported by a series of subplots. In the "Joe and Mary" example, for instance, you could develop a plotline around Mary and a second one around Joe, beginning them separately and then weaving them together as the book progresses. Mary, let's say, is so concerned about social standing because she really isn't what she appears to be. She is hiding the fact that her father is an alcoholic who deserted the family years ago, and her brother is in jail on embezzling charges. Mary has lived all her life without security, and she is determined to get it by marrying a rich man. But in order to do so, she lives a lie—she creates an identity for herself and plays a role.

Joe, meanwhile, is an intelligent man who never finished college because he had to get a job to support his sister, who is chronically ill. Thinking that the only way he can have Mary is to become what she wants him to be, he borrows money from a loan shark so he can get his degree and ultimately enter medical school. Indebted to the gangster, Joe becomes a courier for the mob in a blackmailing scheme against the administrator of the hospital where Joe works.

The main plot, Joe and Mary, has now become a series of complex plotlines: Mary's duplicity and shame, Joe's ill-advised deal with the mob, the administrator's guilt or innocence. When Mary's brother gets out of jail and begins working for the underworld bosses Joe is associated with, the plots are interwoven, and the reader waits breathlessly to find out when and how the complex circumstances of Joe and Mary's lives will work out— or if they will work out at all.

In the final analysis, plot complexity must be commensurate with the magnitude and significance of your book. The amount of complexity your novel can bear will depend, in part, on the length—and on your purposes in writing it. Generally, a shorter novel must be kept simpler, and a longer one will benefit from the texturizing of multiple plotlines and integral subplots.

For a small novel or novella, then, you will want to concentrate on a single plotline with a handful of significant characters who interact with one another. A single plotline cannot bear up under too much intrigue or switchback, or carry too many characters. If your book is simple, keep the plot simple.

For a complex novel, you will probably want to have a couple of parallel plotlines running, as well as subplots within each of the main plots. Consider each of your plotlines as if it were a short novel or novella. Each plotline can usually only bear a handful of significant characters. In a well-developed complex novel, you will find one or two main characters, who carry each subplot, and a group of satellite characters who circle around the main players.

A good example of texturizing a novel through the use of

multiple plotlines can be found in B.J. Hoff's Emerald Ballad series (Bethany House). The first book of the series, *Song of the Silent Harp*, begins in Ireland with a group of characters whose lives have been ravaged by the horrors of the potato famine and the cruelty of their English landlords. Some of the characters emigrate to New York, establishing dual plotlines—"parallel lives." The series then alternates back and forth between the Irish characters and their American counterparts, with the plot ultimately coming together at the end of the series with all the major characters in one location.

Such texturizing does not have to take place on separate continents, of course—the same depth can be achieved by establishing characters in different environments whose lives ultimately intersect for good or ill.

OUTLINING: BLESSING OR CURSE?

Some authors develop detailed and stringent outlines to govern the development of their plotlines, right down to decisions about where the major complications will occur and how many chapters to spend on each subplot. Other writers opt for greater flexibility; they have a general idea of where the book is going, but they feel the need to allow room for unanticipated turns and developments, and for the introduction of characters they hadn't originally envisioned.

A detailed outline has its benefits. When you sit down in front of your computer, you seldom have to worry about where you're going; you simply write the next scene or chapter on the list. But you don't have the option to change directions midstream without going back and reworking your outline. New characters or ideas that come into play during the writing tend to complicate and frustrate the writing process rather than enhance it.

Writing without an outline, or with only a bare-bones structure, gives the author more flexibility and freedom, and sometimes more room for creativity, especially in a character-driven novel. But it also can bring problems: minor characters that "take over" and send the book in an entirely different direction, or unanticipated plot turns that negate, or at the very least complicate, chapters or scenes that have already been written.

The great writers we read and emulate did it both ways. William Faulkner wrote the entire outline for *The Fable* on the walls of his study at Rowan Oak, in Oxford, Mississippi; it is there to this day, open to the view of all visitors who tour his historic home. Flannery O'Connor described her writing process as "sitting down at the typewriter and following her characters around" to see what they would do and say. Even C.S. Lewis contended that the great lion Aslan simply leaped unbidden into his famous Chronicles of Narnia—and the rest, as they say, is history.

Most of the experienced writers I surveyed—Jerry Jenkins, Angela Elwell Hunt, B.J. Hoff and Lurlene McDaniel—report that their so-called "outlines" ranged from a bare-bones idea to a sketchy plot synopsis. "It makes for a lousy proposal," Angela Hunt admits, "but my stories rarely turn out as I originally envisioned them, so only a rough outline does me any good."

Best-selling authors Francine Rivers and Janette Oke, however, do create detailed outlines for their books. "I do an outline in short and then a more detailed 'map,' " Rivers says. "Once done, I put it away. If I get 'lost,' I pull it out to see where the difficulty has arisen."

Janette Oke describes her pattern as outlining "quite extensively. But I also try not to box myself in," she explains, "but to allow for the unexpected to occur while I write. Ideas feed ideas—one must allow creativity to take place."

Of course these writers, unless they are switching to a radically different genre or starting over with an entirely new publisher, usually don't need detailed outlines in order to land a sale. Because of their track record in publishing, acquisition editors eagerly await their next book and will often contract on the sketchiest of ideas. Most of the rest of us are not that fortunate. We may have a great idea, but we have to show some kind of plan in order to sell a publisher on it.

For a book proposal, what we call an "outline" is simply a detailed synopsis, in paragraph form, of the plotline of the story. You may or may not have a chapter-by-chapter timeline and plot plan—in my own writing, chapter summaries usually take shape when I'm about a quarter of the way through the book, and even then they are always subject to reorganization and revision. Editorial committees vary widely in what they need to see in order to be confident enough to offer a contract, but almost every publisher will want some kind of plan or outline for the entire novel, rather than just a few sample chapters.

When it comes to the execution of the plan, however, no one—editor, teacher or fellow writer—can dictate which approach is best for you. If you write without an outline, it is probably to your benefit to have a general idea of where your story is going, even if your plan changes along the way. You will, after all, need that much direction to create a salable proposal. If you are a meticulous planner, go ahead and write your outline, but be prepared to alter it if a brilliant new idea or fascinating character comes along. As Janette Oke pointed out, creativity generates creativity, and the very process of writing may stimulate directions you have never considered.

Whatever decisions you make about your novel—plot-driven or character-driven, CBA or ABA, simple or complex—keep in mind that the *story* must be preeminent. The spiritual truth within you will come out in your novel; you can no more suppress it than you can change the color of your eyes. But it is your story that will captivate readers and keep them turning pages— the story only you can tell as it should be told.

Chapter Five

Miracles, Coincidence and Probability

I believe in miracles. I have, over the course of thirty years as a Christian, even experienced a few firsthand. I see evidence of God's presence and power all around me. But when I encounter miracles in fiction, my hackles go up. All my skepticism rises to the surface, and I mutter under my breath, "Yeah, sure."

I am not alone in my aversion to the miraculous in the pages of a novel. It is one of the potential pitfalls peculiar to the craft of Christian fiction, and one of the issues that makes most editors cringe.

Writers, however—especially young writers—tend to cling to the "reality" argument: "But that's how it really happened! He saw a bright light filling the cell and heard an angel calling to him. . . ."

My response, and the response of a dozen other editors I know, is always the same: "Get out your *Webster's* and read the definition of fiction. What really happened doesn't matter. What matters is whether or not your readers are going to believe it."

Fiction is, by its very nature and definition, a product of the author's imagination. We take a germ of reality—some experience in our own lives or in the life of someone we know, or something we have latched onto through our reading—and out of that experience create a story that goes far beyond what "really happened."

I'll use the example of my first novel in the Home Front series, because I understand from the inside what the process was in developing the book. *Home Fires Burning* is the story of a Yankee soldier and a Southern belle, a young couple from vastly different worlds who meet and fall in love during the early years of World War II. The germ of the novel has its source in my parents' lives—my father was stationed at an army base in Mississippi and met my mother at a USO dance, then was shipped overseas, wounded in France, and ultimately came home to marry her.

That is the basic story, and it's a typically romantic, nostalgic one. As a child, I listened to my parents talk about the war years, about the uncertainties and the difficulties they faced when my father came home in a body cast. And perhaps, even at that young age, I knew this would make a good novel.

But it wasn't enough just to tell their story. I could have done that in a ten-page magazine article. The novel had to be more—richer and deeper, with more complications and an enhanced spiritual dimension. I didn't know firsthand what my parents were like in their twenties; that characterization was derived from my imagination. My grandfather was a headstrong man, but not in any way the manipulating monster developed in the characterization of Robinson Coltrain. My mother's experience was quite different than that of her character in the book—she actually had information about my father's condition long before her character Libba does. But for the sake of drama, I kept Libba in the dark as long as possible.

Fiction is based on truth—the universal truths about human struggle and development, and the common problems we share in learning to trust, love and depend upon God during dark times of our lives. But fiction is not based on what really happened. A novel goes beyond the reality of an event to its deeper, universal significance, which can be shared by a multitude of readers and applied to their own widely diverse life experiences.

This is no excuse, of course, for slipshod research, illogical development or poor characterization. I once read an interview with a popular writer of historical fiction (who shall remain nameless). This author said, "Writing a historical novel is fun. If I don't know something, I just make it up."

No. We don't just make it up.

If we're determined to give attention to our craft, we research all manner of details—what model of car Cadillac was producing in 1943, whether or not the song that runs through a character's mind had actually hit the charts at the time, what kind of shoes the heroine would wear in the summer, what radio shows aired on Sunday evening and at what time.

We don't make up historical details. We make up characters, their motivations and struggles, the complications of their lives, the ultimate resolutions, and the plot twists and turns that keep our readers interested.

And everything we make up as fiction writers must be based on a single principle: *probability*.

ESTABLISHING PROBABILITY

Whether you are writing a character-driven novel or a plot-driven story, the one element that is essential to the "vivid, continuous dream of fiction" is probability.

Not possibility, but probability.

Fiction writers deal with the *impossible* all the time: fantasy, science fiction, the supernatural and created worlds that have no established roots in what we call "reality." But within those unreal worlds, the actions and motives of the characters, and the directions and complications of the plot, must always be probable.

C.S. Lewis's Chronicles of Narnia, for example, is a series of books based on the impossible: a magic wardrobe that lets children into the land of Narnia; a huge and benevolent lion who rules the land; a collection of talking animals, unicorns, elves, fauns and other mythological creatures. It's impossible—no rational human reader would believe that Narnia truly exists. But it is imminently *probable*. For within the boundaries of Narnia, talking dogs still wag their doggy tails, bears are slow and a little stupid, and Mr. and Mrs. Beaver live in a cozy little lodge underneath their dam. Even the impossible characters behave in a probable, believable way.

Probability is the key to believable fiction. C.S. Lewis's beavers are faithful; unicorns are noble, and you don't ride them except in case of emergency; and Aslan is no tame lion. Tolkein's hobbits have furry feet and enjoy roasted eggs at teatime. It's impossible, but it works. We believe it, and we are enchanted.

The principle of probability applies to every aspect of a work of fiction: plot, character, dialogue, setting, spiritual development and resolution. Get into the habit of asking yourself the questions your editor will ask while working through your manuscript:

- Would this character really use an expression like that?
- Does the hero have time to get to the scene of the rescue if he has to drive seventy miles over icy roads?
- How is the house laid out? Could the intruder get in without being heard?
- Why did the lights suddenly go out?
- Why does the heroine begin spouting scripture immediately after her conversion, even though she has no previously established religious background?

In his great work *The Poetics*, Aristotle says that in literature, a *probable impossibility* is more believable than an *improbable possibility*.

We can expect readers to "suspend their disbelief" and accept the impossible, if we have given them sufficient reason to do so. But we can never expect readers to accept the improbable. A character must make decisions according to probable motivation; action must occur in a believable fashion, in logical time sequence and with proper precedence. Readers may be led to believe that pigs can fly, but even flying pigs say "Oink."

COINCIDENCE AND OTHER ATTRACTIVE SNARES

If probability governs the development of plot and character, what happens to your characters and within them will be believable to the reader, even within the realm of the "impossible." Let's face it: Miracles do happen, and coincidence often plays a part in human experience. But in fiction, readers are likely to be suspicious of the miracle that saves the hero at the eleventh hour, or of the coincidence that just happens to place a character in the right place at the right time.

In classical drama, the resolution to a difficult problem was sometimes accomplished by one of the gods sweeping down onto the stage, righting all the wrongs and administering justice to the evildoers. Because the "god" character was often brought on stage in a cart or lowered from above on a rudimentary pulley system, this technique became known as *deus ex machina*: "god out of the machine."

Christian writers, especially, face the temptation to resort to deus-ex-machina endings. We call them "miracles"—the coincidence that is just a bit too coincidental to be believable, the hand of God altering circumstances or changing people in an instantaneous flash of lightning, or the "act of God" (as insurance companies call natural disasters) that frees the hero from an impossible situation.

Manipulating Miracles

In the hundreds of novels I've reviewed and edited over the years, I've seen almost every conceivable manifestation of the miraculous in Christian fiction. I've seen the heavens open and angelic messengers come down to rescue a character facing death. I've witnessed instantaneous answers to prayer, voices whispering in the night, and even dogs and horses leading their masters in the right direction. Certainly, if God could speak to the prophet Balaam through a donkey, couldn't the Lord just as easily use a horse or a dog to warn a character of impending danger? It's possible.

But it's not probable, unless all the dogs and horses in your novel are as articulate and intelligent as the animals who populate Narnia. It's not believable.

We may trust in miracles in our personal lives of faith; we may even have experienced them for ourselves. But in general, when authors manipulate the miraculous for their own purposes in fiction, readers perceive it as a cheap shot and feel cheated out of a rational resolution.

"But part of the Christian experience is the reality of God's work in difficult situations!" writers argue. "I've seen miracles in my own life; why can't I have them in my characters' lives?"

The answer is, you can. But you have to be very careful about how you portray those miracles in your fiction. It's one thing to have an account of a miracle in a straightforward nonfiction book—Jesus turning water into wine at the Cana wedding, for example, or a story in *Guideposts* about an angel who appeared to rescue a child from a burning house. Those stories are not (we assume) fiction, and therefore we are more inclined to give them credence. But fiction is by its very name and nature made up; that is, a product of the author's imagination. To employ the miraculous in fiction the same way you would relate it in nonfiction opens a writer up to a thousand arguments from skeptical readers. In nonfiction, the basic premise is reality—we begin by believing the story is true, and so we are inclined to accept the miraculous turn in the story as also true. In fiction, the basic premise is that the story is made up, so miraculous events come across as less believable.

Consider, too, the Biblical accounts of the miraculous. Did the people at the wedding stand around "oohing" and "ahhing" over Jesus' miracle of water to wine? Probably not. They probably just drank a toast to the bride and groom and didn't give the wine a second thought. The interpretation of the miracle came from the believers who witnessed the event. When Jesus was baptized and the voice of God spoke from the clouds, most people who heard it thought it was thunder, not the word of the Almighty. When Jesus healed people, the Pharisees wrote it off as coincidence or fraud. Even that greatest of miracles, the Resurrection, has for centuries been surrounded by disbelief, doubt and accusations of manipulation.

The point is, most of what we call "miraculous" in daily life is a matter of interpretation. I believe that God works in people's lives all the time, but we rarely see miracles because we rarely have our eyes open to the Lord's activity. When we look for miracles, we see them, even if those around us see only ordinary events that worked out well.

Most daily miracles are simple, unexplained mysteries—the kind of ambiguity common to human life. How did it happen that I met the love of my life a thousand miles from home on a spontaneous, unanticipated vacation trip? How did I escape what seemed to be certain death in that automobile accident? How did I manage to be in the right place at the right time to land my dream job? For the Christian, the answer may lie in the unseen hand of God; for the bystander, it was just the luck of the draw.

As writers, we need to understand that when miracles do happen, they are considered miraculous primarily from the perspective of the one who experiences them—in the case of fiction, the characters involved. To everyone else around, they may be interpreted as luck, a fortunate turn of events or a fluke. If you intend to use a miracle in a character's life, the key to believability is to make sure that your readers make the interpretation of the miraculous for themselves—that they discover the unseen hand of God rather than having it pointed out to them. If your character clasps her hands and raises her eyes to heaven, shouting "Praise God, I'm healed!" then you, as the writer, are imposing the interpretation on your readers and not allowing them to participate in the wonder of the miracle.

Never underestimate the power of deliberate ambiguity in your writing. Tell the story. Show the mystery. And let your readers conclude that a miracle has, indeed, taken place. The dramatic effect will be much stronger and more believable if you let your readers uncover the power of God for themselves.

The Coincidence Crutch

Coincidence is a tricky issue in fiction. Readers may believe without question that the hero and heroine just happen to bump into each other on a crowded subway platform. They may accept a multitude of coincidences that complicate the lives of the characters. But when it comes to resolution of those complications, coincidence is quicksand.

Part of the writer's responsibility is to structure the plot and the character motivations in such a way that the whole novel moves seamlessly—that "vivid and continuous dream" that John Gardner refers to. It's not difficult, as a writer, to paint yourself into a corner by putting your characters into circumstances with no logical exit, or by twisting the plot into a Gordian knot. I've done it countless times—and so have most of the other writers I know. When that happens, we need to go back and rethink the character or the action—to revise, rewrite and work it out, not simply send down an archangel to rectify the situation.

The principle is a simple one: You may use coincidence to get your characters *into* trouble; you may not use it to get them *out* of trouble.

Miracles and coincidence are not the only snares that threaten the fiction writer. As you plan the development of your novel, you should be aware of a number of other traps that present themselves to most authors along the way. Some of these traps apply to any kind of fiction; some of them are particular problems that face writers who include significant spiritual content in their work.

Overly Complex Movements

Even in a long and complex novel, a writer can fall into the trap of making the story unnecessarily complicated for the reader. One novel I edited introduced ten major characters, with all their life history, in the very first chapter! I felt like reminding the author, "You can't tell the players without a program."

Readers should not be required to sit with a pad and pen, writing down settings, character names and plot developments, in order to be able to follow the flow of your story. Multiple setting changes, rapid shifts between plotlines or subplots, or the introduction of too many "major" characters can confuse the reader and make following your plot difficult and frustrating. Don't try to amaze your readers with your ability to juggle; throw out one ball at a time, and let readers get accustomed to the characters and plot shifts gradually.

Simplistic Resolutions

On the other end of the spectrum, some writers make their plots so simplistic that they present no challenge at all to the mental or emotional faculties of their readers. Boy meets girl, boy falls in love, girl rejects him because he's not a Christian, he experiences a wonderful conversion, they marry and live happily ever after. I've read a number of such books, none of them interesting enough to hold my attention—the kind of novel, as one editor friend of mine has said, "that I wouldn't read unless I was paid to do so, and even then it's pretty difficult."

It's not always wise to tie up every thread of your plot neatly at the end of the book, especially if you're writing a series and want your readers to buy book two. Life is seldom neat; it is a messy business with a lot of loose ends. Although you want your readers to feel fulfilled and to have a sense of satisfactory conclusion, your plot resolutions must grow naturally out of the action and characterization of the story itself. Beware of easy answers, especially easy religious answers. Your readers will rise up in righteous indignation.

Pollyanna Plotlines

A third pitfall of plotting the writer faces is the temptation to make things too easy for the hero or heroine. Good fiction is based on *dramatic tension*; unless life is difficult for your characters, you have no story.

Remember Pollyanna, the children's story character? Pollyanna was pert and chipper, ever happy and positive. She always thought the best of people and always knew that everything would work out all right. And it did. Or at least so the stories told us.

The Pollyanna mentality may be fine for a children's book (although I don't know many ten-year-olds in this generation who have such an unrealistic view of life), but it will never work for a novel aimed at adults—even Christian adults.

First Lesson, Religious Reality 101: Life is not easy, and the answers to life's difficult questions are not always simple, even when we believe God is on our side. As Christian writers, we have a responsibility to portray the faith issues in our novels in a balanced, realistic way. Coming to Jesus does not solve all our problems. It gives us hope, certainly, and freedom, and a source of support beyond ourselves, but it does not wipe away all the struggles of human existence.

Those very struggles give life and power to our fiction.

MAKING IT WORSE

I recently edited a book in which the supposed dramatic tension of the story centered around the main character—whether she should engage in a morally questionable activity that would further her long-dreamed-of career. The problem was, there was no problem. The heroine was a devoted Christian who had lived her entire life in obedience to God. There was no question in the reader's mind that she would make the "right" decision, and that God would ultimately reward her for her obedience.

I presented this dilemma to the author, and in a number of telephone conversations and letters we discussed the issue. "Make it worse," I advised her. "Find a way to have a real crisis of faith and honor in this character's life—not just a simple moral speed bump with an already-established answer." To the author's credit, she came to understand why the heroine's conflict was insufficient to support the story line. Eventually she went back and rewrote most of the novel, giving the central character a *real* moral dilemma and circumstances that caused the heroine to question her own commitment to her career. The result? A much stronger book, one capable of holding the reader's interest to the end.

I faced the same kind of problem in the third book of my Home Front series, and found myself (much to my chagrin), having to take my own advice. The primary plotline of *Remembering You* is the story of Owen Slaughter, a soldier who, after an extended stay in a German prison camp, returns to the States with trauma-induced amnesia. My problem was, the war in Europe was over, and thus the main source of texture in the first two novels—the home front vs. the battle front—had been eliminated. I had to find some way to add dramatic tension to the story, particularly to the developing romance between Owen and his sweetheart.

So I began to "make it worse." I sent Owen to his hometown, to a place he couldn't remember and relatives he didn't know he had, on a quest to rediscover himself and find his memories. And in the process, much to my surprise, someone else was waiting for him in Iowa—a high school girlfriend with a six-year-old son she claimed was Owen's child.

The difficulty that builds interest and dramatic tension in a story can come in two basic ways: through plot complications or through character struggle. In plotting, an author seeks to put the character in a dangerous or trying situation, and then make it worse . . . and still worse . . . until the situation is nearly the worst it can be. And just when the characters (and the readers) think they are coming to an escape, something else happens to complicate the resolution even further. The principle? The light at the end of the tunnel is a freight train coming your way.

INTEGRITY AND FAITH

Many years ago, I read a Christian novel that troubled me immensely. Something was wrong, something I couldn't quite put my finger on.

Then I began to look more closely. This particular book was a mystery, a plot-driven novel. But the "spiritual" elements of the story didn't seem to fit. The characters said Grace before meals, made reference to scripture, prayed and attended church services, but all the "religious" elements so prominent throughout the book didn't make one iota of difference in their lives, in the ways they conducted their business within the context of the story.

I took a highlighter and went back through the book, marking every single passage that included some reference to religious activity, and then I read the book again, skipping the highlighted parts. Eliminating the "religious" material made no difference in the story whatsoever, either in the plot or in the development of the characters.

Aspiring novelists at writers conferences often ask the same question: How do you put religious themes and images into your story?

The answer is, you don't.

In the Christian life, we talk a lot about *integrity*, about how our actions should reflect our inner lives and how the fruit of the Spirit grows from deep within us. Those around us can tell whether or not our religious beliefs permeate our lives or are just tacked on for show. There's a word for people who claim to believe one way while living another: hypocrite.

Integrity is important if we expect people to respect our faith and trust our relationship with God. And for the Christian writer, integrity includes how we deal with the spiritual or religious elements in our writing.

The word "integrity" stems from the same Latin base as the word "integrate," and means to make whole or complete by bringing all parts together, indivisible. Integrity in Christian writing means that all elements of the novel, including the religious or spiritual dimensions, derive from within the fabric of the work, and from within our own lives as spiritual beings. We do not "put in" religious elements or images; they grow naturally from the characters and events of the novel.

If you can eliminate the religious aspects of your novel, making it a secular or general novel simply by removing all the God-talk, you have not written a novel with integrity. You have tacked on religious elements for show, to please a CBA publisher or satisfy a Christian reader. It's like pasting paper fruit onto a cardboard tree: It may look good from a distance, at least for a while, but it won't grow, it won't reproduce and it won't nourish anyone who comes to eat from it.

True spiritual content in a novel grows out of the story from deep within, the way sap rises up through the root system of a tree to produce leaves and flowers and fruit. Whatever divine imagery infuses your novel, whatever spiritual themes appear, should come naturally, out of the reservoirs of your own experience with God—and they must fit with your characters' spiritual experience.

Integral Christian faith will show in your work, whether you deliberately plan it or not. It comes out not in overt evangelization, but in a subtle undercurrent of spiritual truth: characters who find hope in the midst of despair, or darkness that is dispelled by the presence of light.

I believe in God, in the power of Christ's presence in my life and the work of the Holy Spirit. Because of that faith, whether I am writing a nonfiction book, a series for a Christian publisher or a novel for the general market, my faith will come out in what I write. It may be proclaimed boldly or whispered quietly, but it will show. I cannot repress it any more than I can stifle my perspective as a woman or disclaim my heritage.

Readers know the difference between religiosity that is pasted on and true spirituality that rises from deep within. They can discern integrity, even if they cannot articulate what it is. And they are looking for real fruit—the kind of spiritual truth that is rooted in reality and natural to the characters and plotlines we ask them to accept.

It's not enough to have characters who pray, preach and sing gospel songs. We must work to create living, breathing spiritual beings who grapple with the hard questions of life and find, if not answers, at least hope in the reality of God's presence in the world.

The Christian writer, above all else, has certain responsibilities, both to the reader and to the work, to present a quality story. A story worth reading. A story not cheapened by easy answers or simplistic resolutions. A story rich in drama and satisfying in conclusion. A story marked by spiritual integrity, meticulously crafted and bearing eternal significance.

Our readers deserve that much, and if we give it to them, our stories can touch not only their minds, but also their hearts and souls.

Chapter Six

God's Word Is a Lamp, Not a Leash

Avoiding Propaganda

Many of us learned the verse as little children in Sunday School: "Thy word is a lamp unto my feet and a light unto my path." (Psalm 119:105, KJV) It's a verse that gives comfort and hope in times of struggle, when we can't see the way and have to trust God in the darkness. It's a good verse for Christian writers, too—a verse that should be engraved upon our hearts, cross-stitched and hung over the door. A verse that can guide and direct our writing. God's word is a lamp.

A lamp provides a limited circle of light, just enough to see the next step. We move into the circle, and the lamp illuminates a tiny bit of what's ahead, just enough to keep us on the path. God's word is not a floodlight, brightening ten miles of highway, or a series of mirrors that enables us to see around the bends in the road. It's not a leash that drags us this way and that, or a prod that makes us go in a particular direction despite our better judgment. It's a lamp: a faint glimmering candle that dispels just enough of the darkness to give us hope and direction.

Our writing should be like that—a candle in the dark. Our plots should nudge our readers gently in the right direction, so subtly that they are unaware of being led, with just enough illumination that they can discover the way for themselves.

Our responsibility as novelists in Christian fiction is not to bludgeon readers with our version of the truth or manipulate them into seeing things our way. We don't shine a floodlight into their eyes and demand that they understand and repeat back the "right" interpretation. We don't collar them and jerk them into awareness. We light the lamp and hand it over, and then let them make their way one step at a time.

One of the greatest temptations for Christian writers is to have a preconceived idea of what great spiritual truths our readers should glean from the work. We desperately want them to understand, and so we set up neon road markers to point the way to the religious "themes" of the novel. "Get it?" we shout. "This is the way a Christian is supposed to live!"

But the purpose of fiction is not to teach a lesson, preach a sermon, convey the message of salvation or set up guidelines for Christlike living. The purpose of fiction is to tell a story. The purpose of reading fiction is to be immersed in the lives and experiences of the characters. Any spiritual insights that take place in the reader happen subliminally, not overtly.

Years ago, when I was teaching English literature in college, I spent several days discussing the poetry of William Wordsworth—a particular favorite of mine and the subject of my Master's thesis. I had several extraordinarily bright students in my class, and for three days we talked about Wordsworth's fine imagery, his mastery of poetic technique, his reverence of God and nature and his deep understanding of spiritual truth. At the end of one class, a hulking halfback stopped me at the door. He scratched his head and frowned. "Ya know," he said, "I don't much understand all the stuff we been talking about, but I do get one thing about this Wordsworth guy. He sure paints pretty pictures with his words."

That football player taught me a new perspective on poetry: Poets paint pretty pictures with their words.

If we want to write quality fiction, fiction that will grab our readers by the heart and not let go, we must never let the *message* take precedence over the *medium*. We must trust our readers to find their own truth in our words, and trust God to lead them, one step at a time, in the way they need to go—not in the way we *think* they need to go.

EMULATING GOD'S DIRECTION

Twenty years ago, I thought I had a pretty good handle on spiritual truth. I was more than willing, both in person and in my writing, to give other people advice on how to live their lives as Christians. I wrote nonfiction books and articles, taught Bible classes and set up study courses to give others the benefit of my vast spiritual experience. I knew how it needed to be done, and

I passed on that knowledge to anyone who would listen.

Today, I'm a lot more reticent to pass out unsolicited advice and tell other people what they should do. Maybe it's maturity. Maybe it's twenty years of seeing my own well-crafted structures fail me. Whatever the reason, I've come to realize that God has individual ways of dealing with individual people. If I trust God in my own life, I must also trust that God is willing and able to lead someone else, even if God's direction takes that person in a way I might not choose to go.

That conviction has resulted in a radical change in my writing, both fiction and nonfiction. The nonfiction I write today is much more open-ended, not telling readers what to do or how to do it, but encouraging them to hold onto their hope, to seek God for themselves and to find their own spiritual paths. My fiction is more realistic, showing the kind of doubts, struggles and spiritual dilemmas all of us face in real life, offering life and hope in unexpected places.

Consider the way God leads us into truth. The Lord does not badger or push us into a relationship, but extends grace and gives us choice: "I have set before you today life and death, blessings and curses. . . . Choose life" (Deuteronomy 30:19, NRSV).

Perhaps the most fundamental demonstration of God's approach to leading us appears in the person of Christ. "The law," John says, "was given through Moses; grace and truth came through Jesus Christ" (John 1:17, NRSV). God *told* us what was expected through the Law; God *showed* us the Divine nature in the incarnation of Jesus Christ.

And Jesus' earthly ministry provides us with an example to follow in our own work. Jesus didn't browbeat people or give them a list of requirements for godliness. He walked among them, lived with them, shared their joys and sorrows, broke bread with them, danced at their weddings and wept at their funerals. He raised more questions than answers—disturbing questions like "Who is my neighbor?" "What does this mean?" "Are you the Messiah who is to come?" And his answers were almost always riddles: "What do you think it means? Who do you say that I am?"

Jesus revealed himself through his presence and allowed people to come to him in their own way—alone or in a crowd, at noon when the well was deserted or at night when no one would see. If our writing does the same—demonstrating truth in our characters' lives and allowing our readers to draw their own conclusions—our work will have a much greater and more lasting impact upon our readers.

The best, most effective novels I have read in more than fifteen years in the Christian publishing industry are not those which loudly proclaim "The Way" or insist that the reader agree with the writer's perspectives on truth, but those that subtly, and with finesse, *demonstrate* the reality of God in the characters' lives. In fiction, as in life, we learn more by example than we do by precept.

SHOWING VS. TELLING

The principle of demonstrating God's grace rather than browbeating people into accepting the truth applies in very practical ways to the creation of Christian fiction. Most creative writing teachers tell their students that one inviolable principle of fiction writing is "show, don't tell." This principle, although basically sound advice, often confuses would-be fiction writers because they are not told how to determine what to show and what to tell.

A few years ago, a filmmaker undertook an ambitious and unusual project. In an attempt to chronicle everyday life, he set up a camera in a family home and filmed all the interactions of the family unit. The result was, as one might expect, a long, tedious and extremely boring film . . . hour upon hour of footage that recorded people walking around, sitting in front of the television and saying "Huh?" and "OK" to each other.

Let's face it—everything in life is not intrinsically interesting. There is a lot of glue that holds the fascinating parts together. And although the glue may be necessary, it is not the stuff of which great fiction is made. As Elmore Leonard, quoted in *The Writer's Quotation Book*, said "I try to leave out the parts that people skip."

Herein lies the principle that governs showing vs. telling: Try to leave out the parts that people skip—or at least relate the information as quickly as possible.

Information Overload

If you attempt to show everything that happens, both in physical action and in the characters' inner struggles, you will probably end up with a twelve-volume novel (the never-ending story) comprised mostly of glue. The "glue" in a story sometimes reads like this:

> John lay on the bed for a long time, his arm thrown over his face, his feet, clad in navy-and-red argyle socks, dangling off the end of the mattress. At last he decided that he had to get up, whether he felt like it or not. He groaned, propped himself up on one elbow and slowly swung his feet over the side of the bed. He felt for his slippers, slid his feet into them and rose. Running a hand through his thinning hair, he went to the window, put his hand to the shade, opened it and looked out. Then he turned away from the window, shuffled across the room, opened the door and stumbled out into the hall.

Only in very rare cases do we really need all this detail about John's every movement. Such detail shows the scene, certainly, but the reader quickly becomes impatient with it and begins to skip over it to get on with the story. If you haven't made a habit of boring the reader with unnecessary details and descriptions of daily activities, when these details do appear in your book, your readers will take them seriously, expecting that there is some reason for them to be there, some clue to the action or character that the reader needs to know.

Good writing is an exercise in elimination. Everything that does not advance your story or develop your characters in a significant way should be cut—brutally and without mercy. Think of your novel as a series of scenes. You will want to *show* in dramatic form those scenes that enhance the movement of the book or enrich the characters' relationships. Background information can usually be told through a character's viewpoint.

The "showing" scenes focus the novel on what is most important to the reader. As John Gardner says in *On Becoming a Novelist*:

> Instead of writing, "She felt terrible," (the writer) can show—by the precise gesture or look, or by capturing the

character's exact turn of phrase—subtle nuances of the character's feeling. . . . The precise gesture nails down the one right feeling for the moment. This is what is meant when writing teachers say that one should "show," not "tell." And this, it should be added, is *all* that the writing teacher means. Good writers may "tell" almost anything in fiction except the characters' feelings. . . . With rare exceptions the characters' feelings must be demonstrated: fear, love, excitement, doubt, embarrassment, despair become real only when they take the form of events—action (or gesture), dialogue, or physical reaction to setting.

Flashback

Writers often resort to flashback in an attempt to show something significant (or not so significant) about a character's background. Sometimes writers think of flashback as an avant-garde addition to their writing, a way to get across important information in an "artsy" manner. But anything out of chronological order is necessarily telling rather than showing, because it is not part of the ongoing movement of the story. Among other problems associated with flashback, the technique removes the reader at least one notch away from the immediacy of the experience.

Another excellent teacher of writing, Carol Bly, advocates the use of chronological order and the avoidance of flashback in her book, *The Passionate, Accurate Story:*

> If a story happens in its chronological order, the reader is free of the interior voice of any character remembering events: For the reader, this means having only his or her self, so the reader feels *there*, savoring the ambiance of whatever strange scenes are offered. C.S. Lewis was right in saying whatever else we want of fiction, we want to be taken away! away!
>
> And fast.
>
> It's wise to think of the flashback as a structure weakener: You can do more of it if other elements are especially strong. If you do too much of it, you have amateurish, self-centered literature. It's like overwatering concrete: You can water it heavily, which makes it easy to mold and handle, but if you do, the mortar-to-sand ratio should be extra-strong.

There are ways, of course, to employ flashback effectively, but if the technique is used, you must take care to be absolutely clear to the reader what you're doing—where the flashback begins and ends, and why it is important at this particular place in your story. Rapid and unexplained shifts irritate readers, and sometimes confuse them. The last thing you want to do in a novel is interrupt the "vivid and continuous dream" by making your reader go back and reread to get your point.

If you absolutely need a flashback scene, you may be able to mark it in the manuscript by the use of italics, a different typeface and/or hiatus marks (a space in the text, usually accompanied by a dingbat, that signifies a shift in time, location or viewpoint). Many publishers, however, are moving away from including long sections of italics in their books, and a lot of editors resist flashbacks for the reasons we've already discussed. A better approach might be to break up the flashback information and include it in shorter segments from your character's viewpoint.

First Person

One additional note about the "showing vs. telling" dilemma: The first-person point of view, by its very nature, confines the author to an inordinate amount of telling rather than showing. Because everything in first person must be filtered through the narrating character's eyes, first-person viewpoint is essentially a "telling" form. The reader is always reminded of the intrusion of the narrative *I* into the story, and thus the use of the first-person perspective can easily interrupt the "vivid, continuous dream" of fiction.

SETTING AND USE OF DETAIL

One of the most problematic issues facing a writer developing a novel is the decision about setting and detail. How much description of setting is necessary and appropriate? How much physical description of characters is needed? And, in a historical novel, how much historical information should be included?

These are difficult questions, and the best answer is not a particularly specific one: You need enough, but not too much. Many writers tend to overuse detail, thinking that their readers will be interested in every angle of the setting, in every historical tidbit that the author has unearthed in months of research and in every nuance of a character's eyes, hair, body stance and gesture. Certainly, the author will know a lot about the characters, the setting, the offstage action and the plot development—information that readers may never see. But if they see too much and are given too much unnecessary information to digest, the book may become, as one editor described it, "The kind of novel I put down and just can't pick up again."

Detail, of course, is the lifeblood of fiction. But it must be *significant* detail that communicates important issues of plot and characterization to your reader. Too much unrelated detail just gets in the way of your story. You don't need to give the reader a close-up view of every leaf, flower, blade of grass and cloud in your opening scene. Even a classic like *Moby Dick* might be improved by a little less attention to whale behavior; the reader of *Ivanhoe* generally doesn't care about the springiness of the turf under the horse's hooves as it gallops along.

Many capable writers lose their readers in the first chapter by opening the novel with vast, intricate physical descriptions of setting or tedious historical background. A few years ago I was asked to edit a historical novel by an experienced writer. When I opened the manuscript, I found myself faced with a 37-page prologue of pure background—the kind of historical information (names, dates, battles and political movements) that puts high school sophomores to sleep in a heartbeat.

I labored over that prologue, finally cutting it down to a streamlined seven pages designed to stimulate readers' imaginations without atrophying their brains. But when the book was released, there was the original 37-page prologue, intact and unedited. The author, I was told, adamantly insisted upon retaining it, even with the admission that most readers would skip over it or get bogged down in it. The writer didn't care whether it would interest the reader or not; it interested him, and that was all that mattered.

But the reader's opinion *does* matter, at least up to a point. I have heard editors say that you have a maximum of five minutes to capture and hold a reader's attention. If the first chapter, or even the first page of the first chapter, doesn't do it, you're likely to lose that reader and hundreds more just like her. As William Zinsser says in *On Writing Well*:

The most important sentence in any article (or story) is the first one. If it doesn't induce the reader to proceed to the second sentence, your article is dead. . . . I urge you not to count on the reader to stick around. He is a fidgety fellow who wants to know—very soon—what's in it for him.

Perhaps that is why the classical writers usually began their epic poems *in medias res*—"in the middle of things." You may not be writing a plot-driven novel that begins on the back of a galloping horse, but even character-driven novels should begin with somebody doing something—preferably something interesting, something that has significance to the development of the story. Necessary physical descriptions of the setting (identifications of where the action is taking place, what the scene looks like and how the surrounding characters relate to the hero or heroine) can be worked in gradually, preferably through the viewpoint of one of the main characters.

Similarly, physical descriptions of people are best kept to a minimum, and are most effectively accomplished through the eyes of another character. Fiction is built on detail—not just any detail, but the kind of detail that advances the movement of the story, reveals significant information about the personalities of the characters and provides necessary dramatic tension. If the hero has a scar that becomes a trademark of his character, describe it. If the decor of the parlor reflects the bad taste of a woman who is supposed to be an elegant society lady, it is pertinent and should be included. But physical descriptions of a granite jaw, sea-blue eyes, Gothic architecture or Danish Modern furniture do not, by themselves, add to the reader's understanding of the book.

We might think of physical description as a travel photograph. If you go down into the Grand Canyon, stand on the bank of the river and have a friend take a photo from the rim, you'll have a lot of physical description, but little significance. You'll have to point to yourself and say, "See that dot? That's me!"

But if your friend takes the photo from the back of a mule or from the stern of a river raft as it goes over the rapids, you have a picture that captures a significant moment of your holiday. Physical description in fiction works best when it becomes part of the backdrop of action or character development, rather than standing by itself in a panoramic view.

When you walk into a room full of strangers, what do you see? Chances are, your mind does not immediately register all the details of the decor, where the furniture is located, what kind of crown molding graces the ceiling or the specific crystal pattern of the champagne glasses. You don't hear clearly articulated conversation, just a buzz. You may notice one woman's bright scarf or one man's bald head, but you don't see everything all at once. You take in detail one bit at a time, processing it as to its importance and retaining only what you really need. If you're an introvert, uncomfortable in social situations, you scope out the location of the nearest exit, seek out a potted plant to hide behind or frantically look for a familiar face. If you're hoping to find a date, you focus on the left hand of the attractive woman in the corner to discern whether or not she's spoken for. If you're allergic to shrimp, you study the hors d'oeuvres table.

The principle is clear: *If the reader doesn't need it or the character wouldn't notice it, don't include it.* If the reader *does* need it, work your description in from a character's viewpoint. Feed your readers physical detail a little at a time rather than overwhelming them with page after page of scenery that won't mean anything to them.

God's word is a lamp unto our feet, a light unto our paths. In like manner, our words—carefully selected detail, historical information, character descriptions, plot developments and subtle spiritual truths—help guide and direct the reader into the imaginative world we have created.

The purpose of Christian fiction is not to leash readers and drag them to the author's perspective, but to offer them images of life and of God's real presence in the world, which will draw them to a deeper insight of their own. We can trust our readers to find in the pages of our work what they need to find. And we can trust God to be part of that process as well.

Writing a gripping novel takes a great deal of work, foresight, planning, flexibility and ongoing development. But if you give attention to the planning up front, you will save yourself frustration and—perhaps—rejection. You will create a "vivid, continuous dream" that captivates your readers and will not let go.

PART THREE

Can These Bones Live?

Chapter Seven

Breathing the Breath of Life

The Birth of a Character

Remember the prophet Ezekiel?
For twenty-two years Ezekiel prophesied to the captives in Babylon, messages of judgment to the false prophets and messages of ultimate restoration. But the promise of a new Israel seemed like little more than a shattered dream. Then one day God led Ezekiel out to the Valley of the Dry Bones. It was quite an object lesson.

"Mortal, can these bones live?" God asked.

"O Lord God, you know," Ezekiel answered—a wise answer, because of course Ezekiel had no idea whether they could or not.

And then before his eyes, under the power of his own words, the prophet watched as the bones rattled, rose up, assembled themselves and took on ligament and muscle and skin. At God's command he called to the winds to breathe into them the breath of life, and they stood up a mighty army (Ezekiel 37:1-14).

Sometimes, as fiction writers, we look at our characters, the people who represent life to our novel, and see only a pile of dry bones. And we cry out, "Can these bones live?"—hoping the answer is "Yes."

Characters are the heart of fiction.

If you intend to write a memorable novel, you must give serious and careful attention to the development of your characters. They are not merely puppets who go through the motions of your plot—if they are, they won't be very interesting. Even in a plot-driven novel, and especially in a character-driven one, fictional characters must live and breathe; they must jump off the page and become so fascinating that your readers can never forget them.

Consider some of the great characters of literature: King Lear,

Othello, Romeo and Juliet, David Copperfield, Oliver Twist, Simon Legree, Hester Prynne and Arthur Dimmsdale, Sherlock Holmes and Dr. Watson. These characters are so memorable that their names have become synonymous with their personalities or choices. They have become *real*.

Whether you are writing a plot-driven or a character-driven novel, you cannot afford to shortchange your readers in characterization. Many a plot-driven novel has fallen short because the author, concentrating on the twists and turns of the action and intrigue, gave little attention to the viability of the characters. And although the plot may have been fascinating, the novel does not stand up under multiple readings because nothing significant is happening within the hearts and minds of the characters.

Without intriguing characters, plot is simply an interconnected series of actions. Readers may care what happens, purely for curiosity's sake, but they won't care much about the people in the novel. Ian Fleming's 007 novels, for example, would still be interesting, but not nearly as memorable, without the presence of James Bond. When characters are used to follow a trail or move through a maze of interesting developments, but have no life of their own, the result for the reader is a temporary interest, not a lifelong fascination.

Characters make the difference between a novel that goes up like a skyrocket but has no enduring value, and one with a long shelf life and generations of readers. Books with memorable characters bear up under a second (or third or fourth) reading. Once the reader knows what the plot resolution is, a novel with one-dimensional characters loses its appeal.

THE RELATIONSHIP BETWEEN CHARACTER AND PLOT

In human life, every person's story is different. The same environment and genetic pool results in siblings—even identical twins—with vastly different perceptions and life experiences. No two people will react the same to a particular crisis, and no two people will demonstrate the same kind of change or growth, even if their experiences appear to be the same.

So it is with characters. Every character will think, act, react and respond in a unique way. Your job as an author is to give your characters such individual life that when they do respond to circumstances or crises, those responses are well-motivated but not predictable, individual but not improbable.

Remember the lessons of probability. If you have a female character who has been put down by men—her grandfather, father, brothers, and ex-husband—all her life, is she likely to fall into the arms of the first man who shows her any attention or respect? She may, if she is desperate for love and unaware of the source of her low self-esteem. But if she has any insight into the causes of her struggles, she is likely to be wary and a little cynical, unwilling to trust too readily. In the first scenario, if she gives herself to a man who is not trustworthy, a man who undermines her in order to maintain control over her, you have potential for drama (and for pain for your heroine). In the second case, if she meets a good man but cannot trust him, you have potential for a different kind of drama.

In most educational programs, before psychiatrists or psychologists can be licensed as therapists or counselors, they must spend time in personal therapy. Part of the reason for this requirement is to give therapists an opportunity to see the process from the other side; part of it, I suspect, is to enable therapists to get to the root of their own issues before attempting to help others resolve theirs.

Therapy might be a good recommendation for a novelist, too—heaven knows most of us could use the help from time to time. But even on a professional level, the more we know about the way human nature works, about the hidden motivations of the heart, the more likely we are to create characters that live and breathe.

The real substance of fiction lies in characterization—not just the *what* of a story, but the *why*. You can have the most carefully crafted plot in the history of the novel, but if your characters walk through their paces woodenly, simply hitting their marks and saying their lines, you won't have a drama worth reading.

In the best novels, the plot is integrally interwoven with the characters—with their motives and actions, with their internal struggles, with their growth and change or their degeneration. Ideally, the plot should be custom-crafted for the characters, so that no other set of characters would be able to do what these characters do.

GIVING YOUR CHARACTERS A REALITY
OF THEIR OWN

The annals of fiction writing are full of stories about characters who just appeared out of nowhere and took over the story, like Aslan, who "leaped unbidden" into C.S. Lewis's *Chronicles of Narnia.* But sometimes, as fiction writers, we stand like Ezekiel over the skeletons of our characters and ask, "Can these bones live?" And we wonder: How do you create characters that breathe, believable people who have a living soul?

One of my favorite books, ostensibly a children's book, expresses some of the deepest truths I've ever encountered about human life and love, about relationships and, by extension, about characterization in the novel. Margery Williams's classic tale *The Velveteen Rabbit* provides amazing insight about reality in human experience. In the story, the Rabbit asks the Skin Horse, one of the oldest toys in the nursery, about becoming Real:

> "What is REAL?" asked the Rabbit one day. . . . "Does it mean having things that buzz inside you and a stick-out handle?"
>
> "Real isn't how you are made," said the Skin Horse. "It's a thing that happens to you. When a child loves for a long, long time, not just to play with, but REALLY loves you, then you become Real."
>
> "Does it hurt?" asked the Rabbit.
>
> "Sometimes," said the Skin Horse, for he was always truthful. "When you are Real you don't mind being hurt."
>
> "Does it happen all at once, like being wound up," he asked, "or bit by bit?"
>
> "It doesn't happen all at once," said the Skin Horse. "You become. It takes a long time. That's why it doesn't often happen to people who break easily, or have sharp edges, or have to be carefully kept. Generally, by the time you are Real, most of your hair has been loved off, and your eyes drop out and you get loose in the joints and very shabby. But these things don't matter at all, because once you are Real you can't be ugly, except to people who don't understand. . . . once you are Real you can't become unreal again. It lasts for always."

If the Skin Horse is right, if becoming real is the result of love, then we as fiction writers need to commit ourselves to loving our characters. That doesn't mean that all our characters are lovable, but that we understand and sympathize with their dysfunctions and eccentricities. Even with antagonists and villains, we must set ourselves to give them a fair shake, to realize and to communicate the motivations behind their behavior.

Becoming real hurts. For the novelist, this means that we cannot shy away from the difficulties and pain in our characters' lives and experiences. Hurting—unrequited love, broken dreams, lost innocence and even death—is part of being human.

And becoming real takes its toll on physical beauty and strength. All the fur gets loved off and you become shabby and loose in the joints. Some of the best, most memorable fictional characters I have ever encountered were not "beautiful" people in the physical sense, not the kind of "handsome hero, lovely heroine" stereotypes we often see in romance novels. They were beautiful from within, because of intangible qualities. And they weren't perfect, either. They were ordinary, struggling people who somehow found inner reserves of faith and strength.

Over the years, one of my biggest frustrations with CBA fiction has been the tendency for Christian novelists to resort to such stereotypes of external beauty and one-sided nobility. As believers in the reality of grace and salvation, we, more than anyone else, should practice what we preach. In God's economy, what matters most is the heart and soul, not the hair, eyes and physique. And yet we continue to create fantasy typecasts of physical attractiveness—a sort of Christianized Barbie and Ken, the quarterback and the prom queen—as if only the "beautiful people" of the world deserve to experience love, faith and fulfillment.

I think our writing should be more balanced than that. I believe we need a good dose of reality in our characterizations—homely or ordinary characters as well as drop-dead gorgeous ones. Men with balding heads instead of granite jaws and cleft chins; women whose sand is settling just a bit in the hip area, whose hair is mousy brown instead of sable, raven or gold. Teens who cry over a pimple now and then. Characters with physical disabilities and challenges.

Despairing of ever finding such a love story, I wrote one into the first book of the Home Front series. In *Home Fires Burning*, Mabel Rae Coltrain, short, dumpy and unattractive, continues to fill her "hopeless chest" with needlework and to dream of finding a man who will come back for a second date. Mabel finds her man, through correspondence with a soldier on the Pacific Rim, but when he comes home to the States, thoroughly in love and determined to marry her, she is shocked. He is not at all what she expected—he's tall, dark, broad-shouldered and handsome. And he doesn't care one bit that she is short and dumpy and not the kind of woman to be an ornament to his good looks. When you're loved, when you're real, you can't be ugly—except to people who don't understand.

If characters are to be real, they need more substance than just their physical attractiveness or their activities on the page— the events of their lives that the reader sees and hears about. In this chapter and the next two, we will look at some techniques you can use to give life and reality to your characters.

- A past history that determines their motives in the present
- A balance of positive and negative qualities
- Inner conflicts as well as outer ones
- Clear motivations for actions and relationships
- Room to grow and change
- Identifiable voices
- Memorable names that fit their personalities

THE SECRET STORY: YOUR CHARACTER'S PAST

When I was in graduate school, I met a law student. He was a quiet, unassuming fellow, tall and dark, with a bit of a sinister look about him, but very gentle and self-effacing. In the course of our friendship, I asked the typical questions about his background, his faith and his family, but he was strangely reticent to talk about himself. Then I heard him give his testimony at a revival.

This sweet, gentle man had spent most of his young adult life imprisoned for his activities as a bombing coordinator for the Ku Klux Klan in Mississippi during the 1960s. Caught after being shot at close range, he had been put in solitary confinement, but eventually escaped from prison. The second time he was arrested, he was left in solitary, and there read the Bible and came to believe in Christ. His life had changed so radically that the warden of the penitentiary lobbied for his release; he was granted early parole and entered law school.

This man was a friend of mine; I thought I knew him. But when I heard his whole story, I discovered that what I *thought* I knew only skimmed the surface of his character. Much deeper, in his past experiences and the transformation of his soul, lay the hidden motivations for his service to God.

A good novelist realizes that each of the main characters has a secret, a hidden past, a biographical history that affects how that character will act, respond and make choices in the course of the novel. Readers, understandably, are intrigued by a character with a secret, and if they suspect a character has something to hide, they will keep on reading until they find out what the secret is. You can use this fascination with the unknown to your advantage—either by hinting at it, or by eventually revealing your character's secret in a moment of crisis.

A great deal of this secret story, of course, will never see the light of day in the pages of your book. But it is important nonetheless. Your character's past, even information the reader never learns, is part of his heritage and his motivation. The more real your characters are to you, the more real they are likely to become to your reader.

Many novelists create whole stories for their characters, apart from their involvement in the present novel. They spend hours writing out elaborate family histories—not only date of birth, parents' names and childhood experiences, but entire family trees for generations back.

This may seem like a futile, fruitless effort, but it can result in a character that is three-dimensional, a person with a past and a future beyond the scope of the book. The more you know about your characters, the more likely they are to have clearly communicated motivations for their actions, and the more probable and realistic they will become.

Creating a hidden history for your characters can dimensionalize them and give them life. But there is one inherent danger in creating a past for your characters—the temptation to try to include too much of the past in the present novel.

Consider human relationships. When you meet new people, you meet them on the turf of the present. All you know about them is what they look like, what they say and whether they seem trustworthy and honest. As you get to know them better, they may or may not reveal to you certain details about their lives. Every piece of information you gather about them—particularly internal, emotional information—goes into your data bank to flesh out your initial evaluation, confirming or undermining your first impressions.

Gradually, over the course of your relationship, you may learn about their family structure, their childhood experiences, their work and educational background, their dreams for the future and their moral convictions. And with every bit of new information, you are better able to understand, and perhaps even to predict, what they might do in a given crisis situation. Is this man gentle and passive, or violent? Is he capable of murder? Is this woman confrontational, or does she let other people take advantage of her? And more importantly, why? What makes this woman docile or angry? Why is she bitter? What makes this man cry? Why does he have difficulty trusting people?

The answers to such questions are the essence of detailed characterization. But you cannot simply dump the information on your reader in an internal monologue, through a character's diary or letters, in an extended therapy session or (a particular trap in Christian fiction) through prayers. You have to give the information as we get it in the development of a new relationship—a little at a time. And some of the information you know as the author may never be revealed in the book. But whether your characters' past histories come out or not, that history humanizes them and makes them real.

THESE BONES CAN LIVE

In all my years of editing, one experience stands out as the landmark example of a living, breathing character. I was working with B.J. Hoff on her Emerald Ballad series, dealing with the character of Finola—a beautiful young woman who, because of a traumatic event in her past, had not spoken since she was a child. "There's something wrong with Finola's character," B.J. told me one day on the telephone. "Something I don't understand. Pray that I'll find out what it is, will you?"

If that sounds a little odd, wait until you hear the rest of the story. I did pray, as promised. The next morning, I called B.J.

and said, "I don't know if it's good news or bad, but I think Finola is pregnant."

A long silence ensued, and at last B.J. said quietly, "Yes. Yes she is. And this baby is going to be the turning point of her spiritual life."

I wasn't the only one who perceived of Finola as a living being. B.J. tells me that, during the course of the series, she received many letters about Finola's situation, and one editor even told her, "I've been praying for Finola."

Our characters *can* live. We can speak the words that summon them to stand upright, to take on ligament and flesh and skin. We can breathe into them the breath of life, the reality of love and the inner beauty and substance that come through faith. With a little work on our part, the Valley of the Dry Bones can become a panorama of life, filling the pages of our books with characters our readers will never forget.

Chapter Eight

Darkness and Light

The Balance of Good and Evil

D id you ever dream of being more like the people we read about and honor in the Bible? Like Abraham, the father of the faith, who trusted God enough to offer his own son Isaac on the altar of sacrifice? Or David, writer of those beautiful Psalms, who was called "a man after God's own heart"? Like Mary, who bore the infant Messiah in her own body? Or Mary Magdalene, the first to see Christ after the Resurrection? Or perhaps like Paul, the great Apostle to the Gentiles, whose words have made the difference between life and death to countless millions of believers?

Think again. Abraham, after all, lied to the Pharaoh and told him Sarah was his sister; this great "father of the faith" got impatient with God's promise and ended up as father to Ishmael as well. David was guilty of both murder and adultery. Mary, along with Jesus' siblings, thought her son was mad and tried to dissuade him from ministry. Mary Magdalene was a woman with a very shady past. And Paul? Paul began his rise up the religious ladder by persecuting believers and participating in the death of Stephen, the first martyr. In later life, Paul proclaimed himself "chief of sinners."

All disciples have a dark side.

You probably do, too, unless the scripture is wrong when it says that "all have sinned and fall short of the glory of God." No doubt you've done a thing or two in your life that you're not particularly proud of. Something which necessitates the grace of God in ongoing forgiveness.

Why should your characters be any different? The characters in your novel are, first and foremost, essentially human. They are not gods or demigods, not superheroes or saints. They are people, and people live with the constant inner battle between good and evil. Even Christ, the Bible tells us, was tempted as we are.

MOVING BEYOND STEREOTYPES

The inevitability of temptation—and for us, as humans, the possibility of giving in to temptation—creates a fascinating dramatic tension within characters. Even the noblest character is subject to the lure of greed, pride or spiritual self-sufficiency. Even the most deplorable villain has moments of tenderness and generosity. The novelist who wants to create living characters will use this dichotomy of the heart to flesh out characters' stresses and motivations.

Consider Steven Spielberg's masterpiece of filmmaking, *Schindler's List*. Schindler wasn't a noble man in the beginning—he was a money-grubbing businessman intent upon using the war to line his own pockets. He exploited everyone around him, and began using the Jews as a cheap source of labor for his factories.

But Schindler had a soft spot in his armor, a place of tenderness and human compassion that grew as the war progressed and the Holocaust was set in motion. He ultimately saved thousands of Jewish lives at the cost of his own fortune, and he was ennobled in the process.

If you are writing for the Christian market, you will want to be careful in your characterization. In the general market, novels are sometimes built around antiheroes, characters whose primary value lies in giving us examples to avoid. These antiheroes are usually struggling, fatally flawed personalities whose choices and decisions get them ever deeper in trouble.

But in the CBA, most publishers (and readers) want their heroes to be strong and moral—or at least to grow into strength and morality. CBA readers want to identify with the good, not with the mediocre or the bad. Thus, your heroes need to be basically strong, facing and overcoming whatever weaknesses they have, and your villains need to be clearly drawn. You may have a villain who seems like a good guy in the beginning, but his deception of the truly "good" characters makes his evil nature that much darker in the end.

Even so, the careful writer will guard against the tendency to resort to two-dimensional stick figures. No one is all good or all bad. Good characters have a point of weakness, and evil characters have a point of goodness. You may use your noble character's weakness as a humanizing agent, or as an opportunity for inner struggle or dramatic tension. You may give glimpses of your evil character's tenderness as a foil, a backdrop to emphasize his evil. But if you create people who are all saint or all sinner, you will inevitably end up with flat, wooden characters who do little more than carry out the action of the plot.

It's essentially an issue of stereotyping—the one-sided "all good" or "all bad" character does not represent the reality of human nature. And for the Christian writer, this is a deeply rooted spiritual issue as well. If we truly believe that we are "sinners saved by grace," we cannot afford to present characters so noble that they are not in need of ongoing grace, or so evil that they are beyond the reach of God's love and redemption.

Previously, in chapter two, we touched on the issue of prejudice—how hidden bigotries can work their way into our writing and undermine our portrayal of the grace and love of God. Such prejudice often reveals itself in characterization and, if we intend to be true to our gifts and our calling, we must guard against it, both in our lives and in our writing.

In practical terms alone, a writer cannot afford to be a bigot. When we allow ourselves to fall prey to prejudice, we cut ourselves off from a rich source of dramatic tension, character development and spiritual truth. We need to be open to the possibility of God's redemptive work in all people and, through that openness, extend the boundaries of our own lives and faith.

Being open to God's work in all people does not mean, however, that you manipulate the story to make the characters think and act the way you, as the writer, would think and act. The tendency to preach in fiction is a grave temptation for the Christian writer, and it often appears most subtly in characterization. If we, as writers, are harsh, dogmatic, judgmental people, our characters will take on the same traits—and they will probably not be very balanced. Who we are inevitably comes out in our writing, and therefore we owe it to ourselves, to our work and to our readers, to grow in Christlikeness and in grace.

POLITICAL CORRECTNESS AND CHRISTIAN LOVE

Many conservative Christians deplore the current trend toward "political correctness." Perhaps in some cases the principle has been taken too far, but in general we can learn from the idea. It will, at the very least, alert us to stereotypes in our characterization.

Most of us, for example, are savvy enough not to pit white against black in the universal struggle of good vs. evil. To portray Anglo characters as heroes and African-American (or Native American, Arab, Mexican or any other ethnic group) characters as evil is nothing short of blatant racism. But do you use images of black and white to denote evil and good? And what about other, more subtle distinctions? Are all your female characters meek and submissive, and all your male characters strong and capable, or vice versa? Are your religious characters upright and noble, while your nonreligious characters are evil and demented—or more indirectly, ignorant and hostile? Or, on the other side of the coin, have you been producing whitewashed stereotypes? In other words, portraying an entire group, class or race as perfect? If, after a long hard look at your characters, you discover one-sided characterizations (either positive or negative) based on race, gender or religion, you are probably guilty of some sort of stereotyping—and you are shortchanging both your characters and your readers.

In chapter seven, we discussed the importance of loving your characters—or at the very least, understanding them and empathizing with them. If you truly know and respect your characters, you will paint them as whole, complex, multifaceted people, not as puppets to do your bidding and project your attitudes.

It's not an issue of political correctness: It's an issue of grace. The Bible tells us, "The Lord does not see as mortals see; they look on the outward appearance, but the Lord looks on the heart" (1 Samuel 16:7, NRSV). God sees each of us as individuals, as humans with free will, capable of both good and evil. If we are wise writers, we will seek to perceive our characters with the same vision not categorizing people according to the outward appearance, but delving into their souls to find the balance of good and evil that will humanize them and give them a point of identity with our readers.

THE VALUE OF INNER CONFLICT

Many of the plot-driven novels popular today rely almost exclusively on external conflict to provide the dramatic impetus of the plot. The hero faces one life-threatening situation after another, each more dangerous and more convoluted than the last, and the reader turns pages breathlessly to find out how the protagonist will get out of this one.

It's a ploy that works—and certainly external conflict is important to your story. Your characters will not truly come alive for your reader, however, unless they have valid and understandable inner conflicts as well. Physical danger, problems to solve and plot twists to negotiate all have their place in fiction, but the real conflict for a living character happens within. Even in a plot-driven novel, external conflict should be mirrored by the struggles within a character's mind and heart.

We might think of the delicate balance between internal and external conflict in terms of flying a kite. For a kite to soar successfully, two forces must be in place: wind against the kite's wings and resistance on the string. The wind is external conflict—the forces of nature or circumstance that buffet the character and threaten to blow him away. The string, the internal conflict, tethers the character to earth and connects him to reality . . . and to the reader.

Readers may not identify with your character's external conflict; they probably have never faced a medieval dragon, been chased by international terrorists or been caught in a prairie blizzard while crossing the country in a covered wagon. But readers *can* identify with the internal conflicts of your characters—the fear of the unknown, the quest to find meaning in the midst of chaos, or the desire to avenge a wrong or rediscover a lost love. The kite string—those internal struggles common to all people—keeps your characters anchored in reality and gives your readers a tangible connection to them.

For the writer of Christian fiction, inner conflict is a rich treasure store for communicating spiritual truth. But the inner conflict for a Christian (or searching) character must be more than the decision to come to Christ, or more than the choice, in the face of adversity, to stand up for what he or she believes in. Too many Christian novels hinge on the salvation of a character: Once the character has come to Christ, all problems seem to resolve themselves, and everything is wonderful.

But in real life, although faith in God makes a profound difference in our perspectives and attitudes, it doesn't solve all our problems. We still struggle with internal conflicts, with doubt and with circumstances that have no easy answers. And your characters, in order to be believable, must live in the real world and face real issues. Easy resolutions do nothing to build character or bring about significant change. And for the reader of fiction, easy resolutions can be downright boring, if not infuriating.

If you want your characters to breathe and come alive for your reader, place them in situations that challenge their inner resources as well as their intelligence or physical abilities. Let their outer conflicts or dangers give rise to equally important internal issues—moral choices, priority evaluations, temptations to sin or decisions about their relationships with God or with other characters. Give them a kite string to hold them in place. Your readers will feel the tug on the string and sense a connection to your characters in their own lives.

GROWING PAINS

Everything that lives grows and changes. Anyone who has ever had a baby knows that when you bring that warm little bundle home from the hospital, you'd better be prepared for a lifetime of nonstop change. Even after that baby is fully developed physically, the process doesn't stop—just ask any parent of a teenager. Human beings continue to change emotionally, intellectually and spiritually throughout their lives. They try and fail, fall and get up, regroup and go on. Your characters, too, if they are alive, must evidence progress (or regression) during the course of your novel.

A character who doesn't change presents little interest for a reader. Especially in Christian fiction, the inevitable changes that occur in human life lend reality to a character. Living characters will reassess their decisions, second-guess themselves, change their minds and decide on a different course of action. They will mature both physically and emotionally; they will grow up. They will also backslide, fail, and get a little dirty in the process.

Crisis, particularly the kind of concentrated crisis often experienced by fictional characters, has a way of changing people, for good or for ill. A person who suffers chronic, ongoing physical or emotional pain will either be softened or embittered by the hurt. A child who has been abused either grows up to be an abuser, perpetuating the cycle, or deals with the abuse and empathizes with other abuse survivors. Stress and hardship bring out the extremes of a personality—either the noble core or the self-centeredness of an individual.

If we want to make our fictional characters come alive, we must allow them room to grow and change. A character (particularly a major character) will not be the same person at the end of a harrowing experience as she was at the beginning. If we try to force her into a mold, to be so consistent with her characterization that she never learns anything from her experience, she will not come across to readers as realistic.

Life changes people. Fictional life changes fictional characters. And the potential for growth, change and maturity in characterization is one of the greatest opportunities a Christian writer has for demonstrating the power and grace of God. But here, as in the issue of inner conflict, the change cannot be instantaneous or simplistic. Growth happens gradually; even when a character comes to a sudden revelation of truth, the outworking and application of that truth cannot come all at once. A character who has "seen the light" about some spiritual or moral issue may have good intentions to change his ways, but in practice, the change will come in fits and starts. Most growth is a "two steps forward, one step back" affair, and lasting transformation takes time.

Beware of incorporating too much change in your characters too quickly. Keep in mind the reality of human life and our human tendency to try, fail, and try again before we finally "get it right." Readers will respond to a character who seems realistic in his efforts to change; a miraculous, overnight metamorphosis is more difficult to swallow.

THE MOTIVATION FACTOR

The single most important question a writer of fiction can ask is the question we all learned by age two: "WHY?" The parent of a two-year-old may become exasperated with the incessant "whys" demanded by that child, but as writers we need to realize that our readers will be asking us that same question—and almost as often.

"Why did Mary decide to break up with Joe? Why did she choose that Ralph character? Can't she see he's no good for her?

And why would she pick up and move to New York with no job and no place to live? It just doesn't make sense. . . ."

In chapter seven, I made the tongue-in-cheek suggestion that we, as fiction writers, might greatly benefit from ongoing therapy. My mother always warned me that anything said half in jest was also said half in truth; I suppose this recommendation is no exception. Socrates gave us the injunction "Know thyself," and for a writer, self-knowledge translates to knowledge of character.

In my estimation, an understanding of human psychology is as important to the writer as an understanding of human physiology was to the artist Michelangelo. Michelangelo was not content to observe the human body from afar and sculpt from that external perspective. He spent hours dissecting cadavers to get below the surface, to understand how the parts of the body were put together and to envision physical reality from the inside out. He made detailed sketches of muscle and bone and ligament, and his research paid off. When he had completed the massive marble figure of the seated Moses, it was so lifelike that Michelangelo reportedly struck the statue's knee with a hammer and demanded, "Now, speak!"

As writers, our research into human reality is not a hands-on dissection of the body, but an understanding—from the inside out—of thought and reaction, of motivation and reasoning. I'm aware, of course, that some Christians are suspicious of psychological research, viewing it as a secular field of study that intrudes onto religious turf. But as a Christian and as a writer, I don't believe we need to be afraid of truth. Michelangelo was criticized for his research by the religious leaders of his day, but no one can deny that his work proclaims the glory of God. For us, as writers, the principle is the same: The more we understand about the way the human mind and heart work, the more clearly drawn and realistic our characters will be, and the more equipped we will be to answer—before they are asked—the "why" questions our readers will raise.

Motivation in characterization is one of the most difficult issues for a writer, because motivation is based on a combination of:

- past influences
- present beliefs

- necessary actions or decisions that face the character at any given moment
- internal changes that are taking place
- the "wild card" factor—the reality that human beings sometimes behave unpredictably

In a good novel, a character's actions are always based on some kind of understandable motivation. The character may resort to an unpredictable action or make a decision that initially seems out of character for her, as long as some kind of motivation for it is revealed—something that leads the reader to say, "Aha! That's why she did that!"

A "good Christian character" who is essentially committed to the truth, for example, may lie under a certain set of circumstances. But if your characterization of Mr. Honesty is based on the fact that he *never* lies, you'd better have a compelling reason for him to be dishonest, or his character breaks down. If Nazi SS troops are pounding on the front door and Mr. Honesty has ten Jewish children hidden in his attic, you can probably make a case for his not telling the truth. But if he lies just to protect his own reputation, or to make himself seem more noble than he really is, his motivations will be called into question.

The underlying principle of motivation is probability. Unless there are extenuating circumstances (like the Nazis at the door), a character should respond in keeping with his basic personality and belief structure.

Let's say we have a character who has had a lifelong struggle with alcohol but has been on the wagon for twelve years. When his wife walks out on him, he may be tempted to drown his sorrows in drink. If he is essentially a weak character who has been abstinent only to please other people and keep his marriage intact, he may well succumb to the temptation and go on a three-week binge. If he has experienced a genuine transformation in his life and is sober because of internal convictions—such as a renewed faith in God—he may be able to face down the temptation and overcome it. The temptation will still be very real, but his response will be different, depending upon his motivation.

Here's where your character's past must come out of hiding. Everybody has secrets—experiences that nobody knows about, hidden dreams, ambitions, fears, frustrations and unfulfilled longings. These inner issues govern a character's motivation for any given action or decision. But when those secret motives affect a character's reactions or responses, it is not enough that you as the author know about them. You must find a way to communicate them to your reader as well—preferably *before* the fact, rather than as an explanation after the fact.

The key question to ask yourself is, "Would this character do that?" If not, then she can't do it in your novel. If the answer is yes, why would she do it? You need to be very clear about the motivational factors that would cause her to make such a decision or take such an action, and you must communicate those motivations to the reader as well.

One pitfall for writers in terms of motivation is a slavish devotion to consistency. If a character never does anything unexpected, if all his actions and decisions are predictable, then he probably is a very dull fellow. Adequate motivation is not based on predictability, but on probability. And probability includes a wide variety of options, any number of which would be realistic in terms of human decision-making.

Suppose we have a middle-aged character, a single mother who is supporting three high-school-age children by herself. She is a woman of deep faith, and has long depended on God to supply her physical and emotional needs. Enter the dragon: a handsome, flashy, wealthy entrepreneur who sweeps her off her feet and offers to "take her away from all of this." What does she do?

- She is deceived, falls for him and alienates her children.
- She sees through him but allows herself to be swayed by his money.
- She rationalizes the temptation because college expenses are looming.
- Her children adore him (and his money) and she gives in because of them.
- She sees through him, resists him and determines to let God provide for her.

Any of these options might be "probable," depending on what direction the plot is going. But whatever course of action she takes, her motivation must be clear to the reader. The reader does not have to agree with her decision or her reasons—in fact, a good deal of the dramatic tension in fiction relies on the difference between what the characters know and what the readers know—but her reasoning must be logical within the framework of her own life experience.

A good author does not want to undermine the potential growth of a character by making that character predictable. But an equally serious trap lies in trying to surprise readers by throwing them a deliberate and premeditated curve. Some authors, without any explanation, manipulate their characters into taking action that is in direct contradiction to their already-established motivations. When confronted with the obvious question about motivation, they defend themselves by saying, "People often do things that don't make sense!"

Yes, people do make decisions irrationally. But in fiction, a hero who acts in an irrational manner will annoy and frustrate the reader. Readers don't like to be able to predict what's going to happen, but they do insist upon being able to *understand* it. The author who allows characters to "do things that don't make sense" alienates the reader from any real identification with the character.

The principle in characterization, as in plotting, is to maintain a "vivid and continuous dream" throughout the novel. If a reader has to stop and reread ten pages in order to follow the plot, the writer has not done her job adequately. By the same token, if the reader gets sidetracked trying to figure out why a character made a decision or took a particular course of action, the writer has not provided sufficient motivation for the character's decision. There may be surprises along the way, and there will most certainly be changes in the characters as they grow and develop or regress. But those surprises should evoke a response of "Oh, yes! I see!" in the reader, not a response of "Huh?" or a sarcastic "Yeah, right."

Characters that live in the reader's mind are characters that have been carefully crafted by the writer to reflect a balance of good and evil, of strength and weakness, of consistency and change. Living, breathing characters exhibit internal conflicts as well as external ones, and those internal conflicts connect them to the readers' lives, making the characters realistic and identifiable.

As Christian writers, we can take a lesson in characterization from the creation story in Genesis. God shaped the environment—the setting, if you will. God formed the mountains, lakes and rivers, and filled the earth with living creatures of infinite variety. But the jewels of creation, the epitome of God's creativity, were the man and the woman. Living beings crafted by God, their lungs filled with the breath of the Almighty. They were not puppets, constrained to obey, but people with minds and hearts, with individual volition, with the freedom to accept God's will or resist it, and with all the internal conflicts that accompanied such a decision.

In like manner, we as writers create gardens—or cities, small towns, factories or prairie dugouts—for our characters. We shape them, breathe life into them and set them on their feet. And if we are wise, we give them free will to act out the drama of human experience—to succeed or fail, to grow or regress, to respond to or resist the call of God upon their lives.

Disciples have their dark side, too. Even the heroes and heroines of our faith were flawed, sinful human beings who struggled to let their faith prevail over their doubt.

We can do no less with our characters. If we are true to them and to ourselves, we will present a balanced characterization of humanity: real people in the real world who grapple with real issues—and in the process give our readers new insights into their own lives and struggles.

Chapter Nine

Hearing the Voice of Truth
Character Identity

I have a number of friends who never identify themselves by name when they call on the telephone. One says, "Hey there!" Another says, "It's me." A third announces herself with a characteristic "Halloo!" And when I call one particular friend's home, I can instantly identify her by her well-known telephone voice—"Mmmm, hello?" Formal introductions are unnecessary: I always know who it is by the speech patterns.

Fictional characters are like that, too. If a character in a novel is well-established in the reader's mind, the reader can instantly mark the character's identity without ever being told the name. Good characters in fiction have a voice all their own.

But how does that happen, when the reader can't *hear* the voice of the character?

IDENTIFIABLE VOICES

In characterization, *voice* does not refer simply to a way of speaking, an accent or a dialect, but also to a pattern of thinking and a unique way of relating to other characters.

Any number of factors affect our characters' voices: their educational background, their relative level of simplicity or sophistication, their internal belief structure, their innocence or cynicism, their emotional attachments to other characters. In a strong novel, each major character (and sometimes minor characters as well) has an identifiable voice, so that readers know immediately whose dialogue they are hearing and whose point of view they are seeing, even without a direct indication of the character's identity.

A character who maintains a facade of brusqueness, for example, will not only speak brusquely but will also think in curt, choppy sentence patterns. A character who is romantic and flowery will have speech and thought patterns to match. An insecure character will probably ramble and backtrack a lot, while a self-confident character will have a firm, direct, positive voice.

Voice can greatly enhance the reader's understanding of a character. If thought and dialogue patterns are consistent with the inner character and personality, the reader gets a clear picture of who the character is. By the same token, if there is a contrast between the inner character and the outward image, perhaps the character has something to hide or is trying to cover something up.

Suppose we have a character who has had to make her own way in the world of cross-country trucking. She may talk tough and present a hard-bitten facade. But when we get into her mind, we find that she is insecure and lonely, and longs to be loved. A core of tenderness that comes out in her inner voice tells the reader that she is not exactly what she appears to be. Thus, when she is confronted with the possibility of a romantic involvement, the reader is not surprised if she leads with her heart and takes the risk to find love. But because she has been conditioned by life to protect herself, it would not be out of character for her to be a little standoffish and cynical in the face of this new experience.

Here, the character's motivation may make a profound difference in the direction of the plot. If she follows her heart and pursues the relationship, she may get her heart broken. But if she stands back and resists love, she may spend the rest of her life wondering what she missed. And her inner voice can reflect what is happening in her heart and mind. If she speaks in short, choppy, "tough-talk" sentences when she's engaged in dialogue, but has a softer, more feminine inner voice when we're alone with her in her point of view, the reader understands that although she may present a crusty facade, she also has a tender side that may affect the decisions she makes and the way she relates to others in the novel.

Either way, the identifiable voice of the character—both external and internal—helps the reader understand her motivation for whatever decision she makes. Readers identify with her because they feel they understand her; they root for her when she takes a chance on love, or feel her disappointment when she has to pull back. And whatever the outcome of her life, they experience it with her, for she is a character who becomes real to them.

Voice is a tricky issue in characterization. It's easy to fall into stereotypes—the western hero who goes around saying "Yup" all the time and thinking in cowboy jargon ("That gal was the prettiest little filly he'd seen in a coon's age, and he wondered if'n he had a snowball's chance in August of ever ropin' her and puttin' his brand on her. . . ."), or the airheaded female lead who can't get a sentence out of her mouth or a thought out of her head without a "mercy me" or a "heavens above!"

In characterization, as in every other aspect of fiction writing, the author must always keep in mind the reality of human diversity. Not all cowboys say "yup" or think of women as "fillies." Not all women simper. For that matter, it can't be said that all people of any classification (gender, ethnicity, race, religion or education) speak, think or respond alike.

The most enlightening experience I ever had with the issue of voice in characterization came when I was editing B.J. Hoff's Emerald Ballad series. I was almost halfway through the editing of the first book before I realized what was so different about this manuscript. B.J.'s major characters, most of them Irish, all had such specifically identifiable voices that each one of them thought, acted, responded and spoke in a manner unique to that character's background, life history and emotional state. When I came to a hiatus indicating a shift in point of view, I did not need to know the character's name in order to identify whose viewpoint the author was employing. Every aspect of the character's voice was evident: thought patterns, particular expressions, and sentence structure reflected that character's particular view of the world and the characters with whom they were interacting. And not once in a five-book series did any Irish character utter the words "Faith and begorra!"

Giving your characters identifiable voices brings them to life in a way that nothing else can. There are, certainly, some techniques for giving characters voices of their own—pet names they use for other characters, a particular word or phrase that is theirs alone, a certain way of focusing on another character's attributes or a uniquely spiritual viewpoint about the events of their lives. But the key to living characters lies finally with the author; if you know and understand your characters and strive to make them realistic in the way they interact with others, the character's voice will come out.

WHOSE VOICE IS THAT?

One of the most difficult challenges for the Christian writer is to find a way to give your characters identifiable voices without making them sound like *you*. When someone responds to my fiction by saying, "Hey, this sounds just like you!" I cringe inwardly, for I know then that I haven't done my job in crafting my characters. But when a reader says, "That sounds just like Thelma Breckinridge," I rejoice, for such a response indicates that I have made Thelma a character in her own right, with her own thoughts, perspectives and unique capabilities.

If a character in a novel "sounds like the author," part of the problem may be that the author has not sufficiently differentiated him- or herself from the characters on the page. Being a writer of fiction is a lot like being a parent: Part of your job as author is to create your characters and then set them free to be independent. But just as many parents have problems letting go when the time comes, many writers can't let go of their characters—they insist on manipulating characters to make them say, think and feel what the author would say, think or feel in any given situation.

It's a delicate balance. Yes, we write out of our own experience and, especially in emotional situations, often ask ourselves, "How would I feel if this happened to me?" But the more important question is, "How would the *character* feel?" And we can't answer that question unless we have sufficiently separated ourselves from our characters.

There's a good deal of role confusion in the world of fiction between the author and the characters—particularly if the novel is written in first person. But even when you have a first-person character, an *I* narrator whose point of view governs the story, that first person *I* is not the author—it is a *persona*, a created character just like any third-person character, separate and distinct from the author.

Readers don't always understand this. Especially in a first-person novel, they often make the erroneous assumption that the central character is the author, and therefore represents the author's perspectives on all the issues and events of the character's life. Such misunderstanding can often give rise to some interesting reactions from readers who become incensed over a character's motives or actions and respond indignantly: "How could the author do such a thing?" Or, in the case of Christian fiction: "How could an author believe that and call herself a Christian?"

Even with a novel written from a third-person viewpoint, the question "Which character is the author?" often arises. The answer, of course, is "none of them." This is fiction, not autobiography, and except in the unusual case of autobiographical fiction, none of the characters in a book represents the author's life experience. Many characters may reflect certain *aspects* of the author—that's almost inevitable—but characters (well-crafted ones, anyway) appear as separate and distinct personalities. It's the author's job, then, whether with a first-person character or a variety of third-person characters, to create individuals who have their own lives, their own attitudes and their own perspectives.

The water becomes rather muddy here when religious beliefs and themes come into play in characterization. It's all too easy for a well-meaning author to manipulate a character into a spiritual role he or she is incapable of bearing just for the sake of getting a "message" across. We need to remember, however, that characters are people in and of themselves. Just as we cannot force our children or our friends into believing as we do, we cannot compel our characters to take on our personal beliefs. Or, more accurately, we *can* force them, but if we do, their faith will seem false and imposed rather than a natural result of their own growth and enlightenment.

If you want your characters to be real, to have identifiable voices and personalities, you must allow them the freedom to believe differently than you believe. You are writing a story about people, not a treatise on spiritual truth. If you insist that all your characters toe the religious party line and adopt your personal values and viewpoint, you will not end up with a novel, but with a sermon illustrated by cardboard cutouts.

Madeleine L'Engle, in her book *Walking on Water*, warns against "falling into Satan's trap of assuming that other people are not Christians because they do not belong to our own particular brand of Christianity." It's true of our characters as well. Faith comes in many varieties, and we, as writers, would do well to explore those possibilities with our characters instead of photocopying our own religious systems onto the people who inhabit our books. As L'Engle says:

> If I cannot see the evidence of incarnation in . . . a book by Chaim Potok or Isaac Bashevis Singer . . . I will miss its significance in . . . the final chorus of the St. Matthew Passion (or) the words of a sermon by John Donne.

Resist the temptation to "convert" all your characters into images of yourself. Let them find their own way to truth and their own expressions of faith. If you give them that freedom— the same kind of free will God has given us—the spiritual dimensions of your novel will be much more real and believable, and much more likely to have a positive impact upon your readers.

NAMING

Names are important.

If you don't believe it, consider whether or not you get just a trifle irritated when someone calls you by the wrong name or spells your name incorrectly. Whenever I'm signing autographs, I ask each person to spell the name before I sign the book, even if the name is "Ann" or "Joe." I want to make sure I get it right, out of respect to the individual. People deserve to be identified by the correct name.

For a long time I didn't understand the source of this irritation—and I wondered about those people who could blithely say, "I don't care what you call me as long as you call me in time for dinner." The fact was, I *did* care. I felt devalued if someone pronounced my name wrong, or used my nickname rather than my full name in reference to my writing. I knew that part of the issue, for me at least, was the need to have my professional name associated with my books in readers' minds. But I sensed, too, that it went beyond just a concern with my work. The name issue struck some deeper nerve in my spirit.

Then I read Madeleine L'Engle's perspective on naming in *Walking on Water*—that naming is at heart a spiritual matter, an incarnational issue.

Naming is one of the impulses behind all art; to give a name to the cosmos we see despite all the chaos. God asked Adam to name all the animals, which was asking Adam to help in the creation of their wholeness. When we name each other, we are sharing in the joy and privilege of Incarnation.

We know this is true—or at least most of us have seen the effects of naming in our own lives and in the lives of those we love. If a girl grows up hearing negative names such as "stupid," "worthless," and "good-for-nothing" applied to her, she is likely to become a woman who thinks of herself as unworthy of affection or respect, even if she is intelligent and industrious. If a young man is told that he'll never amount to anything, that "name" will probably stay with him, either keeping him down or prodding him to disprove it, for the rest of his life. Psychologists call it "self-fulfilling prophecy"—we become what we are named, or what we name ourselves.

Once I began to write fiction, I realized the connection between incarnation and naming. In order to be real in my own mind (not to mention in the minds of my readers), my characters must have names—not just any names, but the "right" names, names that fit who they are and who they will ultimately grow to become.

I have found that I am not the only writer with an obsession about character names. Francine Rivers, best-selling author of *The Scarlet Thread* and the Mark of the Lion trilogy, says "I select names that fit the attributes of the character, so that they live up to—or down to—them. A name fixes an image in my mind about who that person is and how they fit into the story." Jerry Jenkins, author of the blockbuster end-times novels *Left Behind* and *Tribulation Force*, says that his names "must have enough music to be interesting. I think it's fun sometimes to give villains attractive-sounding names and heroes ordinary or even bordering on negative-sounding names."

B.J. Hoff takes the challenge of naming a step further:

The name of a character is absolutely vital for me . . . it's the first step in *defining* the character. Although it's frustrating, I've learned that I may as well prepare myself to spend days finding a character's name that perfectly "fits." I've experienced the folly of going with a name that doesn't seem quite "comfortable," only to realize weeks and chapters later that a character is too vague or nondescript—and the fault will almost always come down to the fact that I should have trusted my instincts about the *name*. I don't know why this should be so, but most writers I know place a great deal of importance on their characters' names.

As Hoff so clearly indicates, naming is no easy task for the writer. But the right name can make all the difference in a character—not only in the *reader's* perception of the major and minor players, but also in the *author's* understanding of the personalities of his characters.

We need to realize, too, that often the name that seems right for a particular character may have a hidden underlying significance, a significance that works its way into the novel so subtly that even the author is unaware of it until it appears on the page. C.S. Lewis's central character in the Space trilogy is a fellow named Ransom. Early in the series, Ransom makes the point that his name does not derive from the same root as the verb "ransom," meaning one who gives himself up for another. Yet as the story develops, Ransom nevertheless becomes a kind of Christ figure, one who gives his life for others. Had Lewis simply named his character and not given the explanation of the name, it might have seemed like a cheap shot—a Messiah character called "Ransom." But because Ransom himself is aware of the irony and comments upon it, the name carries even greater significance for this reluctant prophet.

Memorable characters usually have memorable names—not just unusual or exotic names, but names that fit. The problem for the writer comes with how much information a character's name is intended to convey.

Your setting or time frame may make a difference in the kinds of names you choose. If your novel is set in Victorian times or during the Civil War, you will want to make sure that the names you pick were acceptable names for the era. Most women in the 1800s didn't have names like Brooke or Tracy—they were called Elizabeth or Victoria or Catherine.

Some names carry ethnic connotations: Shug (a corruption of "Sugar") in *The Color Purple*, or Anastasia or Hadassah. But you need to be very careful about stereotypical names. You may well find a girl in the South named Savannah (as in Pat Conroy's *Prince of Tides*), but if you fall back on Sally-Mae or Billy-Bob, you are treading on thin ice. Not everyone in the South has double monikers, and unless you use such names carefully and sparingly, you may be guilty of stereotyping.

One of the best ways to get a feel for appropriate names is to read widely in the genre you want to write in. If you're writing Victorian intrigue, you'll probably come across Colin and Winston and Mariel. If you read Flannery O'Connor, you'll discover Hulga-Joy Hopewell and Bevel Summers and Manley Pointer.

Character names carry significance in a variety of ways. Some writers, particularly in the Christian market, expect far too much from their readers in terms of name interpretation. "Stella" may mean "star," but unless you make a point of emphasizing the meaning in your novel, your reader may not connect with it and may be left wondering why the "shooting star" theme keeps appearing in your book. Beware, too, of attaching too much importance to obscure Biblical names. "Israel" means "he struggles with God," but even educated Christian readers may not be consciously aware of the derivation; instead of expecting a character who struggles with his faith, they may be primed for a historical novel about the development of a Jewish homeland.

Some names evoke a certain kind of aura around a character—a man named Rock, for example, or a woman called Missy. As an author you can use such names to your advantage, but names alone cannot carry the burden of characterization. And as Jerry Jenkins has pointed out, overtly character-oriented names can often be employed ironically—a wimpish, unassertive man named Mr. Power, or a flighty, brainless female called Eleanor Roosevelt Johnson.

In my own writing I have discovered that characters I expect to live up to their names often turn the tables on me. In the third book of the Home Front trilogy, *Remembering You*, a minor character, a pasty, groveling weasel of a lawyer named Orris Craven, appeared almost out of thin air. I chose the name "Craven" quite deliberately; Orris was supposed to be a wormy little character like Dickens' Uriah Heep, a despicable yes-man with no integrity who was willing to do almost anything to ingratiate himself with his boss.

But Orris surprised me. The weasel had a soul—and ultimately developed a backbone to go with it. By the time the novel had ended, Orris Craven had become a character of nobility and honor, and a catalyst for change in another character I had thought was irredeemable.

As you consider the names your characters will bear, you'll want to be careful about the combinations of names, too. If you have three main characters called Barry, Barbara and Benjamin, you're bound to get in trouble and confuse the reader—and maybe yourself as well.

Intentional confusion is another matter. In Elizabeth Goudge's *Green Dolphin Street*, the two sisters are named Marguerite and Marianne. Both of them fall in love with the same man, and when he goes to New Zealand and sends back for his bride, he gets the wrong name and ends up with the wrong woman. The entire plot is built around this misunderstanding, for the husband is determined not to hurt his wife and so decides never to let her know he has made a mistake.

A good character deserves a good name, and the wise writer will spend time and effort to find the right one. Some characters leap into the novel (or into the author's mind) fully formed and with their names attached. In other cases, a fascinating name will be the seed for the development of an equally fascinating character. But if you have characters who are yet unnamed (or badly named), consider carefully how you want to characterize them. If you settle for a common name like Smith or Brown, you may be condemning your character to a life of mediocrity. If you come up with something so exotic or off-the-wall that readers cannot pronounce, remember or understand it, your character may never have a chance for readers to identify with him.

The best name is the name that works, that is memorable and that says something about the character. The right name cannot carry the whole burden of characterization, but it can support and strengthen what you've already done with history, motivation, growth and voice.

FINDING SUITABLE NAMES

Whenever I teach fiction at a writers conference, some aspiring novelist will inevitably ask the question, "Where do you come up with your characters' names?"

Some names, as I have suggested, simply present themselves as the right choice. One of the characters in *Home Fires Burning* is Stork Simpson, the central character's best friend. Initially Stork was so named because he was tall and thin with a hawkish nose. But as his character developed, I discovered that he got the nickname from his army buddies when his girlfriend/fiancee Madge . . . ah, how shall I put this delicately? . . . found herself, in Biblical terms, "great with child." The unwanted pregnancy and resulting shotgun wedding ultimately became a primary motivational issue for Stork as he took over a major role in the series—his guilt, and the desire to atone for his own sin, eventually became the force that drove him to God. Not until Madge showed up with the baby did I discover that Stork's real name was Michael.

I often glean a sense of appropriate character names from reading, although I don't recommend lifting character names directly. I keep a list of interesting names—names of real people from magazine or news articles, and names that occur to me out of nowhere with no specific personality or character affixed to them. Sometimes those names work and sometimes they don't, but keeping the list stimulates other ideas.

Angela Elwell Hunt, author of the best-seller *Tale of Three Trees* and numerous other works of fiction, says she often uses a "baby book" to find appropriate names for her characters. I have used such name books as well, sometimes with success. But again, beware of choosing a name solely for its underlying meaning, because your reader may be oblivious to the significance.

B.J. Hoff also admits to using name books, but she has refined the process by including other factors important to a writer of historical fiction. "I take into account a name's meaning, ethnic origin, etc.," Hoff says, "besides the way it seems to mesh with the appearance and basic personality of the character. Because I work so much with Irish-American characters—and because many Irish family names tend to appear more commonly in certain sections of the country—I try to keep my characters' names consistent with their origins."

Ethnic consistency and historical accuracy are important issues to consider in choosing a name. When I was writing stories set in the heavily Scandinavian areas of southern Minnesota, I often turned to the telephone directories of those small towns, mixing and combining first and last names to come up with characters whose names bore the "flavor" of the Norwegian setting. And on a few occasions, if I was stuck for an interesting name, I would actually scan the spines of the books in my office and adapt those names for my characters. I thought no one else ever did this, until Lurlene McDaniel, best-selling author of young adult novels, told me that she sometimes gets names from her bookshelves as well.

Whatever names we choose, we should make certain the names fit the characters, the location, the ethnicity and the time frame of the novel. Good names—strong, memorable, significant names—will lend reality to our characters and make them live, both for our readers and for ourselves.

Strong characterization is one of the most important issues of focus for the fiction writer. Good characters can carry your plot—and in some cases help to direct it. They give life to the action and enable readers not only to be fascinated with your plot twists, but also to care about the characters, to identify with them, to learn from them and to grow with them. Your people are the life of your story. Pay attention to them, listen to them and care about them. If you don't, your readers will know the difference. If you do, your characters will bring a strength and dimension to your writing you never dreamed possible.

PART FOUR

Can These Bones Speak?

Chapter Ten

Words of Spirit and Life

Effective Dialogue

My grandfather didn't talk much. Oh, you could get him to tell you about his garden, about what was wrong with his pickup truck or about the latest gossip floating around the small town where he lived. But when it came to deeper issues, he was a man of few words.

Once and only once did I get him to open up to me. During a college break, I picked him up and drove him to my parents' home for a family holiday. On that three-hour trip, he talked to me about "real" things—about some of his ambitions that hadn't come true and about his hopes for me, that I would realize my own dreams and not live with regrets of what might have been. Shortly after that trip, he died. And as I stood beside his grave, I was thankful that he had given me such a great gift in the last days of his life—a glimpse into his heart.

Words can conceal or reveal. Dialogue can obscure the truth by focusing on superficialities, or it can cut deep to the heart of a character or situation. In fiction writing, dialogue can be an author's best friend or worst enemy.

All conscientious novelists want their fiction to be realistic. They work hard to create believable characters, gripping dialogue and heart-stopping drama and suspense. But many writers don't seem to understand the difference between *reality* and *realism*. In an effort to be "real" in their writing, they fall into traps that bog down the movement of the story, confuse their readers and clutter up the page.

When we say that we want our fiction to be "realistic," what we mean is that it should be true-to-life, believable. Our plotlines should intrigue and captivate readers; our characters should jump off the page and into the reader's heart.

One of the surest ways to undermine realism in your novel is to be too dedicated to reality. Reality is what occurs in everyday life—brushing your teeth, taking out the garbage, scanning the TV listings to see if there's anything worth watching or trying to maintain your Christian composure when you answer the phone at dinner time only to hear the annoying voice of a garrulous telemarketer trying to sell some worthless product. And let's face it, much of our everyday reality is deathly boring. Realism in fiction is life with the boring parts deleted.

Just as authors often defend an improbable or dreary plotline with the "reality" argument ("But that's the way it really happened!"), they resort to the same logic to defend mundane dialogue ("That's the way people talk!").

It may have happened that way, and people may talk that way, but this is fiction. And the purpose of fiction is to represent truth, not fact. What really happened—or in the case of dialogue, what they really said—may often distort or cloud the importance of the moment rather than illuminating it. A good writer gets beyond the pollution of reality, sifts out the silt and presents the clear, pristine truth—the significance that may be lost among the facts.

Good interviewers know the value of careful word choice. Even in a straightforward question-and-answer interview, the wise journalist will do some judicious pruning before the article goes to press. After all, what subject of a Q&A wants to be quoted as saying, "Well, um, it was, you know, a real great thing to be given the Nobel Prize"?

Articulate writing is an exercise in selection and streamlining—getting rid of the clutter and focusing on the issues, actions and relationships that matter. What you leave out is at least as important as what you put in. If you include all the stuff that really happens but is not germane to your plot or characters, you will end up with a book that barely resembles a novel at all—and one that certainly won't be of much interest to readers.

DIALOGUE: THE REALITY TRAP

The conflict between reality and realism often rears its head in the author's decisions about dialogue. Dialogue is essential to plot development and characterization. Relationships, understandings and misunderstandings, and dramatic tension can all hinge on an effective interchange between two characters. And dialogue serves as an extremely useful tool for the writer. It breaks up long paragraphs of description or the inner workings of the character's mind and puts the relationship between characters squarely out front—*showing* the interaction rather than telling the reader how the characters respond to one another.

One of the main problems with dialogue, however, relates to realism. In everyday conversation, people engage in a great deal of dialogue that has no significant purpose, or at least no purpose in furthering the movement of a novel. We engage in chit-chat, small talk, introductions and general rambling. And although such interchange is "realistic" in the sense that it reproduces how people really speak, it represents a kind of external reality that is not appropriate for a novel. It slows down the pace and can become infuriatingly boring for the reader.

> Marty stopped on the sidewalk and stared at the man in front of him. "Joe!" he said. "How in the world are you?"
>
> "Marty? I haven't seen you in ages."
>
> "I know . . . when was it, five years ago at graduation?"
>
> "No, I think it was four years ago, at our first class reunion."
>
> "You're right. How are you, Joe?"
>
> "Well, I'm just fine, Marty. And you?"
>
> "I'm doing all right, I guess. I'm getting a little arthritis in my left knee, but it's not slowing me down too much."
>
> "Oh, you mean the knee you busted up in that last regular season game?"
>
> "Yeah. Remember, I was in a cast, like, sidelined during the playoffs for the championship."
>
> "Oh, yeah. That was too bad, you know? We could have used you when we were down by seven points."
>
> "Well, it didn't matter much, you know? We won the championship."
>
> "So we did. Great game, too, right down to the final whistle."

Are you asleep yet? If you write this kind of "nothing" dialogue, your reader will be—and soon.

Good writers—successful, "make-a-living-at-it" writers—know the potential and the limitations of dialogue. Lurlene McDaniel, a popular speaker at Christian writing conferences and author of *Angels Watching Over Me*, *Till Death Do Us Part* and many other young adult novels, pulls no punches when she talks about dialogue. "Dialogue has only two purposes," McDaniel says, "to advance the plot or to reveal character traits, weaknesses or personalities." And she should know—she has her own line of young adult novels with Bantam.

Jerry Jenkins, author of *Left Behind* and *Tribulation Force* (co-authored with Tim LaHaye), agrees:

> Dialogue reveals character and moves the story along. It should never be used to prove that the writer knows what normal conversation is like. I skip all the pleasantries. We don't need to hear all those everyday expressions required at the beginnings and ends of telephone conversations, for example. Dialogue is where we cut to the chase.

Judith Pella, best-selling author of the Russians series (Bethany House), is convinced that reality determines the difference between excellence and mediocrity in fiction. "Real people, real situations, real life—written, of course, in such a way that it is a lot more interesting than real life." About dialogue, Pella concludes: "It is the main way for characters to relate to each other, and it can be used to further define characters by what they say and how they say it."

Gayle Roper, fiction author and director of the Sandy Cove Christian Writers Conference, believes that "good dialogue can make or break a novel. It draws the reader in like nothing else." And B.J. Hoff, author of the Emerald Ballad series and *The Penny Whistle*, gives perhaps the most insight into the purposes of dialogue. Hoff says:

> It's easier, I think, to say what *isn't* the purpose of dialogue. Dialogue is not to describe physical appearance. ("Your thick head of raven black hair, with those faint silver streaks at the temples, gives you a rather dignified, if somewhat wicked appearance, Harold.")
>
> Dialogue is not to annoy (or worse, bore) the reader by reciting the ordinary. ("Good morning, Neil Patrick, how

are you today?" said Mary as they entered the office. "Good morning, Mary," said Neil Patrick. "I'm just fine. How are you?")

And dialogue is not to educate the reader, especially in your chosen field of expertise. ("Say, Martin, I was just reading about the warrior codes of the Vikings and the Normans. It was exciting for me to learn that a troubadour in Norse Dublin could demand double the price for entertaining a generous Norseman as for a mean-spirited one.")

It's enough to stress what dialogue should do. Show character. Build the story by furthering action. Reveal emotion. Of all those, I think the delineation of character is the most important.

The verdict is in. The experts agree. Dialogue should be reserved for interchanges that communicate something significant about the characters and their relationship, or the ongoing movement of the plot. In a love scene, for example, dialogue can bring the characters out of their own minds and into interaction with one another. It can demonstrate insecurity, fear, longing or tenderness—any number of emotional responses. In a scene where two con artists are planning their next sting, dialogue can provide necessary information to the reader about the crooks' motivation, their weaknesses, and the possible ways they may slip up and bungle the job.

Beware, however, of trying to use dialogue to fit in information that seems out of place in narration. In historical novels, especially, authors have a tendency to use dialogue to communicate historical data or interpretations of what is going on behind the scenes. Thus we end up with a stilted interchange that sounds like a dry history lesson rather than a genuine interaction between two human characters:

Samantha put both hands on the dining table and stared at Matthew. "You mean," she said, "that you think the South is going to go to war with the North?"

"It looks that way," he said. "I've heard that President Lincoln is about to issue a proclamation, called the Emancipation Proclamation, that will legally free the slaves from their servitude. This will mean financial disaster for Southern slaveholders, who depend upon their slaves for the production of cotton and other products. These slave masters can't make a living without their slaves, and they're bound to go to war to protect their financial interests. Why, do you know that the average plantation owner below the Mason-Dixon line has over three hundred slaves working on his land? Slaves who live in shanties behind the big house. Some of them are house servants and are treated fairly well. They often sleep on pallets in the children's rooms. But the field workers are rarely fed enough to support life, and are often subject to beatings—or worse—if they so much as raise an eyebrow to the overseer."

Dialogue like this is an obvious ploy to inundate the reader with pertinent background material. It disseminates information, to be sure, but it does nothing to move the drama of the novel forward or to texturize the relationships between characters.

Strong, pertinent dialogue creates a scene in which two or more characters have an interchange that significantly furthers the plot or reveals something of their interactions or motivations. Dialogue is by its nature *dramatic*; it represents an active progression in plot or character. The readers are there; they experience the moment of tension or crisis with your characters, and it's a prime opportunity for you to draw them in and involve them in the characters' lives. Save your dialogue for the dramatic scenes: Don't use it to represent chitchat or to communicate background information.

VOICE AND DIALOGUE

Crafting realistic dialogue is a skill more caught than taught. We pick up certain techniques from the kind of fiction we read and, if we read analytically, we can begin to discern what works and what doesn't work—what kind of dialogue seems natural, significant and important, and what kind of dialogue is boring, impotent and useless.

In chapter nine, we talked about the importance of establishing a recognizable voice for each of your main characters. Voice has to do with more than the actual words your characters speak, of course—voice includes issues of motivation, background, attitude and perspective. But a character's voice, those elements that set the character apart from other characters in your novel, must be reflected in dialogue.

Is your character masculine or feminine, educated or ignorant, strong-willed or passive, creative or businesslike, trusting or suspicious? All these factors will play into how that character speaks—what kind of word choice and sentence structure is appropriate for the character, and what kind of attitude is displayed in his or her dialogue with other characters.

In the second book of my Home Front series, *Till We Meet Again*, I introduced a character who took on a life of her own—Libba's Great-Aunt Mag, an eighty-three-year-old widow who lives alone in Memphis and holds tenaciously to her independence. When I first introduced Aunt Mag early in the book, I wanted to show her fire and tenacity in an interaction with Libba, to represent her as a lovable eccentric with an iron will and an incisive wit. Some of that could be done from Libba's viewpoint in her first impressions of her great-aunt, but some of it could only be accomplished through dialogue.

When Libba first comes to Memphis and appears on Aunt Mag's doorstep, she is under the impression that she is coing to the aid of a frail, helpless old lady. She is shocked to find the house filled with an animated group of old women—Aunt Mag's Monday pinochle club—and she quickly learns that Aunt Mag doesn't need as much help as she thought.

> "I—I'm Libba Coltrain," (Libba says.) "I'm here to visit my Great-Aunt Mag . . . Magnolia Cooley. I must have the wrong house." She paused, puzzled. "But the mailbox said—"
>
> "You're in the right place, dearie, never fear."
>
> "But I—is Aunt Mag here? Mother said she was—"
>
> "Ancient, decrepit, and sorely in need of help and comfort?" The broad mouth smiled again. "Indeed she is, my dear. Welcome."
>
> Libba drew back in disbelief. "You're Aunt Mag?"
>
> "In the flesh."
>
> "But you're so . . . so—"
>
> "Alive?" Aunt Mag threw back her head and laughed heartily. "Yes, much to everyone's dismay, I am still able to sit up and take nourishment. People keep trying to con-

sign me to a wheelchair, but so far I've fought it quite effectively."

(Mag takes Libba into the kitchen.)

"Here," Mag said, thrusting a huge crystal punch bowl into Libba's hands. "You can help me make another round of punch for the girls, and we can have us a little chat. Then I'll introduce you." She bustled around the kitchen, pulling orange juice and ice-cube trays out of the humming modern refrigerator. "Equal parts of juice and ginger ale," she instructed as she clattered the ice trays into the kitchen sink. "And there—just above your head in that cabinet—you'll find some red food coloring."

"Food coloring?"

Aunt Mag dumped the ice into the punch bowl and gave Libba a conspiratorial wink. "Makes the girls think they're getting something special." She waved a hand derisively. "Posey Matthews raves about my cranberry surprise. The surprise is, it's not cranberry at all." Magnolia chuckled. "Most of them can't taste a thing anyway, so it doesn't matter."

In this interchange, it was essential to have Aunt Mag's voice come through loud and clear—the aging dowager, just a touch imperious, who grasps life by the throat and refuses to take herself too seriously.

Dialogue can accomplish that kind of characterization and forward movement in a novel if it is significant dialogue rather than just the daily "business as usual" fare.

In order to infuse your character's voice into dialogue, however, you as the writer must know the character well. You must have a clear understanding of not only what words the character would use, but also what kind of attitude and perspective will be communicated through those words. Just as you don't want your reader protesting, "This character wouldn't do that!" in terms of plot development, you don't want your reader to react, "She would never say that!" regarding your dialogue.

This is where an understanding of human psychology serves the author well. Based on a character's background, personality, motivations and belief structures, dialogue will develop that not only reflects words spoken between characters, but also reveals the inner workings of a character's mind.

Dialogue is essentially interaction. If you think about the significant conversations you have with people in your life, you will discover that those conversations are often based on *reaction*. Ralph makes a seemingly innocuous statement about how messy the house is. His wife Martha reacts defensively, launching into a diatribe about how hard she works and how many overtime hours she has been putting in. Ralph comes back with a response of his own: He works hard, too, and shouldn't have to come home to a pigsty. It's a common argument repeated in homes across America, but in fictional dialogue it can do much more than degenerate into a downward spiral of accusation that has no satisfactory conclusion. It can point to a basic philosophical difference between Ralph and Martha. Ralph holds to a traditional view of marriage in which the "little woman" stays home and keeps house; although they need the money Martha brings in, he resents the fact that she isn't available to take care of him. Martha has a more egalitarian view of marriage and expects Ralph to pitch in and do his part. Thus, when this ordinary marital interchange is translated into fictional dialogue, we have something far deeper than a confrontation about housecleaning: We have an underlying dramatic tension that can form the basis of a conflict that will escalate as the plot progresses.

Knowing who your characters are deep down—what brings them joy and gives them pain—is an essential factor in revealing their individual voices in dialogue.

Take care, as you construct verbal interchanges in your novel, to let your characters' dialogue reveal the significant elements of their personality and motivations. Your dialogue will seem real to your readers not because it reflects "what people really say" when they talk to one another, but because it gets to the core of who your people are, bringing new dimension to your characters and their relationships with one another.

DIALOGUE AND THE RELIGION TRAP

For the writer of Christian fiction—that is, fiction with significant spiritual content and evangelical perspective—the task of crafting dialogue presents some particular challenges. In the evangelical world, we are so accustomed to hearing religious jargon that our minds sometimes fail to register it, and thus it creeps into our writing without warning.

Some writers fall into the trap of putting so much God-talk into their dialogue that they begin to sound as if they're preaching a sermon rather than writing a novel—and to be perfectly honest, that's exactly what they're doing. They litter their fiction with prayers, petitions and homilies, and sometimes even with supernatural responses that bear little resemblance to reality.

Let's say you have a Christian family sitting down to dinner together. You want to have significant dialogue going on around the dinner table. Of course they pray before they begin to eat, but is it necessary to reproduce the prayer in its entirety? Only if that prayer contains some important revelation about the character or attitudes of the person saying Grace.

In *Home Fires Burning*, I encountered just such a situation. The main character Libba, a spoiled Southern "princess," has an aversion to housework and lets her cousins Willie and Mabel Rae take responsibility for the apartment they share. In one scene, Willie has had it with Libba's superior attitude, and when they sit down to dinner, her prayer reflects what is going on in her heart. "Bless this food, O Lord," Willie prays, "and the *hands that have worked so hard to prepare it.* Grant that we may be *grateful* for what you have given us, and make us ever mindful of the *needs of others.* Amen."

A simple prayer before a meal—and one that would be extraneous under normal circumstances. But Willie's frustration with Libba comes out in the sarcastic emphasis she gives to the italicized phrases, and although the significance of her prayer goes right over Libba's head, it serves a purpose in the scene—to provide a bit of humor and to give the reader insight into Willie. Willie's not really praying, after all. She's trying to get a point across to her cousin.

Over the years I have edited a number of books in which the author has fallen prey to the religion trap in dialogue. I have seen characters go on and on in long-winded prayers and homilies that serve no purpose in character development or plot movement. And the result of such sermonizing is always the same: It makes the "religious" elements of the book seem tacked on, with no objective except to fulfill a quota of God-language and make the novel fit the description of "Christian fiction."

There are times, of course, when characters do naturally talk to and about God. But we must be careful to construct such dialogue in such a way that it doesn't come across as author intrusion, as a mini-sermon built in to make the author's point or promulgate the author's religious views, or as jargon parroted back from a lifelong immersion in evangelical culture. Dialogue belongs to the character, not to the author, and it must always be consistent with that character's voice, personality and motivation.

Words give spirit and life to our characters. Dialogue—if it's crafted carefully—portrays significant interaction, reveals emotion, lends insight to the character, develops relationship and furthers the plot development.

In fiction, as in life, one principle prevails: If you have something to say, people will listen; if you don't, they'll tune you out. Give attention to your dialogue. Listen. Sift. Find your character's voice and be true to it. Choose wisely. Eliminate the mundane "dailyness" and concentrate on the important and dramatic interchanges.

Dialogue, as Gayle Roper reminds us, can make or break a novel. Evocative, well-constructed dialogue can captivate readers and compel them to identify with the characters, with their hopes, dreams, joys and struggles. Crafting good dialogue takes time, effort and attention, but the outcome is worth the work.

Chapter Eleven

Ain't Gonna Study Grammar No Mo

The Difficulties of Dialect

I grew up in Mississippi. I received my Bachelor's and Master's degrees from Mississippi University for Women, one of the finest small colleges in the nation. I took a Ph.D. at the University of Mississippi, where a portion of William Faulkner's Nobel Prize acceptance speech is engraved on the library wall. Mississippi not only gave us Faulkner, but such literary stars as Eudora Welty, Tennessee Williams and Richard Wright. And yet when people think of Mississippi, they inevitably conjure up images of a backwoods moonshiner spitting tobacco juice out the window of a rusted pickup truck and shooting possum for dinner with a double-barreled shotgun.

Why? I think it's because of dialect. I've always believed you could be dumb as a brick and yet appear intelligent if you have a British accent; on the other hand, a Southern drawl tends to make even a rocket scientist sound ignorant.

In a nutshell, that's the entire plot of Shaw's play *Pygmalion*, better known to most of us as the Broadway musical *My Fair Lady*. Liza Doolittle is a common street girl, an ignorant flower seller with a hideous Cockney accent. But by the time Professor Higgins gets through with correcting her pronunciation and retraining her speech patterns, she passes as royalty.

Dialect can be an important factor in characterization. How a character sounds gives clues to the character's background, educational level and self-perceptions. But dialect can be a dangerous trap for a writer: If we want to write fiction that maintains the "vivid, continuous dream," we need to approach the use of dialect with great caution.

THE DIALECT DILEMMA

In chapter ten, we discussed the difference between realism and reality in reference to dialogue. Reality reproduces the ordinary conversation of ordinary people, and it can be deathly boring in fiction. Realism cuts to the chase, selecting dialogue that furthers the plot or the reader's insight into characters and relationships.

With the issue of dialect, the "reality vs. realism" problem rears its head once more. New writers—and even experienced writers who want to do their own thing—often mistakenly assume that the more realistic a character's inner thought patterns and dialogue are, the better. Thus, they produce dialect that is riddled with distorted spellings, attempting to reproduce the "sound" of a character's speech. They argue that the reader needs to "hear" that the character drops g's from "ing" words, that she pronounces "oil" as "erl" and that she turns i's into a's. And so they come up with dialogue like, "When the moon is brat on a lat nat, ever'thin's gonna be all rat."

I have fought many a battle with well-meaning authors over the use of dialect. For some reason, writers are adamant about keeping their precious, painstaking dialectical constructions. "That's the way the character really sounds!" they argue. "Using dialect is a stylistic technique, not an issue of right or wrong." Perhaps they truly believe that slack language, misspellings, mispronunciations and the like add color and flavor to their dialogue. But by holding onto dialect, they violate the cardinal principle of writing: communication.

Our purpose in fiction is to draw the reader into that "vivid, continuous dream." *Anything* in our writing that causes readers to frown, scratch their heads and go back to read the paragraph a second or third time intrudes into the dream and should be excised.

The use of dialect can be a serious stumbling block in an otherwise credible novel. When readers have to translate every interchange, they find it tedious, time-consuming, wearying work. The writer may sit back smugly, proud of her commitment to reality, but readers don't care about hearing every syllable accurately—they just want to be able to read the book without having to do all the work themselves.

The use (or overuse) of dialect, then, is not a simple difference of opinion about personal style. Dialect inevitably intrudes upon the movement of a story. Whether we like the idea or not, as writers we cannot "faithfully reproduce" the sounds people make and call it dialect.

The fact is, none of us speaks standard English. Every area of the country, every particular location—we might even say every individual—has distinctive pronunciations and phrasing along with grammatical eccentricities. An attempt on the part of a fiction writer to reproduce all of those sounds and structures would result in utter literary chaos. We might as well write every word of dialogue phonetically, to make sure we are being realistic about the pronunciations.

Consider the following "dialogue":

> "M r paigs."
> "M r nawt paigs."
> "O S A R. C m pins?"
> "L I B. M r paigs."

Translation:

> "Them are pigs."
> "Them are not pigs."
> "Oh, yes they are. See them pens?"
> "Well, I'll be. Them are pigs."

As outrageous as this example might seem, some authors' attempts at reproducing the exact sounds of human dialect come across just as ludicrous to a struggling reader who simply wants to get on with the story. Who wants to wade through the dialogue of a German professor who, though an educated speaker of English, says, "Ve vanted to go ta da Embassy Ball vit you, but ve vouldn't be able to vear de vight vardrobe"? Such "dialect" is as contorted as the old Katzenjammer Kids comic strip—but not nearly as amusing. And it makes readers mutter under their breaths, "Hookt own phonics werkt fer me!"

Carol Bly, in *The Passionate, Accurate Story*, discusses dialogue in terms of the difference between "inner realism" and "outer realism" (the distinction I have referred to as "realism vs. reality"). Inner realism is the use of dialogue (and limited words in dialect) to present some significant truth about a character. Outer realism is a slavish devotion to exactitude in the way characters pronounce individual words and expressions. An obsession with dialect does not communicate anything important—except, perhaps, the author's ability to reproduce odd sounds.

Dialect is like ground red pepper—useful for particular purposes, but only in extremely small portions. Too much overwhelms the reader and offends the sensibilities, not to mention bogging down the movement of the story.

A close friend of mine in graduate school was a Ph.D. candidate in pharmacy. He was a bright, intelligent fellow, a brilliant conversationalist and a star student. But his heritage came out in his dialect: He talked about using "balin' war" (baling wire) to hold up the muffler on his old "Spitfar" ('Spitfire) convertible. Had I cast him using those spelling aberrations in fictional dialogue, he would have come across as an ignorant plowhand rather than a gifted intellectual.

Let's face it: Certain speech anomalies and mispronunciations do say something about the education or ignorance, simplicity or sophistication of a character. As Carol Bly reminds us, literature is by nature symbolic, and the words we attribute to our characters symbolize something important about their backgrounds, perspectives, education and social class. We need to keep focused on the purpose of our characterization and not get sidetracked with an external reality that interferes with the story.

THE MORE EXCELLENT WAY

Whenever I teach about dialogue and dialect at writers conferences, the question inevitably arises: "All right, if we want to avoid dialect—distorted spellings and such—how do we get the flavor of a particular character's language across to the reader?"

The answer is simple, and yet not so simple. Like many other issues in crafting a well-written, believable novel, the "best" way to do something is not necessarily the easiest way. Above all, we need to remember our audience: What is easier for the writer (using distorted spellings in dialect, for example) is not always easier for the reader, who has to wade through all that misspelling and translate on the fly.

But there is another way. A better way. If we work at it, we can give the reader the flavor of a character's dialogue through sentence structure and speech patterns, rather than resorting to misspellings and phonetics.

Flannery O'Connor, who writes almost exclusively about

common, uneducated Southern characters, rarely uses dialect. She will occasionally have a character saying "ain't" and "y'all," but those are common usages that don't distract the reader. Instead of burdening the reader with the task of dialect translation, she accomplishes the same purpose—giving a voice to the character and communicating something about the character's background or personality—with a turn of phrase or unexpected usage. In her story, "The River," for example, Mrs. Connin, a simple country woman with an equally simple faith, says, "Well, ain't that a coincident." The misuse of the word "coincident" for "coincidence" speaks volumes about Mrs. Connin's uneducated Southern heritage. O'Connor doesn't have to resort to outer realism; she can, with a turn of phrase or an out-of-place word, pin down the character and catch the rhythms of speech. It's a much more refined—and more effective—technique than phonetic reproduction.

The problem with this technique, of course, is that it takes more time, more effort and more ongoing work than simply reproducing phonetic sounds. We have to study the speech patterns of those around us; we have to listen, to absorb not just the pronunciation of individual words, but also the way those words are put together—the small, seemingly insignificant cadences that comprise an individual's dialect.

Where dialect is concerned, I have a major bone to pick with Hollywood. Because they haven't done their homework, actors and their directors often make the sweeping assumption that all Southerners talk alike. Throw in a few "y'alls" and "ain'ts," drawl one-syllable words out into two or three ("fow-erk" for "fork"), and bingo! Instant Southern accent. What they don't understand is that a broad Texas drawl is quite different from the soft twang of a Georgia peach. That an Alabama socialite's dialect has little in common with the angular expressions of a poor mountain family in the Ozarks. That some Carolinians say "you'uns" instead of "y'all"—and most importantly, that "y'all" is a contraction for "you all," a plural, and is never, NEVER used to refer to one person.

Every area of the country has its own eccentricities of this nature. In Minnesota, the evidence of Norwegian and Swedish influence is rampant, but it goes far beyond the stereotypical "Ya, sure, you betcha" found in Scandinavian jokes about Sven and Ole. Many Minnesotans of Norwegian descent tend to hiss their *s*'s—and so pronounce "Jesus" as "Jessuss." And for once, Hollywood got it right: The 1996 Oscar-winning film *Fargo* finally captured the Minnesota inflections and sentence structure so well that even my Norwegian friends laughed out loud.

If we want our dialogue to sing, to be realistic without resorting to the stereotypes of altered spellings or unpronounceable distortions, we have to pay attention. We have to listen, learn, and reproduce the rhythm and flow of the character's speech rather than taking the easy way out.

This doesn't mean that we never drop a syllable or use a corrupted spelling. Most readers skim right over distortions like "gotta" or "gonna" in an uneducated character's dialogue. Readers can deal with an "ain't" or a "y'all" every now and then. But unless your primary purpose in writing is to frustrate and enrage your reader, you would do well to eliminate most overt dialect from your characters' speech. Drop an occasional *g* from the end of an "-ing" word, perhaps, but don't do it every time. Your character may slur the "it's" when she says "it's not right," but if you render it "S'not right," you are setting yourself up to be the butt of a reader's joke.

If heavy dialect is absolutely necessary to make a point in characterization, there are ways to use it without distracting the reader—to make it work for you rather than against you. In one instance, in *Till We Meet Again*, I faced just such a dilemma. My character Ivory Brownlee, a veteran of World War I and a victim of shell shock, had a very simple approach to life. His speech patterns reflected that—he spoke in brief, almost child-like sentences with an occasional "ain't" or "gonna," but usually in fairly grammatical constructions.

At one point, however, I deliberately used Ivory's dialectal eccentricities to emphasize the simplicity and purity of his faith. At a particularly dark time in his life, he makes a reference to "Jesus being in our *mist*." What he means, of course, is "Jesus in our midst," but he gets the word wrong. Thelma Breckinridge, Ivory's good friend, picks up on the mistake and turns it into a profound theological truth: When the fog is thickest and we can't see where we're going, Jesus is there with us in our darkness, "in our mist."

In a novel I'm currently working on, I face a similar problem.

A young woman named Catherine comes to Mississippi from Minnesota, and to her uninitiated ear, the thick Southern accent is almost unintelligible. I wanted to get across exactly what Catherine was hearing in this first encounter, but I didn't want the reader to have to labor for the meaning. And so I have Catherine's Southern hostess speaking, followed by a mental "translation":

> "Do forgive my forwardness, child. It's just our way; we're all just one big family here. You'll grow accustomed to it, I assure you."
>
> To Catherine's untrained ear, this effusion sounded like *"Dooo f'give mah fowardness, chile. I's jus ahr way . . . yewell grow ahcussomed t'it."* But she caught enough of it to realize that her ebullient hostess had noticed her discomfort, and she blushed.

The reversed pattern—that is, having the hostess speak in normal English and then allowing Catherine to reproduce in her mind the sounds she has heard—establishes the flavor of the dialect and the difficulty Catherine is having with it, without making the reader do a phonetic transcription to find out what the hostess is trying to say. And note: This first brief encounter is the only time in the novel that Catherine makes an issue of the dialect. She may on occasion stumble over an oddly pronounced word, but for the most part, she gets accustomed to the accent and forgets about it, just as we do in normal interaction with people who speak differently.

Imagine, if you will, what a hideous mess it would be if all the Southern characters in the book (that is, everyone except Catherine herself) spoke in phonetically accurate dialect throughout the novel—if every "do" was rendered "doo" and every "for" spelled "fer," and if every slave went around saying, "Yassah, Massah" and "no mo." Not only would the dialogue take twice as long to write and an eternity to spell-check, but it would take three times as long to read. And it would be a fiscal catastrophe as well, because not even the most loyal reader is willing to work that hard.

Rather than spending your time trying to reproduce the sounds of your character's speech, go the extra mile to familiarize yourself with speech patterns instead. Catch the *rhythm* of the dialect and use it to communicate your character's ethnic background, location or educational level. If your readers can hear the unique movements of a character's speech, they won't be concerned about specific pronunciations. If they can't hear it, all your misspellings will merely irritate them and make them feel as if you're taking the lazy way out.

MOVING BEYOND STEREOTYPES

In previous chapters, we have touched on the issue of stereotyping—the mistaken assumption that all people of a particular race, ethnic origin or class behave in a standardized way. For the Christian, especially, there should be no place for that kind of prejudice in our lives or in our writing, and yet we find it all too often in evangelical fiction.

If for no other reason, we need to be extremely careful about dialect because it provides fertile ground for stereotyping. After generations, we have finally begun to move beyond the disturbing caricatures of African-Americans as lazy Step-and-Fetchits, drug addicts, hubcap thieves or professional athletes. We know (don't we?) that all Jewish mothers aren't domineering matriarchs, that Chinese citizens do more than laundry and manual labor, that Native Americans aren't a race of bloodthirsty savages or alcoholics, and that some white men *can* jump. We have learned that femininity can be strong and masculinity can be nurturing, that single career women aren't all frustrated spinsters and that single men don't necessarily live with their mommies.

In addition to guarding against negative stereotyping, we need to be aware of the tendency toward "whitewashed stereotypes" if we wish to offer our readers true and balanced characterization. Even the term White Anglo-Saxon Protestant (WASP) has the capability of packing a nasty sting, and some who claim the name of Christ can on occasion exhibit distinctly un-Christlike behavior. Real Christians don't necessarily live like saints and talk like preachers—at least not all of them, not all the time.

But when we get into the area of dialect, those stereotypes (both positive and negative), seem to assert themselves. Just this afternoon I listened to the "I Have a Dream" speech delivered from the steps of the Lincoln Memorial during the March on Washington in 1963. Dr. Martin Luther King Jr., winner of the

Nobel Peace Prize and acknowledged Moses of the Civil Rights movement, gave this stirring address:

> "I have a dream . . . that someday my four little children will live in a nation where they will not be judged by the color of their skin but by the content of their character. I have a dream today . . . "

But if Dr. King's words were reproduced faithfully, according to his unique style and oratorical delivery, the speech would be rendered:

> "Ah have uh dureeem . . . uh dureeem that one day mah fowah liddle chilrun will live in a nation wheah they will not be judged by the cullah of theah skin, but bah the conteeunt of theah charactur. Ah have uh dureeem today . . ."

Yes, this is reality. This is the way he sounded. But this is not an accurate depiction of the man's intelligence or his passion for his cause. These are not the words of one of the greatest leaders of our time, but the words of a stereotype, words that imply ignorance of the language, words that demean and diminish the power and majesty of the speaker's ideas. The misspellings may accurately represent the phonetic pronunciations in Dr. King's address, but they do not communicate the deeper truths about the man's intellect, calling or intensity.

If your character is ignorant or uneducated or low-class, you may wish to use a few selected ungrammatical sentences or corrupted words to alert your readers to those characteristics. But be wary of resorting to dialect simply to try to make your characters sound real. You may find yourself inadvertently undermining their strengths, stereotyping them and frustrating your readers. It's far better to do the necessary research, get a fix on speech patterns and rhythms, and employ those more subtle identifiers to put the stamp of authenticity upon your characters. Your characters will come alive and your readers will thank you—and your editors will offer prayers of gratitude to heaven on your behalf.

Chapter Twelve

Who Says So?

The Challenge of Attribution

Duriing my years of college teaching, I would inevitably get into battles with students when term paper time rolled around. "I got the quote," they would say when I marked their grades down for insufficient documentation. "What difference does it make who said it?"

It makes a world of difference. When a mob boss tells an enemy, "I'll take care of you," it carries an impact quite the opposite of what a loving mother means when she says the same words to a sick child. When a husband says, "I plead the Fifth," in joking response to his wife's question about whether he took out the garbage, it has a far different impact than when an accused murderer hides behind the Fifth Amendment on the witness stand.

Particularly in fiction—since we have no movement, pitch, tone of voice or visible gestures to indicate the identity of the speaker—clear attribution of dialogue becomes essential. *Attribution* refers to the identification of the speaker in a dialogue interchange—which parts of the dialogue are attributed to which characters. And if we want to craft characters whose dialogue comes alive, the attributions we give them must be appropriate.

WHO SAID THAT?

If fiction is intended to be a "vivid, continuous dream," as writers we need to learn to excise anything in our work that interrupts that dream or intrudes upon the continuity. In drama, we don't have this particular problem—the actors are on stage, in full view of the audience, and there is no question in the audience's mind about who the speaker is. Not so for the written word. On the page of a novel, the author has the responsibility to make it clear who is saying what, and the challenge of doing so in a way that does not disrupt the dream.

New writers—and sometimes even experienced writers who should know better—fall prey to a number of common mistakes in attribution.

The "Said" Syndrome

I remember stumbling across a television show once in which a character was portrayed as an airhead valley girl. Her dialogue went something like this: "And then he says well I don't know, and then she says, like, well you'd better find out, and then he says, you know, like are you saying you won't go out with me unless I do, and then she says . . ."

Some fictional dialogue sounds pretty much the same:

> "I have to go," he said.
> "Do you really have to?" she said.
> "Yes, I do," he said. "I have an appointment."
> "You always have appointments," she said. "You never spend any time with me."
> "I spent time with you last week," he said.
> "But that was only a short lunch, and I haven't seen you since," she said.

In this example, the attributions are certainly clear, but by the time readers gets to the end of the interchange, they've been "said" nearly to death. I've been told that "said" is supposed to be an *invisible* word—a word the reader's eye goes right over without it registering in the brain. But when "said" is repeated over and over with every response, it might as well be written in caps and boldface print. It calls undue attention to itself, and either bores or annoys the reader.

Spice Addiction

Many writers have the mistaken notion that variety is the spice of attribution. Their characters "query" or "interrogate" instead of "ask"; they "expostulate" instead of "say." Mark Twain once commented that since he was being paid by the word, a five-letter word would do as well as a twelve-letter one.

Spice addiction reveals itself in dialogue like this:

"I have to go," he protested.

"Do you really have to?" she queried.

"Yes, I do," he declared. "I have an appointment."

"You always have appointments," she lamented. "You never spend any time with me."

"I spent time with you last week," he countered.

"But that was only a short lunch, and I haven't seen you since," she remonstrated.

In this example, the writer's relative level of self-consciousness is revealed in the use of dialogue attributions, and the reader is left with the overwhelming conviction that the author spends most of his or her free time poring over the *Reader's Digest* vocabulary quiz to learn what "remonstrated" means. Writers who are in love with their own words often fall into the trap of using the "unusual" attribution—attributions rarely used in normal speech, words that bog down the movement of the dialogue and cause the reader to stumble.

Adverb Fixation

Similar to spice addiction, adverb fixation is the author's tendency to use adverbs or adverbial phrases in attribution to communicate something about the speaker's emotions or state of mind. Adverb fixation goes several decibels beyond spice addiction on the annoyance meter:

"I have to go," he said determinedly.

"Do you really have to?" she asked imploringly.

"Yes, I do," he responded emphatically. "I have an appointment."

"You always have appointments," she said whiningly. "You never spend any time with me."

"I spent time with you last week," he countered obstinately.

"But that was only a short lunch, and I haven't seen you since," she said vociferously.

This kind of dialogue provides enough evidence for any writer to be judged guilty of "excessive adverbalization." It's not a felony that carries a prison sentence, but it is a serious misdemeanor that may foster antagonism in your readers.

Description Dependency

A final and most deadly trap for a writer of fiction is the obsession with using dialogue attributions to do the work of narration. In this dysfunctional scenario, the author adds information to the attribution which clearly doesn't belong and which violates the principle of the "vivid, continuous dream":

"I have to go," he said, snapping shut the beautiful oxblood leather briefcase that was given to him by his parents when he graduated from Harvard Law in 1984, the briefcase that always reminded him of how proud his parents would be that he had finally been made a partner in the firm of Clark, Leigh, and Lombard.

"Do you really have to?" she asked, raking a hand through her ash-blonde hair, which she kept long just because he liked it that way, and tightening the belt of the magenta silk robe he brought her from his last trip to Cancun, the trip he had insisted on taking even though Buford had just come home from the hospital and she wasn't even on her feet yet.

"Yes, I do," he said, remembering how much he had once loved her and wondering where the passion had gone since the birth of their son, Buford Jr., nine months ago. "I have an appointment."

"You always have appointments," she said, thinking of how he used to call in late to work just so they could have a leisurely breakfast together on the patio beside the swimming pool they had put in when he had finally gotten his partnership, a lovely kidney-shaped pool with a hot tub at one end and a diving board for little Buford when he got old enough to learn to swim. "You never spend any time with me."

"I spent time with you last week," he protested, looking at his watch and rehearsing the excuse he would give the senior partners for being late to this morning's meeting.

"But that was only a short lunch, and I haven't seen you since," she said, considering the possibility that her mother might have been right when she said she didn't want her daughter to marry a workaholic, even though he would be a good provider and give her all the material things she never had when she was a child because her father was a lazy bum and never held down a job for more than two months at a time.

All the "information" in this dialogue—the fact that the husband has finally won his partnership, his memories of his parents, his questions about his relationship with his wife, his wife's frustrations, her memories of her mother's warning and her father's laziness—may be important for the development of the characters, but it doesn't belong in dialogue attribution. And if you doubt that any author in her right mind would concoct such contorted attributions, count your blessings. I've seen them in manuscripts and even in print, and much worse than the example I've given here. In one particular manuscript (whose author shall remain nameless), I encountered attributions that ran ten to fifteen lines long, with up to nine subordinate clauses. That kind of description dependency, coupled with adverb fixation and spice addiction, makes for a novel that a reader will never forget . . . but for all the wrong reasons.

APPROPRIATE ATTRIBUTIONS

So, you're convinced that you want to avoid the "said" syndrome. You want to recover from your spice addiction, put an end to adverb fixation and liberate yourself from description dependency. You want to create believable dialogue uninterrupted by intrusive attributions. But how do you go about doing it? How do you make your attributions clear without hitting the reader over the head with a two-by-four?

If you want to keep your attributions clean and streamlined, and move the dialogue along, consider the following principles.

The best attribution is no attribution at all. If you think that a constant repetition of "he said/she said" in dialogue is awkward and distracting, you're right. But the answer is not to find a different word—a five-hundred-dollar word—to replace "said." The answer is to construct your interchange so that attributions aren't needed at all. This is most easily accomplished when you have two speakers who take turns speaking:

John looked at Mary and smiled. "Go out to dinner with me tonight."

"Tonight? Oh, I couldn't possibly go tonight! I have to—"

"Nothing you have to do is more important than dinner with me. I'll make it worth your while. . . ."

In the first sentence of the interchange, the author has identified the speakers: John and Mary. John speaks first, Mary answers and then John responds. There is no need for any attributive verbs at all, not even "said." If the dialogue continues, the author can go on indefinitely without any attributions, as long as it is clear to the reader who is speaking.

Writing attributionless dialogue with more than two speakers is a bit more difficult, but with a little care it can be done. The trick is to identify the speaker with some kind of specific action, either before or after the actual quotation.

John looked at Mary and smiled. "Go out to dinner with me tonight."

"Tonight? Oh, I couldn't possibly go tonight! I have to—"

"She has to get ready for her final exams tomorrow." Mary's mother leaned over the upstairs banister and scowled at John. "And besides, why would she go out with the likes of you?"

Without resorting to any specific attributions, we have introduced three characters in the dialogue and made perfectly clear to the reader who is saying what. And we have accomplished another purpose as well—we have characterized Mary's mother. She eavesdrops on other people's conversations, tries to control her daughter's life and doesn't like John one bit. Why she is like this, we don't know; her motivations will have to be revealed in other ways—through her own point of view, perhaps, or through Mary's. But in her two brief sentences, she has revealed a lot about herself.

Attributionless dialogue can work quite well in almost any situation, but you need to be aware of your readers' limitations, particularly if the dialogue goes on for quite a while. I've read otherwise well-crafted novels in which attributionless dialogue goes on for so long that I had to go back to the beginning and count down the page to make sure of who was speaking. You don't want your readers having to go back and do a "one-two-one-two" count in order to identify the speaker. An occasional attribution or a well-placed gesture can solve this problem smoothly, without interrupting the flow of the dialogue.

When attributions are necessary, keep them simple. There are times, of course, when you will have to use some kind of attributive verb to indicate your speaker's identity. But beware of using words your reader will have to look up in his *Funk & Wagnalls.* In general, "said" and "asked" are obvious choices, depending upon whether the dialogue is in the form of a statement or a question. The words "said" and "asked" can be intrusive if they're overused, but they work well as occasional attributions.

Use normal grammatical patterns in attributions. Some writers tend to reverse the natural order of the English language in their attributions—they characteristically write "said John" instead of "John said." But attributions are like any other grammatical structure in your writing—if you vary the word order once in a while, your reader probably won't mind. If you do it all the time, you'll come across as a "literary prima donna affecting a poetic style," and your constructions will call attention to themselves.

Restrict your attributions to auditory verbs. There are some instances in which an invisible verb such as "said" cannot communicate what you need to accomplish in your dialogue attribution. But remember, dialogue is essentially auditory—it should be heard and not seen. Thus, appropriate attributions are those words that communicate some kind of auditory significance: "whisper," "murmur," "shout." Attributive verbs should denote some change in tone or volume—something the reader can hear. If your characters "explode" their sentences or "machine-gun" their words, you are mixing visual images with auditory ones, and the result can be ludicrous rather than dramatic.

Avoid using attributions for description or emotion. Rarely do I find in manuscripts the kind of excess I've described as "description dependency," but by far the most common mistake among young fiction writers is the tendency to use overt description in dialogue attribution. The description may not go on for a page and a half, but even a single phrase or word can disrupt the flow of your novel:

"I've never seen anything quite so beautiful," Maria expostulated wonderingly.

Instead of:

Maria touched the butterfly's wing gently and blinked back a sudden rush of tears. "I've never seen anything quite so beautiful."

Descriptions of a character's feelings, information about the character's past and physical characteristics don't belong in attributions. If a character is "musing," have her stare out the window with a faraway expression on her face; if she is angry, have her frown and narrow her eyes. Don't give her a line of dialogue that "she wondered musingly" or "she spat out angrily."

Overly descriptive attribution falls under the category of *telling*, not showing. When authors resort to adverbs to tell us how the line is spoken (frustratedly, bemusedly, excitedly), they are guilty of author intrusion. They come out in front of the camera and say, "This is the way you should interpret this interchange."

If the dialogue is well written, however, no such interpretation should be necessary. Readers are quite capable of interpreting what they need to interpret, and they will move much more smoothly through your interchanges if your characters reveal themselves, rather than you doing it for them.

Let the character speak; use the words and actions, not the attribution, to communicate the emotional impact of the scene.

A WORD ABOUT THE WORD

For the writer of Christian fiction, one of the most daunting challenges occurs when you want or need to incorporate scripture into your dialogue. How do you have a character quoting a Bible reference without it appearing phony or hyperspiritual?

In the early days of my faith, I was trained with the Navigators Ministry, a campus parachurch organization that stressed the importance of scripture memory. We were taught not only to memorize the word verbatim, but also to commit to memory the exact book, chapter and verse. That might work well with a "sword drill," as some people called those scripture-memory reviews, but when such a principle is incorporated into the ordinary conversation of ordinary fictional characters, the result is at best ludicrous, and at worst propaganda.

A fictional pastor might stand in the pulpit, clear his throat and intone, "In First John chapter four, verses 7 and 8, the apostle says, 'Beloved, let us love one another. . . .' " But when a busdriver, a waitress or a newly converted prison inmate does it, it will undoubtedly raise red flags with your reader.

The key, I believe, is to remember who your character is. Unless the character in question is a professional, direct quoting of scripture may well come across as author intrusion—an attempt to impose the writer's spiritual agenda upon the reader. Most of us ordinary folks, after all, have a limited cache of Bible verses at our command. We may, in moments of joy, crisis, need, or insight, recall certain scriptures and gain comfort and hope from them. But usually our recollections are less than verbatim, and we probably don't know exactly where the verse appears without looking it up in a concordance or going back to a well-marked Bible to find it.

In my own writing, when I have a character recalling a verse of scripture, I almost always paraphrase the verse and give the character only a vague memory of having learned it in Sunday School or having discovered it during a similar crisis in the past. I almost never have one character quoting or reading scripture to another, because I believe that personal discovery leads to deeper spiritual transformation than preaching does.

If we keep in the forefront of our minds the backgrounds, limitations and personalities of our characters, we can determine how (or if) a character would realistically deal with scripture:

- Would the character be likely to know any Bible verses in the first place?
- If she did know them, would she know them by heart, accurately?
- Is this character the type of person to preach to someone else, or to impose her own understanding of the scripture upon another character?
- What motivated the sudden recollection of this verse?
- Does the rendering of the verse seem natural and in keeping with the character?

Scripture can, of course, be used in a variety of ways in your novel. If you have a Pharisaical, self-righteous character, he or she may well go around spouting scriptures at everyone in the novel, but that kind of use of scripture serves to give the character an identity, not to preach to the reader. If you have a new convert, that character may recall a Bible verse or two from somewhere far back in childhood and, depending upon your purposes, the character's understanding or misunderstanding of the verse may provide opportunity for humor, pathos or personal insight.

Whatever your reason for having a character speak the Word, however, you need to make sure that it's in keeping with the character's background and personality. In most cases, that means paraphrasing and refraining from giving a chapter-and-verse reference. If for some reason you quote a verse directly, make sure it's exact and set in double quotation marks. And watch which translation you use: A World War II character will not quote scripture in New International Version!

Even in the case of a preacher or some other character who would naturally think and/or speak in Biblical quotations, you may want to limit the amount of scripture you allow your character to spout. Preachers are human, too—they forget things and get it wrong, and frustrate themselves with their own lack of understanding. Rather than whitewash Christian characters and make them all seem like pure and holy Bible scholars, keep them true to themselves. Your readers will get the point, and they will bless you for your restraint.

Dialogue at its best is realism, not reality. It advances the movement of the plot, enhances characterization and lends authenticity to the writing. If you pay close attention to your dialogue, avoiding dialect, historical lecturing, descriptive attributions, and preachiness, your characters will live, and their words will seem both real and interesting.

PART FIVE

Truth in the Inward Parts

Chapter Thirteen

Only God Is Omniscient

Understanding Viewpoint

F rom an editorial perspective, one of the most frequent and frustrating problems exhibited by novelists is inconsistency in point of view. In both Christian and general markets, we often find highly successful writers who apparently have no concept of viewpoint—or at least no concern about it. They switch point of view indiscriminately in scene after scene. And although most readers couldn't articulate the problem if asked to do so, they sense something wrong because they have difficulty following the movement of the story.

Clearly, a great many successful novelists, both in the CBA and in the general market, get away with murder in their use (or misuse) of point of view, and nevertheless their books appear on the best-seller lists season after season.

But selling a lot of books is not the primary issue: The issue is excellence in writing. Those million-seller books could be vastly improved by careful attention to consistency in point of view. No matter what a novel's sales figures indicate, inconsistency in point of view clouds the characters and causes unnecessary confusion. In short, even a good book can be better if the author pays careful attention to viewpoint.

A writer can get away with almost anything in a novel if the writing is good enough. But if we want to eliminate the stumbling blocks that get in the way of a reader's understanding— those speed bumps that slow the reader down and interrupt what John Gardner calls "the vivid, continuous dream of fiction"— we need to pay attention to viewpoint.

UNDERSTANDING VIEWPOINT

I will never forget the first time I was asked at a writers conference: "What is the most common and difficult problem you encounter in your editing?"

"Inconsistency in point of view," I answered instantly.

People shifted in their seats and glanced at one another apprehensively. For a full minute no one made a sound, until finally one brave soul spoke up: "Ah, what exactly does that mean?"

They don't know, I thought. *They've never been taught about viewpoint, and they haven't the vaguest idea what I'm talking about.*

So we started from the beginning then, and we start from the beginning now.

Perhaps the easiest way to understand point of view in your own writing is to think in terms of *camera angle*. The viewpoint character is behind the camera; everything in the scene, and in the character's emotional response to the scene, is perceived through that character's eyes.

The foundational principle is that every scene in your novel has one, and only one, viewpoint character. During that scene—whether it's a few paragraphs or an entire chapter—all the action that takes place in the scene is filtered through the perceptions of that viewpoint character. Nothing can happen that the viewpoint character is not aware of.

Think for a moment of your own interactions with other people. When you walk into a room full of people, every person, every object and every conversation in that room is filtered through your consciousness. You are the point-of-view character of the scene. You see the physical characteristics of other people, hear their conversations and watch their gestures and facial expressions. But unless you're a Betazoid empath like Counselor Troi on *Star Trek*, you don't hear their thoughts. You don't know what is in their minds except as it is revealed in their words, expressions or actions.

As the viewpoint character, you are very much aware of what is going on in your own mind—your reactions to those around you—but you are not consciously aware of yourself. You don't think about describing your own dark hair streaked with silver at the temples, or the expression in your own startling green eyes. And unless you spill punch on your blue silk dress, you have no reason to give any kind of conscious attention to your own wardrobe. As the viewpoint character, you are the "camera operator," and what you see is what is recorded on film—or in the case of your novel, what is described as taking place in the scene.

That is how point of view operates in your novel. You choose a viewpoint character and stay with him or her through the duration of the scene. And in so doing, you not only give a personal perspective to the action of your book, but you also have the opportunity to deepen characterization and make your characters more real to your readers.

Most writing books I've read carry limited, if any, information on viewpoint. They may give lip service and brief descriptions of different viewpoint options—usually first-person, third-person, or omniscient viewpoints—but they do not go into detail about the techniques of establishing viewpoint.

Maintaining consistency in point of view, however, is one of the most crucial principles for writers to understand and implement in their work. This concept alone can mean the difference between mediocrity and excellence in your writing.

POINT OF VIEW: AN OVERVIEW

When most people talk about "viewpoint," they are referring to the overall perspective of the novel: whether it is written in first person or third person. (If you've been out of school for a long time, "I" is first person, "you" is second person, and "he/she/they" is third person.)

In a novel, first person is the "I" narrator—not the author, but a created character who provides the lens through which the novel unfolds. Third-person point of view is the "he" or "she" perspective—a character (or group of characters) who govern the novel's development. To say that a novel is written in first person or third person is simply a categorization to identify the overall viewpoint of the book.

Writers can choose a number of different approaches when deciding what point of view to use in their fiction. Each option carries with it some benefits to the author and some possible pitfalls.

Omniscient Point of View

Many writers assume that the omniscient point of view (POV) is their best choice. They identify omniscient POV as the "God-narrator," in which the narrator knows all, sees all, and is able to understand and communicate to the reader the thoughts, attitudes and responses of any character at any given time.

This sounds like an easy out. If you as the writer adopt an omniscient viewpoint, you can let readers know what they need to know with a minimum of work—you can simply tell them what is important.

But therein lies the problem. The author who employs omniscient POV throughout the story is telling, not showing. Thus the reader, like the writer, becomes an uninvolved observer, watching what happens and being privy to the thoughts and attitudes of the characters, rather than experiencing the drama of the novel.

The omniscient viewpoint weakens the impact of the characters—their growth and changes, their struggles, their attitudes and opinions. And it often results in problems of anachronism—those subtle, out-of-place little statements or things that the characters cannot possibly be aware of, such as, "Selma didn't know the far-reaching results of her decision, but her actions affected her children for years to come."

What's the problem? Well, if Selma didn't know the results, why is the author telling the reader? And if her decision affected her children for years to come, those years to come haven't come yet—not in the scope of the novel, anyway.

Whether readers can identify the problems of the indiscriminate use of omniscient point of view or not, the result is the same—they feel cheated, as if they have been given some kind of obvious "clue" to a character's motivation rather than being allowed to figure it out for themselves. Both reader and writer become literary voyeurs, peering into the lives and hearts of the characters and making judgments about them based on information they haven't come by honestly.

Only God is omniscient. Only God knows the hearts and minds of all people and can simultaneously "listen in" on mental and emotional processes. And unless God is the viewpoint character in your novel (a perspective I don't recommend), you cannot indiscriminately enter into the minds of all your characters at will.

I've had any number of authors argue with me about this point. "If you tell me I can't use omniscient point of view, then you're limiting what I can do as the author. I can't get into my characters' minds and let the reader know what is going on there."

Well, yes and no. Restricting your viewpoint to one character at a time can be perceived as limiting, but the very nature of the novel is an experiential unfolding of the plot, characters, action and motivations that draws the reader into the drama rather than giving away everything all at once. As authors, we only heighten the dramatic impact of the story by exercising restraint in how much we reveal to the reader at any given time.

And except for first-person point of view, which is limited to one character by its very nature, restricting viewpoint does not limit your ability as the author to get into the minds of your characters—it only means that you deal with one character at a time rather than trying to get into everyone's mind simultaneously. If you want your novel to come across as real, consider that this is the nature of human limitation: I can only know what is in my own mind. I can only discern what is in someone else's mind as that person reveals it to me. I can only understand someone else one step at a time, as that person's character and perspectives are gradually extended to me during the development of our relationship.

Consistency in point of view is not limitation; it is restraint.

It is far better to let the plot unfold for the reader as it happens for the characters, to allow the characters to reveal themselves—and they will, given the chance. This technique heightens dramatic tension and keeps readers involved, because they have the adventure of unraveling the plot at the same time (or just before) the characters themselves do.

There are, of course, legitimate uses of omniscient point of view in a novel, but they are best used sparingly and only for specific purposes.

The Butler's Perspective. Omniscient viewpoint can be used to advantage when the author needs to give the reader a view of the character's world before the character is actually introduced. In the butler's perspective, the author stands outside the scene and describes what is taking place without any significant commentary on the situation—a good butler, after all, knows when to keep his mouth shut.

This point of view is often seen in the opening chapter of a book. The reader is led by an invisible hand up the front walk of a mysterious house. The door opens, and the reader gets a description of the surroundings—the layout of the rooms, the furnishings, the atmosphere of the parlor—as if the reader is being ushered through the house to a meeting with a yet-un-known character. But the "butler" is silent; he gives no insight into the minds, hearts or motives of the character(s) the reader is about to meet, or even about the significance of the drawn curtains and the musty, uninhabited feel of the place. The butler simply opens the door and steps back, letting the reader in. The reader must deduce what the surroundings signify or what kind of character would live in such a dismal place.

The butler's perspective can be used to accomplish a number of important functions in a novel. It gives the reader a sense of setting, establishes an atmosphere and, in some cases, heightens dramatic tension by building suspense. But if the author truly wants to get the reader involved in the development of the story and in the characters' lives, at some point the butler has to open the library door and introduce the reader to the character, where the real story lies.

One warning about the use of the butler's perspective: Although it can be useful in establishing setting and giving the reader a sense of atmosphere, those same functions can be ac-complished—sometimes more effectively—by showing the same setting from a character's point of view. If a character walks up to the house, onto the porch and through the door, we not only see the physical setting, but we have the further advantage of getting into that character's mind and interpreting the scene with the added dimension of the character's reactions—fear, appre-hension, curiosity or courage. When such an introductory scene is taken out of the butler's perspective, it can accomplish the additional task of characterization rather than simply being lim-ited to showing a physical setting.

The Wide-Angle Lens. A second often-used technique in fic-tion is for the writer to pull up and away from the scene to give the reader a kind of "bird's-eye view" of the larger picture. This approach can be especially effective in a prologue or an epilogue, or in an internal scene where the writer wants the reader to have a sense of looking at the scene from the outside. Again, as in the butler's perspective, no significant commentary is offered, only a visual picture from which the reader deduces the importance of the scene and the interaction of the characters. Here the au-thor makes no attempt to get into the characters' minds, only representing what is going on among them from an external perspective.

Perhaps the wide-angle approach is most easily understood in terms of filmmaking. In the movie *Forrest Gump*, for example, the opening scene of the film follows the flight of a white feather up over a town, down side streets and around corners, until it lands at the feet of a man seated on a bench at a bus stop. The man is Forrest Gump, and from that moment on, the movie shifts into Forrest Gump's viewpoint. The film stays with Forrest almost exclusively, except for a few scenes from the perspective of his girlfriend, Jenny. At the end of the film, the feather takes flight again, this time blowing up from Forrest's feet and floating high into the air, taking the camera with it, zooming out into a wide-angle shot from above the trees.

The wide-angle lens, like the butler's perspective, is useful for specific purposes, but if the author tries to keep the wide angle throughout the novel, the result is a book that has little to offer to readers in terms of understanding particular characters and becoming involved in the drama of their lives.

First-Person Point of View

A popular choice in contemporary fiction, particularly in short stories, is the first-person point of view, the "I" narrator. The choice of first person carries with it inherent benefits as well as potential problems.

In short fictional pieces—the short story, novella or shorter novel—the first-person perspective can create a sense of immediacy and identification with the primary character. This viewpoint is often employed in the coming-of-age novel, where the central character's own responses and experiences are of primary interest to the reader, and the events of the plot are significant only in relationship to the main character. In the short story, which is by definition a narrower, more focused genre, the first-person point of view can be effective in spotlighting a single character and relegating other characters and events to subordinate positions.

Authors who choose first-person point of view for a novel necessarily limit themselves to the narrating character's viewpoint. Although a capable writer can sometimes make this work effectively, it is difficult to maintain consistency and interest in a single character for the duration of a large book or a series of novels.

Many writers who choose first-person viewpoint tend to lapse into self-description, where the narrating character spends inordinate time and space describing herself and meditating upon her own responses. Or the central character may inappropriately think about or discuss issues and events she has no direct knowledge of. One of the most challenging editorial tasks in dealing with a first-person novel is to keep the central character *in character* at all times. The first-person narrator, after all, cannot possibly know what goes on behind her back, out of her sight or beyond her earshot. Everything in the novel—every event, every conversation, every emotional response, every relationship twist and every plot development—must be filtered through that first-person narrator's perspective.

Thus, the choice of first-person viewpoint presents the writer with a unique set of challenges. Anything that happens offstage (that is, outside the narrating character's direct experience) must be told rather than shown, and it often takes an extremely creative mind to come up with interesting ways to communicate such happenings to the reader without constantly relying on a "messenger" to bring the news and explain what has happened. Physical descriptions and settings offer similar challenges—most of us, after all, do not spend a great deal of time meditating upon our own appearance or staring in the mirror cataloguing our attractive (or not-so-attractive) physical characteristics.

For example, if the author is committed to staying in character, the viewpoint character in a first-person novel would probably not refer a great deal to his own physical appearance—a man describing himself, for example, as having "rugged, masculine features, an aquiline nose and a strong, determined chin." How many of us, after all, get up in the morning and think of ourselves in those terms? This kind of description usually comes from outside the POV character—from the perspective, say, of a woman who is interested in him as a romantic possibility. And in a first-person novel, this could not be accomplished through a conversation between the woman and her best friend, or within the woman's mind—either choice would be a violation of the point of view. Such a description could only be accomplished through eavesdropping (the first-person narrator overhearing a conversation) or through hearsay (some third party relating the information to the first-person narrator). Either option can easily result in a contrived, unnatural kind of "information dissemination" that interrupts the flow of the story.

Additional problems can arise in first-person viewpoint when the author (or the reader) gets confused about who is who. When an author writes in first person, even though she uses the pronoun "I," she is not writing about herself, but about a character she has created—in literature this is called a "persona." A first-person persona is as distinctly different from the writer as any other created character is, but the use of first person may lead readers to mistakenly assume they are reading about the writer himself. And some writers even have difficulty separating themselves and their own personalities and ideas from those of the novel's persona. Often, particularly in the Christian novel, this role confusion results in the author getting on a soapbox and preaching to the reader, or philosophizing about issues not germane to the novel itself.

The first-person point of view can lend immediacy to the character and reality to the inner issues the character faces. But the limitations of the perspective, and the problems inherent in being true to the characterization, should be carefully considered by the writer tempted to choose a first-person viewpoint. First person can be extremely confining, and unless an author is essentially writing a one character story, it doesn't often work well.

Second-Person Point of View

The second-person "you" point of view is often used in nonfiction—directly addressing the reader and drawing him or her into the discussion at hand. In fiction, however, second person is rarely used today, except in experimental literary forms. In Victorian times, the use of second person was commonplace as an aside ("You, dear reader, must understand that . . . ") but was not employed as a primary point of view, and even in Victorian novels was intrusive and interrupted the flow of the story. For our purposes in twentieth-century fiction, the use of second person should be avoided.

Third-Person Point of View

By far, the most popular approach, and the most workable for most fiction projects, is the third-person "he/she" point of view. In this point of view, the character is addressed from the outside (that is, the author refers to the character as "he/she," not "I"), but that in no way prevents the author from getting inside the minds of the characters and allowing them to reveal themselves.

There are two basic ways to approach third-person viewpoint: *limited third person*, which gets inside only one or two central characters, and *multiple third person*, which employs a wide variety of point-of-view characters, alternating viewpoint throughout the novel. Most authors who write complex, multi-plot novels do best with multiple third-person point of view.

The tricky part here is to make sure that the viewpoint character is properly limited when he or she is onstage and in possession of the "camera." This is the one grave mistake many writers make with point of view: the assumption, often categorized under the catchall "omniscient" term, that they can indiscriminately move from inside one character's mind to inside another character without adequate transition to alert the reader to the change.

Problems like this often arise, for example, in a love scene between two characters: He thinks, *I never dreamed I'd find a woman like this to love me. What will she think when she finds out what I'm really like? Will she still care?*

Then, without blinking, the author switches to the female character's perspective. *He's so wonderful, so noble, so caring* (she muses). *I wonder if he ever feels as insecure as I do?*

The author has combined two points of view—his and hers—without any indication that the camera is changing hands. And readers are often left feeling as if they are watching a ping-pong match instead of experiencing a moment of tenderness.

In every possible point of view, there are certain limitations the author must take into account. If viewpoint can be described as *camera angle*, then someone has to be behind the camera, holding it, panning the scene and taking in the other characters. The someone who holds the camera is the viewpoint character. The *camera operator* (the point of view character in any particular scene) can describe what he or she sees (panning the camera), but cannot get into the minds of the other characters, except by deduction—seeing another character frown, for example, or look away nervously. The people in front of the camera are described and related to in a physical dimension—what they actually say or do.

By the same token, the camera operator can relate his own emotional/mental processes to the reader—what the character thinks about what is going on in the scene—but is limited in physical description of himself. If you're holding a minicam and taking home movies, you see through the viewfinder what is happening before you: You don't see yourself.

The viewpoint character in a scene may see someone else frown, glance aside or fight back tears, and she may *feel* herself do these things. But she will not (if the author is striving for consistency in viewpoint) describe the gleaming white teeth revealed by her own smile or the glimmer in her eyes as the candlelight reflects in her unshed tears. She cannot see the reflection of her tears or the whiteness of her smile, so it is illogical for her to describe them.

In short, the viewpoint character in any given scene, as the camera operator, has the same basic limitations as does a first-person point-of-view character: She can only describe what she sees, what she knows by direct evidence and what she feels within herself.

So, if every viewpoint character has limitations while "holding the camera," how does multiple third-person point of view work in a novel?

In the best-crafted novels, every scene has an *identifiable point-of-view character*, and thus the reader gets the story, the characters' relationships and their emotional reactions to the plot turns from a number of different perspectives. This technique does double duty for the novelist: It advances the plot and characterization of the novel, and at the same time lets the reader get "inside" the important characters and understand something of their motivation from the way they act, respond and react to the other characters.

Let's say we have a death scene: An old, crotchety, bitter matriarch is dying, and her family stands around her deathbed, waiting for her to breathe her last. If the author simply describes the death scene, we have a one-dimensional accounting of an old woman's demise. But if the author gives time and space to get into the minds of several of the primary characters, one at a time, we may discover that Colin, the money-grubbing son-in-law, has pretended to love the old lady only to gain her inheritance, while Angela, the hippie granddaughter, truly loved her grandmother but never found a way to express her feelings. If the old woman dies thinking that only Colin cared for her, we have one plot twist. If, at the moment before her death, she catches Angela's eye and sees true love and remorse there, we have another. And if she holds on long enough to call a lawyer and change her will before the end, we have the potential of a fascinating and dramatic family disaster in the works.

USING POINT OF VIEW TO DEFINE CHARACTER

The writer who understands viewpoint can use it to advantage in a variety of ways. The real challenge of multiple point of view is to endow each character with a specific and identifiable "voice" so that the reader will know immediately, even without being told, who the viewpoint character is in any given scene. There are a variety of techniques for accomplishing this—giving a character a certain turn of phrase, an odd gesture or repetitive motion, a nickname that only he uses for another character or an attitude that differs from that of other characters.

Let's say, for example, that we have a major male character who has been seriously scarred in the war. He seems to be strong and in control of himself, but when he is alone, he unconsciously fingers the scars on his face. He looks at himself in the mirror and thinks wistfully of the woman he was engaged to before the war. When no one else is around, he sits in the dark, staring out the window.

With such a characterization, we have given this man a dimension that could never have been accomplished outside his own viewpoint. We discover that he is not as strong and in control as he likes to pretend; he suffers because of his experiences; he is sometimes uncertain and sad—in short, he is a character who has the potential of eliciting compassion and empathy from the reader.

If a writer is intent upon being true to the point-of-view character, she must put herself in the character's position, behind the camera, and perceive as the character perceives. When referring to his own parents, for example, a viewpoint character usually will not refer to them in his mind as "Fred and Ethel," unless the author wants to stress that he is estranged from them or has a "modern" relationship with them. He will refer to them as "Mom and Dad" or, if he is a highfalutin society type, perhaps "Mother and Father."

One of the greatest challenges to viewpoint consistency occurs when the point-of-view character is a child. It is certainly acceptable, and sometimes quite valuable, to get into the child mind in a novel, but it is essential for the author to maintain the childlike quality of speech and thought patterns while in the child's point of view. That is the difficult part: making a child's viewpoint realistic, stepping back and seeing through a child's eyes, and using a child's limited language to describe situations the child cannot possibly understand or articulate in an adult manner.

In *Remembering You*, the third book of my Home Front trilogy, I found myself facing a challenge unlike any I had anticipated in writing fiction. During the course of the novel, a child is born with Down's Syndrome (called "mongoloidism" in the 1940s). The child was named Angelique, and I found myself fascinated with her. When I came to the epilogue, twenty years later, I knew that to create the kind of empathetic ending I desired, the epilogue had to be written from Angelique's point of view. In order to do that, I had to put myself into the shoes of a twenty-year-old woman with the mind of a five-year-old girl. The sentence structures and vocabulary had to be very simple and the perceptions limited. That brief epilogue took longer to write than any other chapter of the novel. Yet despite the difficulties, Angelique came through for me and provided me with a touching and fitting ending to the series.

One word of warning: Most authors find it extremely difficult to maintain consistency in a child's viewpoint for long stretches in a novel. Unless the novel centers on the child, the best way of using a child's point of view may be to do it in short stints, a scene here and there.

Some writers find various points of view so fascinating that they get carried away. They give a point of view to the dog, the cat, the horses in the stable and even the stable itself: *The horse dashed toward the road, laboring with every breath. Could he make the jump over the fence to freedom? Or would he be caught again, subjected to the cruelty of the trainer he had come to hate?*

Occasionally, writers have been able to get away with writing from the viewpoint of an animal or an inanimate object. But unless there is a compelling reason to do so—unless you're writing the sequel to *Babe* or a canine version of *Look Who's Talking*, or unless you're the next C.S. Lewis writing Narnia stories—the result usually comes across as silly, and the reader laughs at the scene rather than being caught up in it. The best choice is to stay with characters who have the capacity for rational thought and articulation.

A masterful use of viewpoint can add texture and depth to an otherwise shallow and pedestrian scene. Not only does it help advance the plot, it also strengthens the characterization by allowing the characters to speak and think for themselves, and lets the reader in on information about the viewpoint character that the other characters may not know.

Only God is omniscient. For the rest of us, with limited human perceptions and understanding, the best viewpoint is a consistent, limited one that gives readers a chance to get into the minds of our characters and understand them from the inside out.

Chapter Fourteen

Crossing Over Jordan
Negotiating Multiple Viewpoints

braham faced the problem when he said "Yes" to God
and left his home behind to journey to a land God
had promised to give him, a land he did not know.
Moses shared the dilemma when God called him to
lead the Children of Israel out of Egypt into the Promised Land.
How do you get from Point A to Point B most efficiently? How
do you make plans to travel to a place you've never seen (i.e.,
the conclusion of your novel)? How do you cross the wilderness
to get to the land flowing with milk and honey? How do you
organize all these people to get them where they need to go?

As novelists, we face similar questions in our writing: How
do we manipulate multiple characters, scenes, settings and plot
turns in a way that will be coherent to our readers? How do we
get our characters where they need to go in a natural, efficient
manner? How do we handle multiple points of view without
confusing our readers and frustrating ourselves?

As we discussed in chapter thirteen, the best viewpoint option
for most larger, complex novels is the multiple third person point
of view. This approach gives the author the opportunity to develop a number of significant characters from the inside out. In
most cases the novel will have at least two major settings, with
a collection of characters in each setting. As the book (or series)
progresses, the characters will ultimately come together and interact, tying the threads of the plotlines and subplots together.

The logistics of working with a number of main characters in
more than one setting may seem daunting at first, but there are
a few simple techniques that can help you organize your characters and plot developments, herd them across the Jordan and

lead them to the Promised Land with a minimum of time spent wandering in the wilderness.

MANAGING MULTIPLE VIEWPOINTS

The novel, by definition, is a long and complex work of fiction with numerous primary (major) characters and any number of secondary (minor) characters. In most cases, the reader will be most interested in the viewpoints of the major characters, although on occasion inserting a minor character's viewpoint can give a different slant to a scene.

Usually a novel will begin with the introduction of one or two major characters and build from there, adding characters gradually as the plot progresses. Once the plot is underway, new characters who come on the scene have already been introduced indirectly—other characters have talked about them, for example.

Most teachers of fiction recommend that the keystone characters—in a love story, the hero and heroine for example—be introduced early in the book. They may not know each other yet, but the reader can get to know them individually before they come together and begin to be seen as a "couple."

In *Home Fires Burning*, the first book of my World War II trilogy, I began in chapter one by showing the main character, Link Winsom, arriving in Eden, Mississippi, to take up a new assignment at Camp McCrane. This first chapter introduces Link and gives a glimpse into his feelings about being assigned to "the end of the world," and also introduces Thelma Breckinridge, owner of the Paradise Garden Cafe, and Ivory Brownlee, a crazy WWI veteran who plays the piano at the cafe. At this point Thelma and Ivory are both minor characters who will take on more significance as the series progresses.

Chapter two stays with Link as he goes to the base, meets his commanding officer and gets his first introduction to Sergeant Owen Slaughter, another minor character who becomes a major player later on. These two chapters establish Link as the male lead and give the reader a glimpse of Link's perspective of four other characters—but all of the secondary players are viewed through Link's eyes. In time, they will have viewpoints of their own, but for the time being it is most important to establish Link as the central character.

In chapter three, we move to Libba Coltrain and her cousins, Willie and Mabel Rae. We begin with Libba because she is to be the female lead of this book and Link's romantic interest, and we get some insight into her character by the way she interacts with her cousins. One scene in chapter three is from Willie's point of view, to get her responses to Libba and to establish her as a pivotal character in the novel.

In three chapters, then, we have introduced three major characters and five supporting players. We have allowed the reader sufficient time and space to get into the minds of the three main characters, to begin to identify with them and to see the secondary characters through their eyes. Link and Libba's paths do not cross, however, until chapter sixteen, and by then their individual personalities, past experiences and eccentricities have been established—and other characters have been developed as well.

It is usually to the writer's benefit to begin with one of the major characters and give the reader a long, hard look at that character before moving on to another. Sometimes a chapter will be sufficient; in other cases it may take several chapters to introduce a main character, establish some facts about his personality and motivations, and begin building the plot around him. However much time you spend establishing the viewpoint of a major character, the key principle is to remain consistent to that point of view until you switch to another character.

Shifting Point of View to a New Character

There are two main techniques for shifting to a different character's viewpoint without distracting the reader's attention or confusing him: using a hiatus or beginning a new chapter.

Some writers deplore the use of a *hiatus*—usually a space, single line or other marker within the chapter that identifies a shift in viewpoint, time or location. "If an author has adequate transitions," they say, "a hiatus marker shouldn't be necessary. It's a crutch."

Certainly, the hiatus should not be employed as a substitute for transition or to rescue a writer who has painted himself into a corner. But the hiatus as a literary device is extremely useful to identify necessary shifts and avoid excessive explanation or description. Readers are accustomed to the hiatus; when they see a space, text break, line marker or printer's wingding, they understand that some change is coming and are prepared for it.

In general, the hiatus is most useful within a chapter if the author is moving from one viewpoint to another within the same scene. In a love scene, for example, rather than shifting back and forth from the man's point of view to the woman's and back again, one sentence or paragraph at a time, the writer can give a page or two to the man's viewpoint, and then, using a hiatus mark, shift to the woman's viewpoint and get into her mind and emotions. This kind of "parallel thought process" between two characters in the same time frame can be extremely effective, offering the writer the opportunity to show both characters' thought patterns and to build dramatic tension between them with possible misinterpretations, misunderstandings or mutual feelings that are as yet unexpressed.

Another use of hiatus within a chapter occurs when parallel actions are taking place in two different locations at the same time—rather like the split-screen effects in films such as *Pillow Talk* and *When Harry Met Sally*. In both of those films, split-screens were used to represent the lovers, across town from one another in their respective beds, thinking about each other and waiting for the telephone to ring. An author can create the same kind of effect by having two scenes occurring simultaneously in different places; the hiatus indicates a change in location and point of view, and with minimal maneuvering, the author can clearly indicate that scene two is taking place at the same time as scene one.

Hiatus within a chapter can also be employed to show a brief time lapse—the viewpoint character, for example, now alone, a few minutes or hours after the preceding scene with another character has concluded.

Principles Governing Hiatus and Chapter Breaks

The author who uses multiple points of view will want to consider carefully where hiatus shifts and chapter breaks occur within the manuscript. In general, hiatus breaks within chapters can alert the reader to:

- A shift to a new character's point of view within the same scene or time frame
- A brief time lapse (usually less than one day)

- A change of location (usually within the same general locale/city)
- Any combination of the above

Once an author has a grasp of the principles of point of view, the most common error is to use the hiatus indiscriminately—simply inserting a hiatus and shifting to a different viewpoint rather than giving sufficient development time to the point-of-view character. In one manuscript I edited, this tendency resulted in eleven shifts within five pages of text. The author understood that she couldn't change to a different character's viewpoint without a hiatus, so she just stuck one in whenever she took the notion to shift from the man's perspective to the woman's.

In a situation where you have two characters in simultaneous interaction—a love scene, for example, or a stalking scene that moves back and forth between the hunter and the hunted—it is better to stay with the viewpoint of one character and let him or her play out part of the scene, and then shift to the second character. This technique keeps readers from feeling bounced around and gives them a chance to understand the inner workings of one character's mind before moving on to the next. In general, an author should devote at least several paragraphs—a minimum of a page or two—to one character before shifting to another.

It is perfectly acceptable to have a chapter break that picks up precisely where the last chapter left off—same viewpoint character, same time frame and same place. But chapter breaks can also be extremely useful to signal shifts in time or location. When a writer is making radical shifts—moving to another city or country, skipping three months or resuming the viewpoint of a character who has not been onstage for a while—those breaks are probably best handled with a new chapter rather than a hiatus within a chapter. A chapter break signals to readers the possibility of a more significant shift than they expect within a chapter. They are better prepared to follow the movement of the plot if they have a moment to catch their breath before being whisked away to a new location or being plopped down inside the mind of a character they haven't heard from in a while.

Chapter breaks should generally be used for:

- Long-distance location changes—another city, county or nation
- Introduction of a new major character
- Reintroduction of a character who has not been seen recently
- Major time lapses—a different day, month or year
- Shifting to a subplot or parallel plot
- Any other major change that might cause confusion for the reader

MAINTAINING CONSISTENCY IN POINT OF VIEW

Once you understand the principles of point of view, it is a relatively easy matter to determine whether or not you are maintaining consistency in viewpoint. As you revise and rewrite (you *do* revise and rewrite, don't you?), identify the viewpoint character in each scene. If you can't identify your point-of-view character, it's a sure bet your readers will be confused.

When you've identified your viewpoint character, check to make sure that there are no lapses and that everything within the scene is consistent with the camera angle of the viewpoint character. Does the character give inappropriate information about himself, such as physical descriptions that are impossible to see from his camera angle? Does she slip into the mind of other characters in the scene, revealing things about them that are impossible for her to know? Put yourself in the character's place. Is everything that happens in the scene, within the character himself and around him consistent with his point of view? Keep in mind: Although you are writing in third person, when you are focusing on one character's POV, the effect is the same as if you were writing in first person—everything that happens within the scene must conform to the viewpoint character's perspective.

Now focus on the details of the scene, the logistics of entrances and exits of other characters or, perhaps, of your main point-of-view character. Remember that the viewpoint character cannot know what is taking place before she enters the room or after she has exited.

Consider the following scene, and try to identify what is wrong with this picture.

> Elizabeth lay on the couch with her hand over her eyes. She had a pounding headache that was rapidly building into a migraine. If it got too much worse, she'd never make it to her job interview—or if she did, she'd be no good once she got there. And she couldn't afford to let this once-in-a-lifetime opportunity pass her by.
>
> Randall came down the stairs and stood in the doorway behind her. He couldn't see her face, but he could tell by her breathing that it was a bad headache—really bad. Without a word he slipped to the bathroom, wet a washrag with cold water and returned.
>
> Elizabeth didn't hear him come in until he placed the cold cloth on her forehead. "Randall, is that you?" she murmured, her eyes still closed.
>
> He nodded. "You'll be all right, darling. Just rest."

The viewpoint character in this scene is Elizabeth, identified from the first sentence of paragraph one. We find her alone in the living room, lying on the sofa, and we get immediately into her thoughts—her concern about the upcoming job interview and the effect her migraine might have on her performance.

But if Elizabeth is on the couch with her hand over her eyes, how does she know that Randall is coming down the stairs and standing in the doorway? How does she know that he can't see her face, but knows by her breathing that she is in pain? How can she know that he slips to the bathroom to get a cold cloth for her head? And once she is aware of his presence beside her, how, with her eyes closed, does she know he has nodded in answer to her question?

These are issues that the ordinary reader might not catch on a first reading—or even on a second. But there is sufficient viewpoint confusion here to keep the reader from being sure just whose perspective is being represented. If Elizabeth, as the point-of-view character, is alone in the room with her eyes closed, she might hear Randall's footsteps coming to the door and then disappearing again for a moment or two; she might even hear the water running in the bathroom and deduce that he was getting a cold cloth for her head. But she wouldn't know those things for sure—and she certainly wouldn't have any way of knowing what was in his mind at the time.

The point is, the author has responsibility for knowing more about what is going on in any given scene than the reader does. If you give close attention to developing consistency in point of view, your readers may not identify what you've done—they will simply read on. If your viewpoint is confused, they will notice that something doesn't seem right, and they may quit reading altogether.

Perhaps the key principle that the writer needs to remember in dealing with point of view is simply this: *Don't make your reader work unnecessarily.* This does not mean that an author should "write down" or condescend to readers; it only means that if readers have to struggle to follow where the author is leading, the author may not be doing a very good job at guiding them.

Good fiction writing is not a game of cat-and-mouse or hide-and-seek, where an author puts her reader through rigorous mental gymnastics just to follow the trail to the end of the book. As John Gardner says, good fiction should be a "continuous, vivid dream" in which the reader gets caught up in the flow of the story. It is the author's responsibility to eliminate anything that interrupts that flow—including, and perhaps especially, inconsistency in point of view.

Consistency in viewpoint is an invisible art. You will probably never get a fan letter that says, "I just love how you maintain consistency in point of view." But you will get letters that say, "I get so caught up in your characters; I feel as if I really know them." And whether or not there is any direct correlation between your handling of point of view and the sales figures on your royalty statements, you will have the satisfaction that you have done a great service to your characters, to the flow of your novel and to your readers. You will have done your part to raise the level of excellence for the industry as a whole.

PART SIX

Humility and Exaltation

Chapter Fifteen

The Invisible Servant
Keeping Your Ego in Check

A young novelist, just completing the initial book of her first historical fiction series, asked her editor, "What about my style? I mean, I hear a lot about style and voice . . . do I have an identifiable voice in my fiction?"

The editor's response: "Concentrate on communication right now; you'll find your voice eventually."

It's good advice. Some authors are so concerned about establishing their "turf," their personal style, that they ignore (or abandon) the principles of clear communication. The result is muddy, obscure writing that demands an inordinate level of concentration from a reader—a reader who is, quite frankly, unlikely to work that hard.

If our writing is to be a "vivid, continuous dream" that draws the reader in, our first priority should be clarity. Professional writing is, first and foremost, readable writing—a plot that makes sense and develops logically, characters who act according to understandable motivations, and resolutions that do not frustrate or cheat the reader.

Writing "readably" does not mean that every novelist needs to adopt the sparse, clean style of Hemingway. But every novelist does need to examine their work for stumbling blocks that will trip readers up—intrusions that will make readers balk, argue or scratch their heads in disbelief.

If you want to guard against those speed bumps that slow your readers down and irritate them, you need to have a clear understanding of the difference between uniqueness in your writing style and rebellion in your attitudes. The "rules" of good writing are there for a reason, and the reason is communication. Unless there is a compelling argument in favor of breaking the rules or diverging from commonly accepted grammatical and literary standards, you will do best to observe the conventions rather than swimming against the tide.

STYLE AND SELF-CONSCIOUSNESS

Someone once said that "Imitation is the sincerest form of flattery." But in writing, imitation is the surest path to mediocrity. Extended stream-of-consciousness might have worked for the literary fiction of William Faulkner or James Joyce, but it is death to mainstream fiction. The refusal to capitalize letters gave e.e. cummings a visible edge in modern poetry, but the imitation of that style by other writers simply seems juvenile. Emily Dickinson used dashes in place of traditional punctuation marks such as the comma and the period, but she . . . well, she was Emily Dickinson. You're not. Neither am I.

For our purposes, developing an individual style and finding a unique and memorable voice has little to do with obvious "gimmicks" or with overt imitation. Reading a work that is filled with individualistic ploys is rather like watching a bad B-movie in which the actors all put on a syrupy Southern drawl or affect a nose-in-the-air phony British accent. The audience quickly tires of the sham, and soon begins laughing at the performance rather than becoming involved in it.

Any number of mistakes can interfere with the "vivid, continuous dream." All of them represent author intrusion and should be eliminated.

THE INVISIBLE PUPPETEER

A friend of mine used to direct a children's puppet ministry at a local church. She insisted that her puppet team carry their puppets to and from practices and performances in a pillowcase, and that they stay hidden behind the puppet stage during the act. Nothing spoiled the magic and wonder of puppets, she maintained, like seeing a "dead" puppet or catching glimpses of the hands or heads of the puppeteers.

By the same token, nothing destroys the "dream" of good fiction like seeing the author come out from behind the stage to stand in the spotlight.

The goal of good fiction is to write so that your readers completely lose sight of you as the author and immerse themselves in your characters and plot. In our discussion of point of view, we examined the importance of consistency in viewpoint—keeping the point of view character *behind* the camera. The same principle applies to the author. If the author intrudes upon the scene, the spell is broken and the magic disappears . . . just as if the director of a film were to keep walking in front of the camera, making comments to the audience or interpreting the scene.

Avoiding author intrusion is an important issue of professionalism, but for the Christian writer, it is a spiritual issue as well. Jesus made it very clear that "the servant is not above the master" and that Christ's purpose in coming to earth was to exemplify servant leadership to all who would follow. For the writer, servanthood means the willingness to get out of the spotlight and into the background, and to let the work speak for itself.

Authors who are self-conscious or self-absorbed—either with their ideas or with their use of the language—will inevitably intrude upon their own stories. Such author intrusion makes itself visible in a number of common problems.

Philosophical Tangents

Most authors write out of their own set of philosophical assumptions—issues that are important to them and ideas that beg to be expressed. But when an author's own philosophical bias begins to be obvious to the readers, the motivations of the characters take a back seat, and the author takes the stage.

Philosophical tangents often center around controversial issues that the author feels strongly about . . . war, for example, or abortion, euthanasia, or the treatment of the elderly. The intrusion occurs when the author loses sight of the character as a separate individual. The dividing line between the author and the character blurs, and the character takes on the author's perspective—and the author's issues.

Such topics, in and of themselves, may be valid material for fiction. It is perfectly legitimate to create characters who have their own issues, and to allow them to express their opinions. You need to make sure, however, that such expressions are in keeping with the character's personality and motivations, with the time and setting of your novel and with the plot developments. A character in Victorian England, for example, might well express opinions about child labor, but would certainly not have a hobbyhorse about legalized abortion. Any philosophical expression that hinders the movement of your story, or conflicts with your time frame or characters' motivations, is probably a tangent and needs to be cut.

Gratuitous Religion

Most CBA writers are acutely aware of the problems inherent in gratuitous sex, violence and profanity. But few Christian authors are equally concerned about gratuitous religion. Religious elements in your writing become gratuitous—that is, excessive and unnecessary—when they are imposed on the story from the outside rather than developing from the inner structure of the plot or characterization.

Gratuitous religion, often called "sermonizing," is the religious version of the philosophical tangent, and it is a particular danger for Christian writers. Many writers of spiritual fiction, intent upon having the "strong Evangelical content" often demanded by CBA publishers, give themselves excessive leeway for sermonizing. They create Christian characters and then fill their minds and mouths with pat answers, long and eloquent prayers, or expository dissertations upon their favorite Bible passages. As a result, what was initially designed as a story becomes an extended sermon. Characters become mere mouthpieces for the author's religious perspectives, and plot development gets lost in the author's hidden agenda.

Philip Yancey refers to such intrusion as "content idolatry." When the "message" of the book takes precedence over the story, you no longer have a true work of fiction—you have religious propaganda masquerading as a novel. If you feel compelled to instruct your readers on how they should live, what they should believe and why they should believe it, write nonfiction. If you're going to write fiction, concentrate on the story and eliminate your religious biases.

As Christian writers, we need to remember that true faith is an inward working, not an outward show. Just as the produce of a tree is generated from below ground, with nutrients coming up through the roots and trunk and eventually resulting in blossom and fruit, so spiritual life comes from within. If faith is an integral part of your characters' lives and motivations, it will make itself plain as the book progresses and it will be an important part of the novel. If it isn't, adding religious elements will be like pasting paper fruit on a cardboard tree.

Purple-Patch Writing

Excessive description—particularly flowery, simile-laden writing—is called a "purple patch," and generally indicates the author's overfondness of language for its own sake. In the novel, language is a tool, not a decoration; purple-patch writing has the effect of embellishing a log cabin with gilded ceiling molding and Baroque murals.

> Jacob stared long into the reddening sunset until his corneas ached with the breathtaking beauty of the cloudshapes shifting across the sinking ball of flame. Life was like that, he thought—an ever-changing wonder of light and shadow, constantly renewing itself with each new misty dawn. One never knew what the brightness of a fresh sunrise would bring, what kind of illumination the pastel hours of an unknown day would draw in their wake. One could only trust that after each darkening evening, life would renew itself in hope, like the bud of a morning glory lifting its face to the sun.

Authors who include such passages in a novel leave the reader with the feeling that they are writing to hear themselves spin out beautiful phrases, to lift themselves into a literary euphoria rather than to communicate to the reader or to advance the movement of the plot.

If you find yourself enchanted with your own expression, lost in the wonder of your own words and expressions, it's probably time to get out the red pen, shift into your brutal self-editing mode and begin to cut.

Inconsistency in Point of View

We've already dealt extensively with point of view problems, so we won't belabor the idea here. But you should remember that if you get in front of the camera (or allow your viewpoint character to do so), you will intrude upon the scene and distract the reader from what is really important—the story.

Inappropriate Humor

Humor, like religious content, must grow naturally out of the characters or the situations in which they find themselves. Some authors tend to try to inject humor into their writing to lighten a tense moment, or simply to disarm the reader with laughter. Humor can be a valuable tool for a writer, but only if it is used appropriately and within the context of the story.

Most of us have had the uncomfortable experience of listening to a preacher or speaker who tried to loosen up the crowd with an opening joke that had little or nothing to do with the subject of the sermon or speech. Such humor falls flat because it is not natural—it is not generated from either the subject matter or the speaker's personality. In writing, similarly, humor will only work if it is spontaneous, arising from the situation or from the character. Any other attempt at using humor will be an intrusion and will distract the reader from the movement of the novel.

The essential principle for the novelist is to keep yourself out of sight. Let the characters, the action, the drama and the significance of events in your novel carry your theme, and trust your readers to make the appropriate applications. Like the comedian who constantly asks the audience, "Get it?" the author who intrudes upon the story offends readers and makes them feel inferior. If you continually try to guide the reader into the "correct" response, you will come across as a bore, a pedant or a condescending elitist.

Author intrusion indicates that a novel has not been well-crafted from the beginning, and that the reader needs help to understand it. If you have done your job as a writer, your novel can stand alone, without your explanations or apologies. It will have sufficient strength of character and plot to speak for itself. The author's job is to start the ball rolling and then get out of the way.

CUTTING THROUGH THE FOG

Many years ago, at one of my first writing conferences, a workshop leader led his group in what he called "Evaluating the Fog Factor." Using a complicated mathematical formula, he led us through an evaluation of our own writing, counting the number of syllables per word, the number of words per sentence, the number of clauses per sentence and the number of sentences per paragraph. I have long since forgotten the formula, but I remember the principle: *subdivide and streamline.*

Many writers never give a thought to the amount of "fog" in their writing. They blissfully construct one long, involved sentence after another, heaping clause upon clause and phrase upon phrase until the poor reader has to put one hand on the subject and the other hand on the verb even to figure out what the sentence says. The reader finally begins to skim over the dark, crowded paragraphs, turning pages, hunting desperately for a section of dialogue—or at least a little white space.

If you want to write mainstream fiction, you have to keep your fog factor low. Most readers are not university graduates or Ph.D. candidates. They read for entertainment—or perhaps for inspiration and enlightenment—and they have little patience with sentence structures that make them feel ignorant.

This doesn't mean that all your sentences have to be simple ones. It does mean, however, that you should carefully evaluate your writing to see if those long, complex sentences can be broken up, and if your precious parallelisms can be expressed more directly. You can get by with the occasional complex sentence or inverted expression: "Never did Alicia imagine that she would experience such a crisis." But in general, simpler is better.

Inflectional languages such as French create grammatical constructions through inflectional endings. A subject has one kind of ending, and a direct object has another. Thus the order of the words in the sentence is irrelevant—a reader can easily discern the grammatical relationships by word endings.

English, however, is essentially a "word-order" language. The chronological order of your words indicates their meaning. "John hit Ralph" means something entirely different than "Ralph hit John." The more you contort your sentences with elaborate internal structures—subordinate clauses, participle or gerund phrases and the like—the more difficult they will be for your reader to follow.

Your personal style is no excuse for zero-visibility fog. If you're not communicating, you're not fulfilling your primary purpose in writing.

Personal style comes into play with another common problem demonstrated by young (or recalcitrant) writers—the need for *sentence variation.* Most writers seem fixated on a particular style of sentence, and their writing suffers because of the lack of variety. You can't build a four-hundred page novel on simple three- or four-word constructions (subject, verb, object). Neither can you construct every sentence with complex variations (subordinations, parallelisms, introductory gerund phrases and so on).

The careful, dedicated writer will make an effort to match the type of sentence to the character's point of view and speech patterns. An uneducated farmer will not fill his dialogue with sixty-dollar multisyllabic words; a college professor will probably not speak in short, chopped-off phrases.

Many untested writers fall back on familiar patterns to help them through the difficult problem of physical action:

> Going to the doorway, Gerald paused and turned. Looking straight into Ophelia's eyes, he gave her a glance that told her of his anger. Then, turning his back on her, flinging open the door and striding onto the porch, he stalked off into the night.

You can take a passage like this and make it flow more smoothly simply by varying the sentence patterns:

> Gerald stalked toward the door. With his hand on the doorknob, he turned and glared at Ophelia. She knew he was angry—angrier than she had ever seen him. But he said nothing. Instead, turning his back on her, he flung open the door and disappeared into the night.

In fiction, there is a place for everything: sentence fragments, elaborate structures with graceful parallel constructionseven the occasional introductory gerund or participle phrase. But if you find that every other sentence is a fragment . . . or a complex structure with three semicolons and two dashes . . . or a simple, direct, three-word construction, it's time to begin revising.

DEALING WITH "THE BIG THREE"

For the novelist in the CBA market, a final style issue arises over the use of "The Big Three"—profanity, sex and violence.

Profanity

Most CBA publishers tend to be extremely skittish about the use of profanity in the novels they publish—even if the character who uses bad language is an evil person for whom such expletives come naturally. For the writer, the profanity prohibition can present a ticklish problem. Do you simply say, "He swore," and let the reader fill in the blanks? Do you replace the offensive word with some kind of minced oath, like "Blast!" or "Shucks"?

Perhaps we can get a clearer perspective on the issue by looking at some common patterns in secular fiction. In some contemporary novels and movies, profanity abounds: the "F-word" in every sentence or two, and characters who speak in scatological metaphors and describe their enemies and friends alike with references to questionable parentage. In our generation, profanity has become little more than a cliché, a fill-in, a cheap shot by an author who doesn't want to work at finding a more appropriate expression. The profanity or obscenity becomes at best distracting, at worst ludicrous.

But it's not always that way. When we examine the work of other writers in the general market—even wildly successful commercial writers such as John Grisham—we do not find that kind of broadside use of profanity. Characters sometimes curse, but their cursing communicates something significant about their personalities or the intensity of the crises they face. Good writers don't use profanity simply to titillate or shock the reader.

Mystery writer Mary Higgins Clark, a resounding success story in the general market, provides an example we, as Christian writers, might to do well to emulate. As a young widow with several children to support, Clark began writing mysteries at her kitchen table at night. A devout Catholic, she determined that she would not descend to the baser elements of secular fiction, but would write books that any of her children could read and be proud of. Clark's novels to this day contain very little that could be considered offensive to any reader, and yet her success is unparalled—she is the reigning monarch of mystery and suspense.

In the Christian market, we should be at least as capable as secular writers of avoiding offensive language. As one friend of mine jokes about popular films, "You know, I've often heard people, Christian and otherwise, complain about the foul language in movies. But I've never once heard anyone say, 'Hey, that was a good film, but they just didn't use the F-word often enough to suit me. I really missed it.' "

Through adequate character development and dramatic dialogue, we can communicate intensity of emotion without resorting to profanity or obscenity. Our readers won't miss it in the least, and our publishers will thank us.

Sex

Sex in Christian fiction presents a different kind of problem. For whereas "good Christian characters" don't (or perhaps shouldn't) swear, good Christian characters do have legitimate sexual desires and acceptable ways to fulfill those desires. The key for the Christian writer is to allow characters to be human without demeaning or exploiting the holiness of sexual union. Every publishing house will have its own concept of "how much is too much" in regard to sensuality and overt references to sex. But no matter how much freedom you are allowed as a writer, it's usually best if the bedroom door stays firmly closed during intimate moments. You may refer to your characters' sex lives, but if you show them in intimate interaction, you are bound to get in trouble.

Violence

Violence presents less of a problem in Christian fiction than sex or profanity, although some editors and readers (myself included) wonder why publishers are not more concerned about it. Action novels and historical fiction (especially novels based in wartime) inevitably contain a certain level of violence. But it behooves the Christian writer to be considerate of the sensibilities of the reader. Graphic descriptions of physical violence (war wounds, shootings, rapes, etc.) usually serve no purpose except to incite the reader, and seem inappropriate for Christian fiction. Violence against women is especially offensive. Yes, it happens, and yes, it is a tragedy. But giving explicit descriptions of rape, sexual violation or domestic abuse has no redeeming value. It simply makes the reader cringe, and may result in heated letters to your publisher.

The decisions about the use of profanity, sex and violence may ultimately lie with the publisher rather than the author. But from the writer's perspective, evaluations of what to leave in and what to take out should be based on necessity and appropriateness. If there is no significant argument for including them, they are probably gratuitous and should be eliminated.

An aside on the issue of including or deleting the Big Three from your novel: Each writer must decide individually which issues are important enough to fight about. But you will be wise to heed the counsel of your editor and publisher if you want to succeed with your fiction in the CBA. Publishers understand the market, and you may find that the readers of your novels tend to be more conservative than you are personally—or even than your editor is.

The biblical principle here is not to offend the "weaker brother or sister" if you can, in good conscience, avoid doing so. Some authors have been known to dig in their heels and refuse to compromise on minor issues, and their books suffer because of their stubbornness. If you take the advice of your editor to heart, you will avoid undermining the potential ministry of your books—and your future as a Christian novelist.

Your personal style and voice as an author will depend in part upon your background and education, and in part upon the level of readership you are aiming for. Your job, however, is not to defend your style at the expense of your story. If you write professionally, commit yourself to excellence and listen to your editor's advice, your own voice will eventually make itself known. You will become an "invisible servant" serving God, your gift, and the work with faithfulness and distinction. And you will be valued for what you do best—writing a readable, compelling novel, a "vivid and continuous dream" that brings your readers back for more.

Chapter Sixteen

Ongoing Creation

Revision and Rewriting

R emember the popular buttons and T-shirts of years ago that proclaimed, "Please Be Patient, God Isn't Finished With Me Yet"? I always wanted to have a custom button made bearing my own private version of that sentiment: "God is an Editor."

Whether we believe that Creation was accomplished in six days or six billion years, one truth we cannot deny—the Creator has never stopped creating. All created life exemplifies the inevitability of change. We are born, grow up, grow old and die. As we mature, our thought patterns develop, our spiritual insights deepen and our priorities shift. Winter melts into spring; the chrysalis breaks open to reveal a caterpillar transformed into a butterfly. The process of creation and re-creation—editing, if you will—goes on.

I experienced the reality of this inexorable change and growth in a vivid way not too many years ago. I decided that one of my first books, long out of print, needed revitalization, a new life. A publisher was interested in the possibility of a new edition. And so I went back to it, intending to tweak it here and there, add a chapter or two and be done with it.

But when I began to review what I had written nearly ten years before, I quickly concluded that the project was utterly impossible. My own perspectives, not to mention my writing style, had changed so radically in those ten years that I felt as if I were reading the work of a stranger. I had grown. I had deepened. I couldn't just "fluff it up" and recycle it again. It no longer represented who I was, what I believed or where I stood in relationship with God.

God is an editor. If we claim the name of Jesus Christ, we

must acknowledge that our Lord has both the right and the responsibility not to leave us alone, but to continue to work in our hearts and minds to conform us to the Divine Image.

The principle is one that we can—and must—apply to our writing.

THAT DIRTY OLD "R" WORD

Just last night, at a Lenten supper at my church, a woman at my table began to ask me about my writing. I'm always reticent to talk about my work, partly because I'm an introvert, and partly because I'm uncomfortable with the way most people perceive my work as some kind of "glamour career" that sets me apart from "normal folks."

Unable to evade her insistent questions, I summarized briefly what I do for a living. Then the question came that made me smile. "So, you write books. Do you do rewriting, too?"

I wasn't quite sure what she meant—whether she wanted to know if I edited other people's books, supplemented my income with ghostwriting or simply did more than one draft of a book. But I answered, "All serious writers rewrite. That's the biggest part of the job."

We don't want to hear it, of course. We'd like to think—and some authors seem to believe it—that our words come down from On High and fill the page with inspiration without needing the slightest alteration. But it's not true, not even for the most successful among us. The biggest part of the job is revision.

Rewriting takes many forms, depending upon how an author works, how much prewriting is done and how meticulous the writer is in the first draft. Some writers fly through the rough draft as quickly as possible, just "getting it down on paper" and worrying about the details later. Some authors labor over each chapter, revising each scene, each paragraph and each sentence to get it "exactly right" before moving on. However you do it, whatever method works for you, you must do it. No one, not even the brightest, most gifted star in the literary galaxy, gets everything perfect on the first pass. Or the second. Or the third.

Some writers I've worked with resent the implication that their writing needs revision. They've done the work, they claim—forged through from Prologue to Epilogue, and presented a "finished" manuscript. Now it's the editor's turn. No matter what they've left out, slid over or muddled, it's the responsibility of the editor to "fix it."

No. It's the editor's job to fine-tune, raise questions, catch inadvertent errors, check facts and polish the manuscript into a publishable work. It's your job as the author to present a manuscript that represents the best writing you are able to produce at any given moment in your career. If you offer less than the best—slipshod research, sloppy writing, a confused chronology, unresolved plot twists or underdeveloped characters—you do not honor yourself, your publisher, your gift or the God you serve.

REVISION AS SELF-PRESERVATION

There's a biblical principle at work in revision, a principle that applies both to our spiritual lives as Christians and to our professional lives as writers. In Luke 14:7-11 (NRSV), Jesus told the story:

> "When you are invited by someone to a wedding banquet, do not sit down at the place of honor, in case someone more distinguished than you has been invited by your host. . . . But go and sit down at the lowest place, so that when your host comes, he may say to you, 'Friend, move up higher'; then you will be honored in the presence of all who sit at the table with you. For all who exalt themselves will be humbled, and those who humble themselves will be exalted."

Revision can be humbling work. When I go back and begin to rewrite, I am often embarrassed at the mistakes I have made—employing the same phrase twice in a paragraph, changing the color of a character's eyes or using the wrong name. I find scenes out of sequence, viewpoint inconsistencies, inaccurate historical data and sentences that just don't make sense no matter how many times I read them. But far better to humble myself and do the rewriting before I submit my manuscript, rather than have an editor find those same errors and wonder what in the world I was thinking. Or worse, get smug letters from readers who delight in catching my mistakes.

Once the initial creative work is done on a novel, it's time for the author to switch into a brutal self-editing mode—to examine every character, every plot turn and every sentence to make sure it all fits together in a continuous whole. Whether we enjoy the work of revision or not, self-editing is self-preservation. If we humble ourselves, we will not need to be humbled by some source outside ourselves.

FROM CREATOR TO CRITIC

One of my favorite comic strips shows Snoopy the Writer on top of his doghouse, pecking away at the keys. "Edith wouldn't marry Ralph because he was too fat," the first frame says. In the next frame, the Great Canine Author continues: "Ralph tried, but he couldn't stop eating, so Edith broke up with him." Third frame: "It was a shame Ralph couldn't have his cake and Edith too."

The final frame of the strip shows Snoopy doing his victory dance on the roof, thinking, "It's a wonderful feeling when you know you've written something *really good*."

It is a wonderful feeling—and let's admit it, we've all felt that way. You're reading along in the chapter you've just created, and suddenly you experience what B.J. Hoff calls "the angel touch." Chills run up your spine, tears spring to your eyes and you wonder, "Did I really write that?"

Creative people need that kind of encouragement. We need to see, now and then, that we are capable of writing something *really good*. But we need to balance that awareness with the sobering thought that we are also capable of writing something *really bad*. And when it comes time for revision, we need to have our antennae out to identify what is really bad, or mundane, or simply not as good as it could be.

For many writers, the inherent dichotomy between writing and self-editing is a difficult juggling act. It's like living out the nightmare of Dr. Jekyll and Mr. Hyde—Jekyll the writer is a passionate, creative, energetic soul who derives great joy from the process. The alter ego Hyde is a nasty, critical, nit-picking so-and-so who tears Jekyll's precious work to shreds.

Revision, however, does not necessarily have to be an experience in self-imposed schizophrenia. I learned this lesson from a friend who used to do wood carving. She would take a block of teak, pare it down to a rough shape, and then begin the "real" work of carving—painstakingly slicing off paper-thin curls until a more recognizable form appeared. But the carving wasn't finished just because you could tell what it was. She had to put in the fine detail, sand it, apply stain and varnish, and then sand it down and varnish it again. And when it seemed finished to me, she would run expert fingers over the contours, find a rough edge that needed a bit of additional work—and get out the sand paper again.

Rewriting is the "detail, sand and varnish" stage of the novel—the time when we set aside the creator in us and let the critic come forward to center stage. And if we truly want to continue to grow and develop as writers—not just get books in print and cash royalty checks—we need to pay close attention to cultivating the critic as well as the creator.

But how do we go about cultivating the critic within? What elements are most important in the process of rewriting and revising?

Time

It takes months—sometimes years—to write a novel. That kind of extended time span inevitably results in details forgotten, questions unanswered, needless repetitions and rough edges that need to be carved away. But although it may take you months to write your novel, it takes your greatest fan only a few hours to read it. And that reader will notice if your character has blue eyes on page 37 and brown eyes on page 337.

You need to build into your schedule time to read your novel as others will read it—in one or two sittings, straight through. I strongly recommend doing this with a printed manuscript in front of you rather than trying to do it on the computer screen. You need to be able to see whole pages at a time, to flip back and forth between chapters, to mark pages with sticky notes and write in the margins. Despite all the blessings of modern technology, there are times when a red pen and a dog-eared corner can be more effective.

As you read through the entire manuscript, you will notice places where the flow is not quite right, where the dialogue is rough, where the chronology doesn't seem to fit and where the word choice is all wrong. Mark those places and go back to them later. For now, your job is to read, to get the whole scope and sweep of your novel as if seeing it for the first time.

Once you've read through the entire book, you can begin to go back and make necessary changes. Some writers do this in stages—doing the "big rewrites" such as reorganizing or rewriting whole scenes or chapters first, and then returning to deal with details such as word choice, sentence structure and historical facts. Some writers do it all at once, giving attention to one chapter or scene at a time. The method is less important than the final result.

Objectivity

Time is a factor, too, in gaining sufficient distance from your work to see what needs to be changed. If you spent your school days doing "all-nighters" and finishing your term papers right before the bell, reconsider your working patterns. The deadline for your finished manuscript—the one written into your contract—does not indicate the date on which you type in the last word and write "THE END" on the final page. It is the date you present a finished manuscript to the publisher—a manuscript that has been meticulously written, rewritten, revised and corrected.

It's good to have a cooling-off period of a week or two, perhaps a month if you can manage it, where you lay the manuscript aside and leave it alone. When you come back to it fresh, you will see many changes you might not have caught if you had gone immediately into rewriting.

If you have a friend who knows something about fiction and is willing to give you input on your first draft, take advantage of the offer (and buy your friend an expensive seafood dinner in repayment!). A writer's greatest blessing is the objective eye of an honest critic.

If you don't have such a friend, you can be your own judge. Get away from your novel, and when you come back to it, don't just sit down and scan through it looking for obvious errors. Read it aloud, painstakingly. When you stumble over a sentence, mark it for rewriting. When you furrow your brow in a frown, put a note there to reevaluate the scene. When you come to a paragraph that has more alliteration than "Peter Piper picked a peck of pickled peppers," get relentless with yourself. Slash and burn, if need be. Better for you to do it now than for your editor to have to do it later. Better for you to do it now than to lose readers because of muddy or unclear writing.

You're a writer; you have a more vivid imagination than most people. Imagine yourself as your reader, coming to this book for the first time. Look for places that the reader might fall by the wayside. Don't make excuses or explain away those vague passages. You won't be there to explain it to the reader. Your novel has to stand on its own, without rationalization or clarification. Rewriting is your opportunity to make this book work.

Attention to Detail

The process of revision demands careful attention to the details of your work—not just whether or not you have gotten from Point A to Point B without falling into a pit or painting yourself into a corner, but whether the whole book flows in that "vivid, continuous dream" John Gardner recommends. To that end, you should pay attention to a number of major factors in your novel:

- Logical plot development and timing
- Realistic characterization
- Significant dialogue
- Logical chronology
- Consistency in point of view
- Sufficient conflict and dramatic tension
- Believable resolution

In addition, your revision should include attention to less obvious issues:

- Variety in sentence structure
- Word choice
- Repeated phrases
- Use of hiatus
- Chapter division and dramatic chapter endings
- Scene shifts and transitions
- Accuracy of historical data and timeline

As you begin the process of revision, you might want to consider writing out a separate timeline and a list of characters (including their significant physical attributes and relationships) just to double check your own chronology and plot development. Such a list will be a blessing to your editor and may save you a good deal of grief. If Teresa finds out she's expecting in chapter three, two months after the wedding, and in chapter fifteen, six months later, gives birth to a full-term baby boy, some reader will be sure to write a furious letter to your publisher accusing you of advocating sexual immorality in your major character.

If you're writing historical fiction, you have the additional responsibility of making sure your historical facts and references are accurate. Since you will check and double-check these facts anyway (yes, you will—it's part of the job of revision), it would be a considerate gesture to supply your editor with a list of that information—the date *Gone With the Wind* won all those Academy Awards, the last year the Packard automobile was made and so on. Even a passing remark, such as a character humming a popular tune, should be checked. If it's 1944 and the song wasn't released until January 1945, you'll have egg on your face if you let it slide.

I keep a number of reference books and a good CD-ROM encyclopedia within easy reach of my computer desk. That way I can check facts as I work, make notations in my manuscript if necessary, and assure both myself and my editor that I've been thorough about my research.

Go ahead, humble yourself. It will hurt less now than it will later. Do the hard work of revision, and save yourself from embarrassment and humiliation. Do it immediately, before someone else gets the chance to do it for you by catching some appalling error that has made its way into print. Do it for yourself, for your editor, for your loyal readers, for your publisher and for the sake of your integrity as a writer. Do it because you're a professional.

Just do it.

If you humble yourself, you'll be exalted. Some editor down the line will attach a note to the galley of your manuscript saying, "I feel guilty getting paid for this job because you just didn't leave me anything to do." Some up-and-coming young writer will send you a letter declaring, "Your work is my example of how to do this right." Some publisher will send you another contract and say, "I wish we had a hundred authors as committed to excellence as you are."

Well, maybe. But whether that happens or not, you will have

the satisfaction of knowing you have submitted a manuscript that represents the very best novel you can produce at this point in your career. Next year you'll be better; five years from now even better than that. But for today, this is the shining example, the well-crafted manuscript. The one with your name on it.

Creation is not the end of the process; it's the beginning. In the image of our Creator, we continue the work of ongoing re-creation. We revise, refine, reorganize and rewrite. And at the end of the day we, too, can rest and say, "It is good."

Chapter Seventeen

The Visible Celebrity
Getting Ready for Success

I*t Could Happen to You.* The movie, released in the summer
of 1994, explored a fantasy: A struggling beat cop wins
four million dollars in the lottery. All his dreams have come
true; this windfall will free him from trouble and struggle
for the rest of his life. But his troubles have only begun.

That same premise supported the popular 1960s TV series,
"The Millionaire." Ordinary people, blessed with financial
riches beyond their wildest dreams, face a different kind of challenge—wealth and fame may corrupt the noblest of hearts.

We find the problem in publishing, too—even in Christian
publishing. Fame and fortune (even a little fame and moderate
fortune) can have adverse effects upon our souls. Despite the
best of intentions to remain humble and grateful, it's not always
easy. We need to plan for success *before* it becomes a reality.

For the Christian writer, planning ahead for success is especially important. In our market, well-known writers are often
exalted on the pedestal of public opinion. They receive fan mail,
are sought out for autographs at CBA and writing conferences,
and can find themselves perceived as "experts" on matters they
know little about.

It could happen to you. But before it does—before your head
swells from all the acclaim and your credit limit skyrockets—
you might do well to establish a contingency plan, to prepare
yourself in advance to avoid the pitfalls of success.

RESISTING THE PRIMA DONNA/
FRANKENSTEIN SYNDROME
The most deadly snare for any writer is the temptation to buy
into your own PR, to believe the flattery of the press release and

conclude that you are, indeed, the brightest, the best, the most incredible writer to come on the scene in decades. If you think you are irreplaceable, sooner or later you'll begin to act like a "star."

Editors deal with them all the time—writers who experience a little success and then, as if lightning has struck the primary brain cells, become monsters overnight. Such authors ask for the world and expect to get it. They forget their humble beginnings: the editors who gave them advice and direction; the publishers who took a chance on them when they were nobody; and the families and friends who loved them, supported them and endured, without complaint, the temporary insanity that inevitably accompanies a writer's frantic attempts to meet a deadline.

At its worst, the Prima Donna Syndrome results in heartbreak, broken marriages, lost children, emotional struggle and spiritual chaos. At its mildest, it produces frustration, confusion and migraines for editors and publishers—and a terrible reputation for the writer.

Perhaps the best way to avoid the Prima Donna Syndrome in your own life is to remember, before success comes your way, that Christ has called us to be servants, not lords. Writing is servanthood; we are servants to the work, to our readers and to our craft. Certainly we want to succeed, but success is best measured by the character, not by the checkbook.

As a wise writer, how do you plan for success so that it won't make you into a monster?

Keep your priorities in order, and your heart humble.

Writers have a peculiar problem with priorities. Because we work inside our heads, the work is always with us. We eat, sleep and dream writing. Every new experience holds the potential of being incorporated into a chapter of the next book. The computer is always there, beckoning with its single penetrating eye. We could work all the time, if we wanted to—or even if we don't want to. Especially if some editor sits at the other end of the Federal Express line, eagerly awaiting the new manuscript.

But a great deal of living goes on beyond the office walls, and we need to emerge once in a while and experience it. We need to savor and value life for its own sake, not just for its research potential.

Our spiritual lives will not take care of themselves just because we happen to be writing about spiritual truth. One of the great dangers for the Christian writer is to let writing *about* God take the place of growing in our relationship *with* God. Our experience of faith may ultimately find its way into our books, but that is not the primary reason we need to grow spiritually. We must nurture our souls and allow God's grace to work in building our character, whether or not the truths we discover ever make their way into print.

Our relationships of love and service—with spouses, parents, children and friends—must also take precedence in our lives. If we give ourselves to our loved ones grudgingly, as if they are an imposition upon the "really important stuff" we have to do, they will come to resent our work, and we will end up resenting them. Like the workaholic pastor who neglects his family and his personal spiritual life in order to "minister the Word of God," writers who fail to keep their priorities in order will ultimately hurt themselves and those around them.

Jesus gave us two overriding commandments: love God and love others. The career call—whether it is missions work, evangelism or fiction writing—comes third.

Successful writers can avoid the Prima Donna Syndrome if they have a few trusted people around them—people who understand and believe in their work but are nevertheless courageous enough to tell them the truth. Cultivate relationships with people who care enough about you and your work to be honest with you—a trusted editor, perhaps, a fellow-writer or a few intelligent, thoughtful friends. Listen to them. Make yourself accountable to them, and ask them to keep an eye on your character as your career begins to flourish. If you begin to show signs of exalting yourself to a position of royalty, they can help bring you back to earth—back to your loved ones and back to your God.

The best writers, and the ones editors love to work with, are writers who remain humble and teachable no matter how successful they become. The writing life is an unending journey; we never "arrive," and if we're wise, we'll keep growing and always remember where we came from.

PROFESSIONALISM: DEALING WITH PUBLISHERS
You're doing your best. You work hard, meet your deadlines, and have a relatively successful track record in sales. You avoid

being a petulant, whiny author who thinks she should be carried around on a satin cushion. You don't make a pest of yourself. You try to keep your expectations low. But sometimes you wonder: "What, exactly, does an author have a right to expect from a publisher?"

A good publisher knows that authors do have reasonable requests, and most houses will make every effort to conduct their business in a way that will make authors want to continue publishing with them. Occasionally you may discover (the hard way) that your publisher simply will not give you straight answers, pay royalties on time or fulfill promises—in such a case, you may need to cut your losses and look elsewhere. In general, however, most publishers concur that authors have certain needs and rights that must be considered.

Reasonable Deadlines

Writers work in different ways and at different rates. Some authors can produce ten or twenty pages a day, while others consider themselves fortunate to finish a book in eighteen months. The temptation for an up-and-coming writer, or a writer who is greatly in demand, is to agree to an unworkable deadline for the sake of getting a contract signed. Your reputation will be in jeopardy, however, if you consistently miss or extend your deadlines, so it is to your advantage to be honest about how quickly you can produce a finished manuscript. Most publishers will allow you sufficient time because they want a quality book, but if they press you to work at a pace that frustrates you, you will need to hold the line and set a deadline that is workable for your own writing style and speed.

Fair Contracts

In the CBA, you don't necessarily need an agent to get a fair contract, but you do need a little business savvy. The more in demand your writing is, the more you can ask for—higher advances, greater royalty percentages with quicker escalation clauses, perhaps even assurances of certain kinds of marketing. All contracts are negotiable—until they are signed. Once your signature is on the dotted line, the negotiations are over. So it's wise to scrutinize your contracts carefully, perhaps even to get legal advice on them, before you sign. Don't let your eagerness to publish blind you to the realities of business. (For more detailed information about contracts, you might do well to seek out more expert advice. Donald Maass, in *The Career Novelist*, has an excellent chapter on Contracts & Income.)

First, you need to be aware when you're negotiating contracts that just because a publisher bears the name "Christian" does not mean the publisher is looking out for your best interests. Publishing houses are in business to make money, and their standard (or boilerplate) contracts are usually weighted in favor of the publisher, not the author. Most writers look at the basic financial offer: the advance and royalty payments. But other issues may radically affect the success of your career, including details such as:

- Subsidiary rights (translations, foreign sales, multimedia rights)
- Termination (going out of print) and reversion of rights to you
- Linking contracts (tying up your royalty on this book until you've satisfied the advance on the next one)
- Option clauses (requiring you to give first chance at your next book to this publisher)
- Transfer of rights (when the publisher is bought by another company)
- Reserves against returns (the publisher holding back a percentage of your royalty to offset returns of your book)

In the Christian market, other factors come to play in contract negotiations. Some publishers, for example, still include a "moral turpitude" clause in their contracts—a statement that the publisher has the right to refuse to publish a book if any "morally questionable" activity is discovered in the author's personal life. Philosophically, I believe the morals clause implies a lack of trust in the author; in business terms, such clauses are usually so vague as to be meaningless, and they are virtually unenforceable. Many writers I know deplore those clauses. As one author said, "It's God's job to keep me moral, not the publisher's."

As an author, you do have the right to expect your publisher to offer you a fair contract. But be advised that you also have the responsibility to educate yourself and to negotiate wisely. As long as you conduct yourself professionally and negotiate with good business etiquette, your publisher should not resent your attempts to get the best deal possible.

Advances Commensurate With Projected Sales

Advance money accomplishes several purposes. It buys time for the writer, it demonstrates the publisher's belief in the salability of the project and it encourages advertising and publicity (a publisher will invest marketing dollars to earn back his original investment on a high-advance book). As you gain some prominence in the market, you can expect your advances to escalate with each book project. But bear in mind: Advances are usually offered on the basis of sales projections. A novelist who has sold 200,000 copies of her first book will be offered more than a writer who has sold 20,000.

Simultaneous Submissions

In our market, an author has the right to submit a proposal to more than one company at a time, as long as the proposal is clearly marked as a simultaneous submission. Simultaneous submissions save time for the author and alert the publisher to the fact that other houses may be vying for the same project.

Some general-market publishers refuse to consider simultaneous submissions—they want an exclusive look at your manuscript without the pressure of other possible bids playing into the contract negotiations. But CBA publishers are usually a bit more flexible. For the sake of your reputation, however, you may want to avoid putting competing publishers into bidding situations. I had two offers for my Home Front series, but rather than pit one company against the other, I evaluated each offer and made my decision, and then negotiated with the publisher for the contract I wanted. That approach helped keep the doors open with the second publisher for possible projects in the future.

Honesty and Forthrightness

An author has the right to expect honesty from the publisher— forthright answers, an honest evaluation of where the book comes in the publisher's priority list for publicity and advertising, what is being done to sell the book and how enthusiastic the publisher is about the prospects for success. Unless you insist on learning everything by (hard) experience, the best way to discover which publishers tend to be honest in their dealings with authors is to *ask*. Talk to other writers about their experiences; listen carefully to the warnings that filter through the grapevine. If a publishers has a long history of disgruntled writers, take heed.

Updated Information About Books in Progress

Authors have the right to know what is happening to their books—where the manuscript is in editing or production, when the book will be released and what the updated sales figures are. A reputable publisher should provide this information on a regular basis, and should not be defensive about answering an author who calls to check on the progress of the book. In an attempt to keep the lines of communication open, most publishers will try to connect the author with . . .

A Warm Body In-House

Most authors need to have a contact person within the publishing company (usually the acquiring editor, or in some cases the line editor who is responsible for the manuscript). Some publishing companies actually have an Author Relations Liaison, a person whose job it is to keep up with authors and make sure their questions are answered. But for the most part, these tasks are performed by the editor who works most closely with the author. If you are uncertain who your in-house contact will be, ask—both about editorial contacts and about a contact person in publicity and marketing. If the publisher does not give you a contact person to deal with, you may get the runaround when you have questions that must be answered.

Marketing Information

More is involved in the success of a book than good writing and quality editing—much more. Authors with a little experience know that no matter how good a book is, it won't get to the public without some effort at marketing. Although you do not have the right to demand unlimited resources in marketing and advertising, you do have the right to know what will be done to market your book. If you are a relatively unknown writer, don't expect a media blitz or expensive trade and consumer ads, and don't buy a new wardrobe for the Oprah Winfrey show. But do ask what the plans are, and do cooperate with marketing and publicity personnel to get the word out about your masterpiece.

Promises Fulfilled

One of the biggest complaints among authors about their publishers is the tendency for publishers to make promises they can't—or won't—fulfill. As an author, you have the right to expect promises to be kept, but the reality is that publishing houses and personnel change. The editor who acquired your manuscript may be working in another house by the time your book is in print. The publisher may experience a shift in priorities that results in less attention being given to your manuscript. Only what is written into your contract is legally binding on the publisher, but if the company has integrity, they will not promise what they can't deliver.

On-Time Decision Making

The wheels of publishing often grind slowly, and the inevitable delays can become a serious frustration for a writer. But you do have a right to reasonable efficiency in the decision-making process. "Reasonable," of course, is a relative term, depending upon the inner workings of the house. Some publishers make contract decisions fairly quickly—within two or three months of initially reading a proposal. Others take longer—up to a year— a situation that lends support to simultaneous submissions. If you have presented a proposal and have heard nothing within a month or two, you are certainly within your rights to check with the editor to find out where your project is in the decision-making process. If your book is already contracted, and decisions are still pending on title, cover design, distribution date or other details, most publishers will make every effort to keep you apprised of the decisions as they are made. If you need to know, ask.

Quick Turnaround on Advance and Royalty Checks

The issue of money is often a touchy subject with writers— asking for a check seems like begging for a handout. But if you have contracted for a book, you have earned that advance or royalty check, and you have a right to speedy payment. The method of payment is a subject pertinent to your contract negotiations. Some publishers divide the advance check in thirds—a third at contract, a third when you finish the manuscript and a third on publication. Most, however, deliver half at contract and half upon completion of the manuscript—a much more equitable division, considering the fact that it may take up to a year for the final product to be completed. Once your contract is signed and returned (or in the case of your second advance check, after the manuscript is delivered), you should receive your advance check within thirty days. If you have questions about your publisher's turnaround time, ask. And make sure you know how long it will take for your finished manuscript to be deemed "acceptable"—that may affect how soon your check is cut.

The frequency and timing of royalty statements are also subjects that may be negotiated. Some publishers want to pay annually, but they will send semiannual or even quarterly statements and royalties if you insist. Semiannual statements are the most common. Many publishers will write into their contracts a grace period of up to ninety days after the statement date before the check is overdue. The ninety-day clause is fairly common, but most reputable publishers make an effort to issue statements and checks as soon as possible after the closing date. If your statements or checks habitually come more than ninety days after the statement period ends, you have the right to raise the issue with your publisher.

Professional Courtesy

As an author who works hard to meet deadlines and conform to the publisher's needs, you have a right to expect a certain amount of loyalty and consideration in return. But while you may have to confront a publisher occasionally, keep in mind that your ongoing success as a writer may depend in part on how you deal with problems. If you have a complaint, a calmly worded, professional letter or telephone conversation will usually have greater effect than a hysterical, demanding, confrontational style. Keep your cool, listen, stand firm when necessary, and you will be perceived as an author who is professional, reasonable and easy to work with.

EDITORS—WHO NEEDS 'EM?

Max Perkins. Not a household name, or a common answer for the "Final Jeopardy" question. Yet Max Perkins may have had more positive influence on the development of twentieth-century American literature than any other individual.

Max Perkins was an editor—according to the title of his biography, "an editor of genius." In the 1930s, Max Perkins mentored some of the most brilliant stars on the literary horizon—people such as Thomas Wolfe, whose manuscripts reputedly arrived at the publishing house in trunks . . . thousands of pages that had to be sifted and cut and transformed into workable manuscripts. And Marjorie Kinnan Rawlings, who won the Pulitzer Prize for her novel, *The Yearling*—a book that would never have been published without Perkins' help and encouragement.

Who needs editors? All writers need them, no matter how well-known or widely published, no matter how wealthy, successful or competent. Any writer who claims not to need editing is sadly deluded—or outrageously egotistical.

Editing at its best is a silent servanthood. A good editor is the unsung hero of the best-seller and the writer's most faithful friend. Still, many authors fall into a deadly trap, a snare that can hinder their development—and their success—as writers. They approach an editorial relationship from an adversarial stance, thinking that this person on the other end of the telephone and the other side of the manuscript has some hidden agenda—that she is a frustrated and unsuccessful writer who takes out her hostilities on someone else's book. But this is rarely the case. Most editors simply want what the writer wants—to make the book the best it can possibly be.

The problem is that writers are often too close to their manuscripts to see the inherent problems or the rough edges that need to be chipped away. Writing is a kind of birthgiving, and no one likes to be told their baby is less than perfect. The editor's job, however, is to point out the imperfections—to raise questions, to spot inconsistencies and to call the writer to task on inaccuracies or careless writing.

The editor—a good editor—takes a rough rock and polishes it to gemstone quality. She cannot make a diamond out of quartz, but she can make the quartz shine brilliantly. In order to make it shine, however, she must chisel away the unnecessary fragments, carve out new facets and put the manuscript to the grindstone.

Sometimes the process hurts. But writers who are more interested in the quality of the book than in the fragility of their own egos will welcome such painstaking work.

Give your editor the benefit of the doubt. Listen. Rewrite. Polish. Revise. Remain teachable. A capable editor is a blessing, not a curse. An editor who gives your work time and attention can help mold and shape you into a writer of excellence. If you want to hone your skills, cultivate your talent and become the best writer you are capable of being, take a step back from your personal connection to your manuscript and heed your editor's advice. Pray for a Max Perkins. If God answers your prayer, it will be the greatest gift your writing has ever known.

THE POWER OF READER RESPONSE

In the CBA, many fiction writers (and some nonfiction writers) develop a following—a group of faithful readers who often perceive themselves as intimately involved in the work of the writers they admire. If you are fortunate enough to develop a presence in the market, you *will* get letters from readers, and it is important to be prepared to handle that reader response.

We sometimes chuckle and make jokes about people who watch television soap operas—those viewers who become so caught up in the characters' lives that they write long, impassioned letters to the actors, pleading, "Please go back to your wife and children! They need you." But be warned: Such obsession doesn't necessarily limit itself to the soaps. In fiction, particularly in series fiction, readers also become very involved in the characters' lives, and often write to the author to find out what happened to Colin or whether Maxine's baby is going to live. Sometimes readers even try to get involved in plot development: "You can't let Jonathan die!"

As flattering as such response may be, it can whirlpool into a dangerous undertow for the unsuspecting writer. The fact is, you can't please all the people all the time—and you shouldn't even try. Input from readers can encourage and motivate you, but it can also distract you from your original vision for your books.

Only the author, after all, can know whether or not Jonathan has to die. As sad as it may be, if Jonathan's time is over, he must be laid to rest. Public opinion cannot determine the author's direction.

The extreme of such reader fanaticism, no doubt, is reflected in Stephen King's best-seller *Misery*. A famous novelist, injured in a car accident, is rescued by "his biggest fan" and taken to her home to recuperate. While he is still unconscious, she reads the manuscript of his recently completed novel and discovers that the hero, her favorite character, is killed in the course of the plot. This madwoman holds the author hostage and tortures him, forcing him to rewrite the story so that the hero lives.

We hope, certainly, that we never meet a fan like that. But even the most gracious of admirers can divert an unwary author from her original purpose and wield an enormous—and often inappropriate—influence over the writer's directions.

At the opposite end of the spectrum is the reader who functions as a couch critic, constantly inspecting every book for errors or signs of theological heresy. Such readers seem to delight in pointing out an author's mistakes and can, if taken too seriously, undermine the writer's confidence. We need to listen, of course, to helpful criticism. But we do not have to allow our sense of calling to evaporate under the harsh light of a reader's belittling scrutiny.

Most reader letters can be handled by the author, and the personal touch enhances a writer's reputation. But if you receive an angry letter or a letter from a questionable source, you may want to refer such correspondence back to the publishing house for response.

On one occasion I received a fan letter, postmarked from the state penitentiary, from a man incarcerated for unknown offenses. I was gratified by the knowledge that my ministry in writing had reached into a prison. But at the time I lived alone in a small town, and I felt acutely uncomfortable with the prospect of this man knowing my whereabouts. My course of action—which turned out to be a wise decision—was to refer the letter to my publisher. The publishers fielded the man's questions, sent him a complimentary copy of the book and saved me a great deal of uneasiness.

Recently I received another such letter—this time from an

inmate who described himself in great detail and suggested that we might want to strike up a romantic relationship. Although I usually answer all reader letters that come my way, I decided that this might be one instance in which silence was the better choice. I did not want to take the chance of inadvertently encouraging this gentleman, only to have to deal with a much more complicated situation later on.

An author who responds graciously to readers' letters develops a reputation for being a kind, humble and generous soul. But many fiction writers find that they don't want readers to have access to their private lives—their home addresses and telephone numbers. In that case, you may want to invest in a ream of tasteful stationery that does not include your residence and phone numbers.

Since readers are the lifeblood of fiction sales, we need to value them and treat them with respect. But we do not need to allow them to set the course for our writing—either positively, through flattery, or negatively, through criticism. We serve God first, and God's call and direction upon our writing should be our primary concern.

SCHEDULING FOR THE LONG HAUL

Once you get a reputation for being a writer who delivers quality manuscripts, you are likely to be inundated with offers. Many beginning writers perceive such a situation as heaven itself, but popularity brings it own set of pitfalls. Instead of scrambling to produce an acceptable proposal and praying for some editor to take notice, now you face a whole new realm of possibilities—and problems.

A common complication among writers in demand is the tendency to overwrite—to take on too many projects, to commit to several different series for different publishing houses. It's an understandable trap; if you've scraped and struggled for years, you know that the same stream of offers that floods in today could dry up tomorrow. You tend to hedge your bets, to try to do everything, just in case the tide of financial security ebbs out again.

But each of us has a limited store of creativity at any given time. If we spread ourselves too thin and push ourselves too hard, the writing is bound to suffer. The quality will go down and, although the sales figures may not reflect it, we will no longer be doing our best work.

It's important, therefore, that writers know when to say "No"—or at the very least, "Later." Be honest with your publisher about how long it will take you to write a book and how prolific you can be. Don't sign a contract for a project due in six months if it will take you ten months to finish it.

Some writers in the Christian market tend to be extremely prolific, producing a major novel every six months or so. Especially with a series of novels, you may face pressure to produce at a faster rate than you're comfortable with. But if you're rushing to meet your deadlines, exhausted and ignoring your loved ones in the process, something is wrong.

In order to have a long-term, successful career as a fiction writer, you need to know your own patterns and pace yourself accordingly. Many writers who are touted as extremely productive—those authors who produce multiple series for several different publishers—are actually turning in rough drafts instead of finished manuscripts. They may produce and sell a lot of books, but the quality of their work suffers, and they never truly reach their full potential as writers.

In addition to the actual timing of book projects, another scheduling question arises for the up-and-coming writer in relation to publicity. Once your name is known and your reputation begins to be established, you will more than likely be inundated with offers to speak. Writing conferences, business luncheons, women's groups and book signings can take up an inordinate amount of time. Speaking engagements provide a good platform for publicizing your work (and an opportunity to sell books directly), but at some point you will have to decide how much speaking you can do without cutting into your writing schedule.

Writers have differing attitudes toward speaking and publicity engagements. A few writers are natural speakers and good teachers; others hate the very idea of getting up in front of a group. Some writers complain that when they speak, they feel as if they are lurching backward in time—they've already finished that book and moved on to the next, yet they have to keep on talking about a subject they've already exhausted in print.

If you generate enough success in writing to be in demand as a speaker, you will have to make your own decisions about speaking and publicity, based on your priorities, your available time and your natural abilities. But if you want to keep on writing, you'll need to make sure that writing is high on your priority list—and that may mean saying "No" to some of the speaking engagements that come your way.

Scheduling for the long haul is no simple task. It takes foresight and planning, the ability to set priorities and to turn down offers that look attractive. However, if you prepare yourself ahead of time to make those difficult decisions, your choices will be based on your principles rather than on the pressure of the moment. And your writing will be better, because you've learned what to accept and what to decline.

A WORD ABOUT AGENTS

In recent years, with the burgeoning of literary agencies serving the CBA market, a lot of controversy has arisen about a writer's use of an agent. An agent who knows the markets, believes in your writing and represents you faithfully can certainly be an asset to your career. An agent can keep a finger on the industry's pulse and be aware of publishers' needs, freeing the author from the unnecessary distraction of finding the right publishing house and negotiating a good contract. The agent can serve as the author's representative when disputes arise with a publisher. And because an agent represents a number of authors, the agent may have more leverage with a publisher than the individual author does.

In the general market, you need an agent just to get a reading in most of the large New York houses. In the CBA, however, a well-informed author can survive quite well without representation. Most CBA publishers will work with agents, but many prefer the personal connection with the author—not only in editorial situations, but in contract negotiations and problem-solving.

If you decide to contract with an agent, do your homework before signing on the dotted line. Research a prospective agent's reputation and record by asking for a list of the authors he or she represents. If you know any of the authors on the list, contact them and ask them how satisfied they are with their representation, or talk with editors you trust about the agents they respect and enjoy working with.

In entering a relationship with an agent—as with any business arrangement—it pays to be a little skeptical in the beginning. Find out if the agent can deliver what she has promised: Ask for details about contracts she has negotiated and publishers she has worked with. Promises are only good if they are backed up with action.

Agents can sometimes get more advance money and better perks for their authors, but not if they're overcommitted or fail to represent you aggressively. An agent who has a long list of heavyweight authors will inevitably spend more time and energy on those writers who have the potential of making the greatest amount of money. Sometimes, regrettably, the newer author or the author whose earning potential is primarily in the future gets lost in the shuffle.

If you want to publish both in the general market and in the CBA, look for an agent who has a proven track record in New York. Many CBA agents *want* to cross over into the general market, but simply do not have the contacts to make the necessary connections in the New York houses. The CBA and ABA markets are very different, and an agent who is quite capable and well-informed in one may not be able to sell your work effectively in the other.

Success is not a dirty word for the Christian writer, nor is ambition contrary to faith. The fact is, your "ministry" as a writer of spiritual fiction is directly linked to success in the market. If your books don't sell, your story doesn't reach the audience it is intended to uplift and encourage.

The Christian writer, however, needs to prepare in advance for the pitfalls of success. Writing is not just a job; it is a vocation, a calling. No matter how successful you become, your callling will only be fulfilled to its highest potential if you keep your head about you and remain humble, teachable and grateful to those who have supported you. With your priorities in order, as you give attention to your spiritual growth and your relationships with significant people in your life, your writing will be balanced, and you will develop a well-rounded career that gives glory to God.

APPENDIX A: SAMPLE PROPOSAL
FOR A NOVEL OR SERIES

Simultaneous Submission

If you are submitting the proposal to more than one publisher at a time, put the words "Simultaneous Submission" at the top of your title page. It alerts the editor that other houses are considering your idea.

TITLE OF YOUR NOVEL

Book 1 in the _____ Series

(if you are doing a series and have a series title)

A Proposal Presented to
Solomon Richfellow Christian Publishers, Inc.

By

Your Name
Your Address
Your City, State, Zip Code
Your Telephone, Fax #
Your Email Address

Your Social Security Number

If you are represented by a literary agent, put "Represented By" and the agent's name, address and telephone number in place of yours.

Title of Your Book Proposal   Page #
Your name

I recommend using a header so that your name and your proposal title are on all pages of your proposal. That way if anything gets out of order or separated, it can be easily identified.

Title: Your Book Title
Series: Series Title (if you have one)
Author: Your name

Genre/Type: **Historical**   **Romance**   **(Contemporary,**
Mystery, Western, etc.)

Long, long ago in a galaxy far, far away . . . .

Here give a brief synopsis of your novel. Make it as creative and as representative of your writing as you can. Do not simply reproduce the first few pages of your book, but summarize without overwhelming. Write your synopsis in present tense:

When Jody McAlister comes to Copperhead Crossing, she is seeking peace and tranquility, and she thinks she will find it in this pastoral setting. She takes up residence in her grandmother's old farmhouse and begins to work on her novel. She has no way of knowing, however, that just across the valley a mild-mannered schoolteacher is planning the destruction of the entire human race. Against her better judgment, Jody becomes romantically involved with him and must face the consequences of being an unwitting accessory to his diabolical plot.

Be sure to include specific characters—their names, motivations, and the spiritual significance of the events in the novel. Include any important subplots and how they are connected to the main plot.

Audience: Summarize who your are writing for, including age and demographics, and why you believe your book will appeal to them.

Market Analysis: Demonstrate your familiarity with other books in this genre—why your book is similar to, but not a clone of, others in the category that are selling. What makes your book different, but not *too* different?

Series Plans: If you have planned sequels to this book, give a one paragraph summary of the other books in the series.

Length of Manuscript: Estimate the approximate length of your book.

Delivery of Manuscript: Estimate when you will be able to deliver the book. Give yourself a reasonable deadline, such as "Within nine months of contract date, or at a date agreed upon by author and publisher." If the book is finished, put "Immediate" or "Upon Request."

About the Author: Here include a brief bio, and keep it professional. Include any life experiences that might pertain to your credibility as the author. Do not give your complete resumé—no one cares that you flipped burgers at the Beef Palace—but do include significant publishing credits if you have them.

TITLE OF YOUR BOOK
Chapter Summaries

Begin your chapter summaries, if you have them, on a separate page to divide them from your proposal. If you don't have chapter summaries but you do have an outline—part divisions, for example—you can summarize the main plot movements that way.

Part 1: CREATION
Chapter 1: In the Beginning

If you're far enough along in your development to propose your book, you should be able to give at least a rough outline of the major movements of your plot and the major developments in your characters. Be sure to include major plot twists, character motivations and spiritual implications. A CBA publisher is going to want to know how God plays a part in your book and in the lives of your characters.

♦ ♦ ♦

When you finish with your chapter summaries, next include the sample chapters (preferably no more than three). Most publishers want to see the beginning of the book, how quickly you grab the reader and what your writing style is like. If you have a prologue, include it as well.

You should treat your sample chapters not as part of the proposal, but as a portion of the novel itself—this means new page numbering, beginning with page 1. Put a header on each page that will identify the title and author of the work. I also include the chapter number in the header in case the pages get separated.

I usually also include a title page for the book itself, as if I were presenting the whole manuscript. This title page looks like the proposal title page except the words "Proposal presented to" and the "Simultaneous Submission" line.

When you have done all this, write a brief cover letter (on your professional letterhead) to the editor who has asked to see the proposal. (You *have* already sent a query letter or discussed your idea with a publisher who expressed interest, haven't you?)

Keep your letter short and to the point:

Thank you for your interest in the fiction project we discussed last week at the Imminent Rapture Christian Writer's Conference. Enclosed, as you requested, is the full proposal for my series, including chapter summaries and three sample chapters.

I look forward to your response. . . . If you need any additional information, please do not hesitate to call. . . .

Sincerely yours, etc.

Put the proposal and sample chapters into a file folder labeled with your name and address, and send it flat in a 9×12 mailing envelope. **Do not staple the pages together.** Unless it is a rush job, Priority Mail or FedEx Two-Day delivery is usually sufficient. Mark the outside of the envelope "Requested Material" so it won't get lost in the slush pile. Include a SASE (self-addressed stamped envelope) for return correspondence. If you want your manuscript returned, include a SASE mailing envelope.

Need I say it? DO NOT SEND YOUR ONLY COPY. Send your proposal on disk *only* if the editor requests it that way. Later, your publisher will probably want the final manuscript both on disk and hard copy.

APPENDIX B: AUTHOR'S CHECKLISTS FOR PLANNING, DEVELOPMENT & EXECUTION

Prayer, Planning and Preparation
Why are you considering publishing in the Christian market?
- ☐ Good opportunities for new/developing writers
- ☐ Editorial assistance
- ☐ Personal attention
- ☐ Acceptance of spiritual truth
- ☐ Good potential for financial success
- ☐ Sense of God's calling

In light of the distinctive features of CBA fiction, does your writing include:
- ☐ A clearly articulated Christian worldview?
- ☐ A familiar setting/historical time frame?
- ☐ Universal themes?
- ☐ Action orientation?
- ☐ Viable Christian characters?
- ☐ A strong Evangelical perspective?

What types of writing most interest you?
- ☐ Historical novels
- ☐ Romance
- ☐ Nostalgia
- ☐ Supernatural/Prophecy novels
- ☐ Westerns
- ☐ Intrigue
- ☐ Suspense
- ☐ Mystery
- ☐ Gothic
- ☐ Coming of Age
- ☐ Contemporary Character novels
- ☐ Short Stories

Where would you place your own writing on the "readership base" pyramid (see page 32)?
- ☐ Elitist
- ☐ Literary
- ☐ Sophisticated

☐ Mainstream
☐ Popular

List your top three choices of publishers who currently produce the kind of novel you envision yourself writing.

_____

_____

_____

Who would your contact be if you were to submit a query or proposal to those publishers?

_____

_____

_____

Check your proposal to make sure you have included:
☐ Plot synopsis
☐ Chapter outlines (if available)
☐ Possible sequel ideas
☐ Identification of genre and target audience
☐ Brief biographical note
☐ Sample chapters
☐ Projected completion date

If the editor requests it, are you willing to:
☐ Submit a completed manuscript for evaluation?
☐ Discuss changes in direction/plotline?
☐ Revise and rewrite?
☐ Respond positively to editorial advice?

If your proposal is not accepted, what will you do?
☐ Give up writing forever.
☐ Take your masterpiece to an editor who appreciates your genius.
☐ Publish it yourself.
☐ Seek out professional advice about changes that need to be made.
☐ Re-evaluate your proposal and prepare it for another publisher.
☐ Pray.

If your proposal is accepted, what will you do?
☐ Celebrate with a steak dinner.

☐ Run up a huge long distance bill with calls to family and friends.

☐ Work like crazy to finish the book and meet your deadline.

☐ Seek out your editor's guidance.

☐ Cheerfully revise, rewrite and polish.

☐ Keep learning and growing as a writer.

☐ Pray even more.

Stories, Sermons and Sunday School

What kind of novel do you intend to write?

☐ Plot-driven

☐ Character-driven

What length/complexity do you envision?

☐ Short novel with a single plotline and a limited number of characters

☐ Complex novel with multiple plotlines, several subplots and many characters

Briefly describe your main plotline/subplots:

_____

_____

_____

_____

If you have outlined your novel, list the major turns and complications of your plot:

☐ _____

☐ _____

☐ _____

☐ _____

If you are not outlining, give a brief summary of the way you see your novel developing:

_____

_____

_____

_____

If unanticipated actions or unplanned characters take you by surprise, you will:

☐ Ignore them.

☐ Spend time developing them and see where they lead.
☐ Write them down somewhere else and wait to see if they will work.
☐ Let them lead your novel into a new direction.
☐ Get distracted from your original plan and purpose.

As you plan the development of your novel, check to make sure you have avoided:
☐ Overly complex movements and settings.
☐ Simplistic resolutions to complex problems.
☐ Pollyanna plotlines or characters.
☐ *Deus ex Machina* endings.

Concerning the "telling vs. showing" dilemma, check to make sure:
☐ Every scene you've "shown" advances the plot or develops a character.
☐ You have eliminated unnecessary action or movement.
☐ You have "shown" rather than "told" your characters' feelings and emotional responses.
☐ You have eliminated unnecessary flashbacks.
☐ Your characters' physical descriptions come from a character outside themselves.

Concerning your use of setting and detail, check to make sure:
☐ You have eliminated excessive and unnecessary historical data.
☐ You have used physical descriptions of characters to capture some significant factor of their personalities rather than simply giving a catalogue of features.
☐ You have focused on setting details that capture an important moment or establish some essential meaning.
☐ You have limited your use of "panoramic shots."
☐ You have eliminated any description of character or setting that does not directly advance your plot or the development of your characters.

Can These Bones Live?

Considering the relationship between characters and plot, remember:
☐ Characterization is strongest when characters are uniquely suited to plot.

☐ Every person's story is different, and every character will react differently.
☐ To be credible, characters must respond to their situations:
  ☐ individually, but not improbably.
  ☐ believably, but not predictably.

To personalize your characters and give them life:
☐ Give them a past.
☐ Give them a balance of positive and negative qualities.
☐ Give them inner as well as outer conflicts.
☐ Give them room to grow and change.
☐ Give them clear motivations for actions and relationships.
☐ Give them identifiable voices.
☐ Give them names that fit.

Motivation in characterization is based on:
☐ The character's past influences.
☐ The character's present beliefs.
☐ The necessary actions or decisions of the moment.
☐ Internal changes or conflicts.
☐ The "wild card" of unpredictability.

Name your characters based on:
☐ Historical accuracy.
☐ Regional or local customs.
☐ National or ethnic patterns.
☐ Sound and meaning.
☐ Memorable structures.
☐ Possible irony (when appropriate).

When naming your characters, avoid:
☐ Stereotypes.
☐ Excessively obscure meanings.
☐ Ordinary or common names.
☐ Similar or overlapping names.
☐ Excessively exotic names.

Can These Bones Speak?

Concerning the "reality vs. realism" dilemma:
☐ Remember that fiction is about truth, not fact.

☐ Focus on what is important rather than "what really happened."

☐ Prune away the irrelevant issues.

Concerning your use of dialogue:

☐ Eliminate chitchat or small talk.

☐ Eliminate "historical information" speeches.

☐ Make sure your dialogue presents significant forward movement in plot or characterization.

Check your dialogue to eliminate:

☐ Deliberate misspellings or phonetic transcriptions of words.

☐ Any focus on "outer realism" rather than "inner realism."

☐ Attempts to reproduce dialect patterns that do not directly contribute to characterization.

☐ Any dialectical speed bumps which slow the reader's progress.

Instead of faithfully reproducing dialects:

☐ Learn the rhythms and patterns of your character's speech.

☐ Employ those unique patterns to give your character life.

☐ Use only the occasional misused word or phrase to identify character.

Concerning attributions:

☐ Use no attributions if possible.

☐ When attributions are necessary, keep them simple.

☐ Use only descriptive attributions that relate to tone and volume.

☐ Avoid adverbial attributions.

☐ Do not use attributions to communicate characters' emotions.

Only God Is Omniscient

Overall point of view selected for your novel:

☐ First Person

☐ Limited Third Person

☐ Multiple Third Person

If the viewpoint is First Person, check every scene to make sure:

☐ The central character has a distinctive voice and identifiable attitudes
☐ The character does not think about or discuss issues that he/she cannot be directly aware of, such as:
  ☐ historical events, or results of events, that have not yet occurred.
  ☐ action that has happened or is happening elsewhere.
  ☐ other characters' internal thoughts, attitudes or motivations.
☐ Every scene represents the camera angle of the first-person character.
☐ Any judgment or evaluation about other characters is based on deduction from visible signs.
☐ The character does not lapse into sermonizing or philosophizing about issues that represent the author's favorite hobby horses.
☐ The character's speech and thought patterns are commensurate with his/her age, social class and maturity.
☐ The character's actions and thoughts are probable, consistent with his/her personality and motives.

If the viewpoint is Third Person (Limited or Multiple), check every scene to make sure:
  ☐ Primary characters' points of view are introduced early in the book.
  ☐ Omniscient viewpoint (i.e., the butler's perspective or the wide-angle shot) is used sparingly, and only for introductory scenes, broad-span visuals, and scenes where no specific character's point of view is appropriate.
  ☐ Initial introductions of characters are given sufficient space for development.
  ☐ Every point of view shift is marked by a hiatus within a chapter or by a chapter division.
  ☐ Each viewpoint is given sufficient development (one to two pages) before shifting to another character's point of view.
  ☐ Radical shifts in time, location or viewpoint come at chapter breaks, not within chapters themselves.
  ☐ Parallel scenes (two characters within the same scene or time frame) occur within the same chapter or in sequential chapters.

☐ For each viewpoint character in a given scene, the criteria for a first-person point of view (as listed on the previous page) have also been met.

Humility and Exaltation

Author intrusion interrupts the "vivid, continuous dream" of fiction. Check your own fiction to make sure you have eliminated:

☐ Philosophical tangents.
☐ Sermonizing/gratuitous religion.
☐ Flowery "purple patch" descriptions.
☐ Inconsistency in point of view.
☐ Inappropriate humor.

Evaluate the relative "fog factor" in your own writing. What kinds of sentences do you most commonly use?

☐ Simple sentences
☐ Sentence fragments
☐ Introductory clauses
☐ Compound sentences
☐ Complex sentences
☐ Parallel sentences

Regarding the use of profanity:

☐ Is it absolutely necessary?
☐ Is it a cliché, a lazy way to avoid real characterization?
☐ Is it appropriate to the character/situation?
☐ Will your readers be offended?
☐ Will your publisher refuse to let it go through?
☐ Is it worth fighting for?

Regarding the use of sexual references and sensuality:

☐ Is it designed primarily to titillate?
☐ Is it consistent with the character?
☐ Is it modest?
☐ Is it inappropriately intimate?
☐ Have you invaded the sanctity of the bedroom?

Regarding the use of violence:

☐ Is it absolutely necessary and appropriate to the scene?
☐ Have you been discreet about the use of graphic details?

☐ Have you avoided explicit descriptions about violence to-
ward women?
☐ Do your violent scenes describe rather than incite?
☐ Have you been considerate of your reader's sensibilities?

The Essential Work of Revision

Give yourself plenty of time to:
☐ Schedule in time before your final deadline to rewrite.
☐ Let the work "cool off" before beginning revisions.
☐ Read through the entire manuscript as an ordinary reader
would.
☐ Mark problem areas for later attention.

Maintain objectivity by:
☐ Having the manuscript read by a trusted (and honest) friend
or colleague.
☐ Reading the manuscript out loud.
☐ Avoiding explanations, rationalizations or excuses.
☐ Being brutal with your own shortcomings.

Pay attention to details like:
☐ Logical plot development and timing.
☐ Realistic characterization.
☐ Significant dialogue.
☐ Believable chronology.
☐ Consistency in point of view.
☐ Sufficient conflict and dramatic tension.
☐ Believable resolution.
☐ Variety in sentence structure.
☐ Word choice.
☐ Repeated phrases.
☐ Use of hiatus.
☐ Chapter division and dramatic chapter endings.
☐ Scene shifts and transitions.
☐ Accuracy of historical data and timeline.

For yourself and your editor:
☐ Keep a running timeline of major events.
☐ Create a character list including physical descriptions and
personality traits.

☐ Check, double check and provide sources for historical references.

The Invisible Servant/The Visible Celebrity

Before you become successful and well-known, commit yourself to incorporating the following truths into your life:

☐ Writing is a calling, not a job. Your first responsibility is to be faithful to God.

☐ Maintaining a strong spiritual and family life is of utmost importance.

☐ Relationships are valuable for their own sake, not just for research purposes.

In order to avoid the Prima Donna Syndrome:

☐ Keep your priorities in order: God, family/friends, occupation.

☐ Cultivate relationships with trusted supporters who will tell you the truth about yourself, and warn you if you start to adopt unreasonable attitudes.

☐ Remember that you never "arrive" as a writer; good writing is an ongoing process of growing and learning.

Appropriate expectations for a positive relationship with your publisher include:

☐ Reasonable deadlines.

☐ Fair contracts.

☐ Advances commensurate with projected sales and sales records.

☐ Acceptability of simultaneous submissions.

☐ Honesty and forthrightness.

☐ Updated information on books in progress.

☐ An available contact person in house.

☐ Clear and direct marketing information.

☐ Promises fulfilled and mistakes corrected.

☐ Reasonable time frame for decision making.

☐ Appropriate issuing of checks and royalty statements.

In terms of your relationship with your editor, commit to:

☐ Avoiding an adversarial relationship.

☐ Responding positively to editorial advice/changes.

☐ Trusting your editor's commitment to making your book the best it can be.
☐ Putting a bridle on your ego.
☐ Appreciating your editor's skill and hard work.

Concerning reader response and fan mail:
☐ Steadfastly maintain your own vision for your book.
☐ Do not allow flattering reader response to swell your head.
☐ Do not become discouraged by negative reader response.
☐ Do not allow reader pressure to decide the direction of your work.
☐ Refer questionable letters back to the publisher for response.
☐ Respond graciously and humbly.

Questions to ask yourself regarding long-term scheduling include:
☐ How quickly can you produce a finished manuscript?
☐ Are you able to work efficiently on more than one project at a time?
☐ Do you feel rushed, harried, frustrated or cut off from your loved ones?
☐ What writing pattern or schedule produces your best work?
☐ How do you feel about speaking and publicity engagements?
☐ What proportion of time are you willing to spend in speaking?
☐ How will speaking and publicity offers affect your concentration and focus on your writing?
☐ Are you willing—or able—to turn down offers when it is appropriate to say "No"?

Concerning the possibility of signing with an agent, consider:
☐ Can you (or do you want to) represent yourself within the CBA?
  ☐ Do you understand contracts and negotiations?
  ☐ Do you have a clear idea of which publishers might be right for the kind of writing you are doing?
  ☐ Can you handle disputes firmly, professionally and reasonably?

☐ Do you have contacts in the publishing houses you would like to work with?

If you think you need an agent, why do you want one?
☐ Career management
☐ Breaking into the ABA
☐ Contract negotiations
☐ Follow-up and marketing momentum
☐ Dispute settlements
☐ Better advances and royalties

If you intend to pursue representation, find out:
☐ Other authors represented by the agent.
☐ The agent's sales record in the CBA and ABA.
☐ The agent's experience with publishers.
☐ The agent's reputation in the industry.
☐ The number of authors represented by a single agent.
☐ Whether the agent believes in your work.
☐ What kind of writing the agent represents best.
☐ Whether the agent will market your work aggressively.
☐ The agent's experience in dispute settlement.

In general, how do you perceive your writing?
☐ A ministry
☐ An opportunity to evangelize
☐ A hobby
☐ A job
☐ A money-making proposition
☐ A permanent career
☐ A passion/addiction
☐ A vocation or calling from God

APPENDIX C: ESSENTIAL BOOKS
FOR THE SERIOUS WRITER

This is a partial list of good sources for writers who want to improve their craft. There are others, of course, that might be added to this list, but I have found these books to be particularly useful and inspirational.

Basic Resources You Shouldn't Be Without

Chicago Manual of Style. The definitive word on style issues, and the standard for most publishers' individual house style.

Glazier, Stephen. *Word Menu.* Given to me as a Christmas gift, this volume from Random House has proved to be one of the most often-used books in my library. It's a reference book that organizes language by subject matter—a combination of dictionary, thesaurus, almanac and glossary—and the most accessible word book I've ever found.

Stuart, Sally. *The Christian Writers' Market Guide.* This essential tool provides not only the names and addresses of Christian book and magazine publishers, but also topical lists of which publishers accept what kinds of writing. Also included are helpful articles from industry professionals, and other information useful to both beginning and seasoned writers.

Strunk, William, Jr. and E.B. White. *The Elements of Style.* This little classic offers elementary rules of usage and an accessible guide to clear expression and communication.

Writer's Market (current edition). A guide to general publishing, which also includes listings for religious publishers. Updated annually.

Zinsser, William. *On Writing Well.* Zinsser's book is ostensibly about writing nonfiction, but its principles are invaluable for a fiction writer as well. The book is well-organized, entertaining and informative.

Practical Books for the Aspiring Novelist

Bly, Carol. *The Passionate, Accurate Story*. This volume is a little difficult to obtain (it's from Milkweed Editions in Minneapolis), but it is an incisive and instructive book on the craft of fiction. Bly's approach is based on the short story, but the principles apply to novel writing as well.

Maass, Donald. *The Career Novelist: A Literary Agent Offers Strategies for Success*. One of the best books I've read recently on planning for long-term success as a fiction writer. Maass has experience on all sides of the desk—as an editor, as a novelist and as a literary agent. His practical approach to the business of writing and career-building has helped me understand how to get where I want to be ten years from now.

McCutcheon, Marc. *The Writer's Guide to Everyday Life in the 1800s* and *The Writer's Guide to Everyday Life from Prohibition Through World War II*. No writer of historical fiction should be without these titles from Writer's Digest Books. They are an invaluable source of information about all the little details that go into historical fiction.

Noble, William. *"Shut Up!" He Explained: A Writer's Guide to the Uses and Misuses of Dialogue*. This book is worth buying just for the title, but what's between the covers is even more valuable. Noble provides clear, understandable discussion of the uses of dialogue, and although I disagree with his perspectives on dialect, I recommend his book.

Sloane, William. *The Craft of Writing*. A witty, concise, sensible treatment of the techniques that comprise good writing. His chapter on "Fiction Is People" is worth the price of the book.

Books to Inspire, Encourage and Inform

Charlton, James, ed. *The Writer's Quotation Book*. I have a whole shelf of little books like this one—collections of quotations and witticisms about the craft of writing. This inexpensive paperback is illustrated with nineteenth-century woodcuts and provides hours of entertainment, inspiration and fun. The perfect companion when you're feeling a little cynical or struggling with writer's block.

Gardner, John. *The Art of Fiction, On Becoming a Novelist* and *On Moral Fiction*. I believe that even more than his own fiction, John Gardner's teaching on fiction is his greatest gift to the world. He is informative, humorous and incisive in his perceptions. *On Becoming a Novelist* is a book that inspires my teaching and my writing, and I often read it just for the sheer pleasure of being in the company of a mind like Gardner's.

Harper, Howard V. *Days and Customs of All Faiths*. Although the title is a bit misleading—"all faiths" to this writer is mostly variations on Christianity, with a few Jewish traditions thrown in for good measure—this old volume is the kind of book that fascinates writers. It's a day book that chronicles the customs, feasts and celebrations of saints for every day of the year. Look for it (or something like it) at a library sale or used bookstore.

Lamotte, Anne. *Bird by Bird*. A humorous, witty, well-written book for writers, subtitled "Some Instructions on Writing and Life." Not a practical handbook, but a rich resource and well worth the price.

L'Engle, Madeleine. *Walking on Water: Reflections on Faith and Art*. This slim volume from Harold Shaw Publishers changed my life and my career directions during a summer trip to England. L'Engle's spiritual insights, as well as her perceptions about the value of creative endeavor, are unparalleled. I read this book at least once a year, just to remind myself what my writing is all about.

O'Connor, Flannery. *Mystery and Manners*. A nonfiction book that has all the verve and audacity of O'Connor's fiction, this series of lectures gives profound insights about what it means to be a spiritual writer. Read it and reread it.

Sayers, Dorothy. *The Mind of the Maker*. A highly motivating book with great spiritual depth and professional expertise.

Welty, Eudora. *One Writer's Beginnings* and *The Eye of the Story*. The first is a kind of "professional autobiography"; the second, a series of essays on the craft of writing. Both are entertaining, instructive and humorous in that inimitable Welty style.

INDEX

More Great Books for Writers!

1998 Writer's Market: Where & How to Sell What You Write—Get your work into the right buyers' hands and save yourself the frustration of getting manuscripts returned in the mail. You'll find more than 4,000 listings loaded with submission information, as well as real life interviews on scriptwriting, networking, freelancing and more! *#10512/$27.99/paperback/1088 pages*

1998 Novel & Short Story Writer's Market—For years, fiction writers have relied on this trusted guide to the best opportunities to get fiction published. You get more than 2,000 listings, including accurate, up-to-date information on each market to help you find the right publisher for your work. *#10525/$22.99/paperback/656 pages*

The Writer's Digest Guide to Manuscript Formats—Don't take chances with your hard work! Learn how to prepare and submit books, poems, scripts, stories and more with the professional look editors expect from a good writer. *#10025/$19.99/200 pages*

Grammatically Correct: The Writer's Guide to Punctuation, Spelling, Style, Usage and Grammar—Write prose that's clear, concise and graceful! This comprehensive desk reference covers the nuts-and-bolts basics of punctuation, spelling and grammar, as well as essential tips and techniques for developing a smooth, inviting writing style. *#10529/$19.99/352 pages*

How to Write Attention-Grabbing Query & Cover Letters—Use the secrets John Wood reveals to write queries perfectly tailored, too good to turn down! In this guidebook, you will discover why boldness beats blandness in queries every time, ten basics you must have in your article queries, ten query blunders that can destroy publication chances and much more. *#10462/$17.99/208 pages*

How to Write a Book Proposal, Revised Edition—Get your nonfiction published as you learn the basics of creating effective book proposals with experienced literary agent, Michael Larsen. From test marketing potential book ideas to creating a professional-looking proposal package, you'll cover every step that's essential for breaking into the publishing market! *#10518/$14.99/224 pages/paperback*

Building Fiction: How to Develop Plot & Structure—Even with the most dynamic language, images and characters, no piece of fiction will work without a strong infrastructure. This book shows you how to build that structure using such tools as point of view, characterization, pacing, conflict, and transitional devices such as flashbacks. With Jesse Lee Kercheval's guidance, you will build a work of fiction just as an architect would design a house—with an eye for details and how all the parts of a story or novel interconnect. *#48028/$16.99/208 pages/paperback*

Writing the Private Eye Novel: A Handbook by the Private Eye Writers of America—Discover pages of advice on writing and publishing PI novels—from authors whose fiction flies off the shelves. You'll find 23 tip-filled chapters on topics that include plot structure, character development, setting and short stories. Plus, specific advice on finding ideas, keeping readers on edge, creating slam-bang endings and more! *#10519/$18.99/240 pages*

Elements of the Writing Craft—Apply the techniques of the masters in your own work! This collection of 150 lessons reveals how noted writers have "built" their fiction and nonfiction. Each exercise contains a short passage of work from a distinguished writer, a writer's-eye analysis of the passage and a wealth of innovative writing exercises. *#48027/$19.99/272 pages*

Writer's Digest Handbook of Making Money Freelance Writing—Discover promising new income-producing opportunities with this collection of articles by top writers, editors and agents. Over 30 commentaries on business issues, writing opportunities and freelancing will help you make the break to a full-time writing career. *#10501/$19.99/320 pages*

The Writer's Digest Dictionary of Concise Writing—Make your work leaner, crisper and clearer! Under the guidance of professional editor Robert Hartwell Fiske, you'll learn how to rid your work of common say-nothing phrases while making it tighter and easier to read and understand. *#10482/$19.99/352 pages*

The 30-Minute Writer—Write short, snappy articles that make editors sit up and take notice. Full-time freelancer Connie Emerson reveals the many types of quickly written articles you can sell—from miniprofiles and one-pagers to personal essays. You'll also learn how to match your work to the market as you explore methods for expanding from short articles to columns and even books! *#10489/$14.99/256 pages/paperback*

Writing to Sell, 4th Edition—You'll discover high-quality writing and marketing counsel in this classic writing guide from well-known agent Scott Meredith. His timeless advice will guide you along the professional writing path as you get help with creating characters, plotting a novel, placing your work, formatting a manuscript, deciphering a publishing contract—even combating a slump! *#10476/$17.99/240 pages*

Writer's Encyclopedia, 3rd Edition—Rediscover this popular writer's reference—now with information about electronic resources, plus more than 100 new entries. You'll find facts, figures, definitions and examples designed to answer questions about every discipline connected with writing and help you convey a professional image. *#10464/$22.99/560 pages/62 b&w illus.*

Writing and Selling Your Novel—Write publishable fiction from start to finish with expert advice from professional novelist Jack M. Bickham! You'll learn how to develop effective work habits, refine your fiction writing technique, and revise and tailor your novels for tightly targeted markets. *#10509/$17.99/208 pages*
